CARA LEA BURNIDGE is
assistant professor of religion at
the University of Northern Iowa.

A Peaceful Conquest

A Peaceful Conquest

Woodrow Wilson, Religion, and the New World Order

CARA LEA BURNIDGE

The University of Chicago Press
Chicago and London

Cara Lea Burnidge is assistant professor of religion at the University of Northern Iowa.

The University of Chicago Press, Chicago 60637
The University of Chicago Press, Ltd., London
© 2016 by The University of Chicago
All rights reserved. Published 2016.
Printed in the United States of America

25 24 23 22 21 20 19 18 17 16   1 2 3 4 5

ISBN-13: 978-0-226-23231-7 (cloth)
ISBN-13: 978-0-226-23245-4 (e-book)

DOI: 10.7208/chicago/9780226232454.001.0001

Library of Congress Cataloging-in-Publication Data

Names: Burnidge, Cara Lea, author.
Title: A peaceful conquest : Woodrow Wilson, religion, and the new world order / Cara Lea Burnidge.
Description: Chicago ; London : The University of Chicago Press, 2016. | Includes bibliographical references and index.
Identifiers: LCCN 2016008495 | ISBN 9780226232317 (cloth : alk. paper) | ISBN 9780226232454 (e-book)
Subjects: LCSH: Wilson, Woodrow, 1856–1924. | Wilson, Woodrow, 1856-1924—Religion. | Protestantism—Political aspects—United States. | Social gospel—Political aspects—United States. | Christianity and politics—United States—Protestant churches. | Protestantism—United States—History—20th century. | Protestantism—United States—History—19th century.
Classification: LCC E767.1 .B87 2016 | DDC 973.91/3092—dc23 LC record available at http://lccn.loc.gov/2016008495

♾ This paper meets the requirements of ANSI/NISO Z39.48-1992 (Permanence of Paper).

To Rosebud

Contents

Acknowledgments

I have had the good fortune of being surrounded by generous colleagues and friends who have shared their time and wisdom with me as I wrote this book. The strengths readers may find in this work are a direct result of their collegiality. A few pages will not adequately convey all of my gratitude to those named here, but I am delighted to have the chance to do so in print.

This book simply would not exist without Amanda Porterfield's simple and thought-provoking question, *Have you given any thought to Woodrow Wilson?* At the time, I had not. Our conversations inspired me to think about him and his historical context until the present work took shape. I am grateful for her patience with early drafts and her uncanny ability to understand what I mean to say before I am able to fully articulate it. Likewise, Amy Koehlinger's wisdom and constructive criticisms lingered with me as I conceptualized this project and its argument. Discussions with John Corrigan made this work sharper as we thought through historiographical trends and disciplinary distinctions together. John, Amy, Amanda, and their families taught me that scholarship thrives when placed in perspective. I cannot thank them enough for demonstrating this through their scholarship and for encouraging me to do the same.

I first learned how history is a conversation among historians at the Department of History at Washburn University. Grateful does not begin to describe the appreciation and admiration I have for my mentors, Alan Bearman, Kim Morse, and Tom Prasch, and the fellow historians they produced, Jess Rezac, Jennifer Wiard, Darin Tuck, and ReAnne and Brandon Wentz. I would also like to thank the Department of Religion at Florida State University and all of my colleagues who consider Dodd Hall their intellectual stomping ground. Conversations with Mike Pasquier, Joseph Williams, Laura Brock, Monica

Reed, Brooke Sherrard, Shem Miller, Frank Pittinger, Emily Clark, Adam
Park, Kirk Essary, Brad Stoddard, Michael Graziano, Tara Baldrick-Marone,
Charles McCrary, and Andrew McKee have challenged and encouraged me
in equal measure. They, along with Jeffrey Wheatley, Steph Brehm, and T. J.
Tomlin, have contributed to a life of the mind that extends well beyond the
walls of the ivory tower. Likewise, the Religion in American History blog,
established by Paul Harvey and continued through numerous contributors,
shaped, and continues to shape, my conception of our subfield and what it
means to belong to this guild.

For this work, I would like to thank the White House Historical Association for a generous research grant, which allowed me to visit the Woodrow
Wilson Presidential Library and Museum in Staunton, Virginia, as well as the
Library of Congress and Woodrow Wilson House in Washington, D.C. I am
especially grateful to Peggy Dillard, who directed me to boxes filled with letters neither of us knew what to do with at the moment. They gave me plenty
to consider long after I left Staunton.

As this work developed, I benefitted from feedback from several scholarly societies and academic conferences where I presented portions of this
work, including the American Academy of Religion, the American Historical Association, the Society for Historians of American Foreign Relations,
and the John C. Danforth Center for Religion and Politics. The idea for this
project was first introduced to a wider audience at the 2012 meeting of the
American Society for Church History where Tisa Wenger provided valuable
feedback for considering the relationship between religion and secularism.
At the 2013 meeting of the American Historical Association, my copanelists,
Mark Edwards, Malcolm Magee, and Caitlin Carenen, helped me to place
this project in relationship to the study of religion in U.S. foreign relations.
Andrew Preston's comments, as well as his body of work that inspired the
panel, continue to be a significant influence on the ways I think about religion and diplomatic history. Two early risers and engaged audience members who attended our AHA panel, Ray Haberski and Sylvester Johnson, were
invaluable to moving this project forward. Ray's infectious enthusiasm for
the history of ideas was instrumental in introducing me to the Society for
U.S. Intellectual History. I cannot speak highly enough about the benefits of
belonging to a scholarly community that approaches intellectual inquiry and
collegiality with equal vigor. Sylvester Johnson, along with Tracy Leavelle,
later welcomed me to the Religion and U.S. Empire Seminar. Their guidance,
as well as the support of the entire group, helped to bring this book into conversation with other scholars thinking about the United States in relationship to the rest of the world. Edward Blum, Emily Conroy-Krutz, Jon Ebel,

Jennifer Graber, Heather Curtis, Sarah Dees, and Charles Strauss gave more than their fair share of time reading drafts and thinking through concepts with me.

Chapter 2 in particular resulted from "Presidents at Prayer," a panel at the 2013 meeting of the American Society of Church History, which was later published in the society's journal, *Church History: Studies in Christianity and Culture*. Chapters 4 and 5 took their present form after the 2014 SHAFR Summer Institute on Wilsonianism and Its Legacies, a seminar Mark Lawrence and James McAllister designed to bring together scholars of Wilsonianism. I am grateful I was able to be a part of the extended conversations with Ross Kennedy, Mary Renda, and Christopher McKnight Nichols. Kyle Lauscerettes, Charles Laderman, David Fields, Matt Jacobs, and Michelle Geitschel were especially helpful conversation partners for being so patient with my insistence upon nonstate actors and their cultural influences.

As I revised this manuscript, I began working at the University of Northern Iowa, where the Department of Philosophy and World Religions welcomed me as one of their own. I am especially grateful to Jesse Swan, Jolene Zigarovich, Elizabeth Sutton, and Leisl Carr Childers for their interdisciplinary collegiality. If teaching the liberal arts is valuable because it moves beyond disciplinary boundaries, then so too is our research and writing.

Finally, I would not have been able to complete this book without the love, support, and patience of my family. Greg Crawford never had a doubt, even when I had plenty to go around. Hugh, Shannon, Lucy, Thea, and Felix Crawford brightened my days when nothing else could. Tom Kirkland weathered the storms alongside me when neither of us knew the way forward. Timothy Leffert and Jason Novotny—in their infinite wisdom—encouraged me (sometimes through coercion or bribes) to put the books and devices away. Mike, more than anyone else, read drafts and edited them. Most important of all, he and Syrio put it all in perspective for me.

Introduction

This is a council of peace, not to form plans for peace—for it is not our privilege to form
such—but to proclaim the single supreme plan of peace, our relation to our Lord and
Savior, Jesus Christ, because wars will never have any ending until men cease to hate
one another, cease to be jealous of one another, get that feeling of reality in the brotherhood of mankind, which is the only bond that can make us think justly of one another
and act righteously before God himself.

— WOODROW WILSON[1]

President Woodrow Wilson believed the Great War presented the United
States with an opportunity to build its empire. Speaking to the Columbus,
Ohio, chapter of the Chamber of Commerce in February 1915, he announced,
"America now may make a peaceful conquest of the world."[2] Wilson was sure
that the nation could, but he wondered if Americans would. He invited these
local businessmen, the pillars of U.S. economic interests, to play a role in
developing a new age for the United States in the world. As these Chamber of
Commerce members shipped their goods to faraway lands, he explained, they
would also transport their ideas. Those services—a combination of material
goods and intangible ideas—could improve the lives of countless people. This
purposeful enterprise, he promised, would also allow the United States to be a
"mediating influence" in the world. Wilson explained, "The American spirit,
whether it be labeled so or not, will have its conquest far and wide," ushering
all toward a global rebirth.[3]

To Wilson, this conquest was unlike any that had come before it in world
history. Whereas past empires gained power and territory at the expense of
weaker peoples and nations, the United States sought friendly, disinterested
relations with all nations through global commerce and mutual "serviceability." In these interactions, Americans did not seek their own self-interest
but rather acted in the interest of a global good. To that end, Wilson contended, Americans offered a "spiritual mediation" in which the essence of
America transformed peoples of the world, tapping into a universal feeling
that all humans could naturally possess but only Americans fully embodied.
By U.S. citizens being good Americans—citizens who served others before
themselves—the rest of the world would see that the spirit animating Americans was embedded within the hearts of millions the world over. So long

as the nation "preserved her poise" during this time of crisis, this American impulse "will assert itself once and for all in international affairs."[4] Wilson imagined the Great War as presenting the moment through which Americans could inspire a global transformation.

Wilson revealed several of his assumptions about humanity and world order in this speech. He demonstrated his optimism about the human condition—human beings were naturally good and could improve over time. His optimism in humanity carried over to his assessment of social order. Wilson presumed that history was a story of progress leading to the betterment of society. He considered human effort to improve individuals and their communities was not only possible but was also the best means for making the world a better place. He also believed the United States to be an exceptional nation. American exceptionalism, for Wilson, derived from the country's unique genesis in world history (a birth of a nation founded upon the consent of the governed) and its living democracy, a form of government that continually changes (i.e., progresses) according to the will of the people. These certainties about the United States and its citizens were not matters of politics, economics, or law alone, but products of an invisible spirit cultivated through American culture and history. That spirit, he believed, existed as a result of Providence, a creation of God's design to fulfill God's will.

The same day he met with Chamber of Commerce members, Wilson also spoke at the annual meeting of the Federal Council of Churches (FCC). Established in 1907, the FCC began as a movement to "Christianize" America. German Baptist minister Walter Rauschenbusch best explained what this form of activism meant in his book *Christianizing the Social Order*.[5] This effort was not intended to lobby for "God" or "Christ" to be included in any legal documents, oaths of office, or pledges of allegiance. It did not mean making the United States a theocratic state or coercing citizens to attend church. Rather, Rauschenbusch explained, "Christianizing the social order means bringing it into harmony with the ethical convictions which we identify with Christ." This mission would be achieved when "the institutions of social life" reflected what he believed were the highest moral principles found in humanity.[6] These principles did not necessarily belong to Christianity alone, but for Rauschenbusch and the FCC, one could "find their highest expression in the teachings, the life, and the spirit of Jesus Christ."[7] The figure of Jesus, then, supplied their notion of the most basic element of Christian identity and action: selfless, disinterested service to others.

Those converted to this cause called themselves "social Christians," and their theology became known as the "social gospel." They distinguished themselves from other Protestants by conceptualizing a theology of the New

Testament Gospels that applied this ethic of service evenly to both individuals and society. Social Christians developed their own sense of applying Christianity through lived experiences of agitating for, implementing, or enforcing state-based reform. They shared an effort to make biblical concepts manifest in temporal, secular laws. This did not mean a formal legal establishment of a specific religion; rather, social Christians wanted to cultivate a proper civic morality, a more perfect Christianized union. Sincerely held individual beliefs mattered to social Christians, but they mattered only inasmuch as they contributed to the common good, or what Rauschenbusch and Wilson would separately describe as being "serviceable" to others.[8]

Wilson's presidency, and the outbreak of Europe's war, appeared to these Protestants as a chance to fulfill their Christianization efforts through U.S. action in the world. In their interpretation of scripture and history, Christianity presented a new conception of social engagement through the figure of Jesus, a model of service in which great individuals cared for the least among them to create a mutually beneficial society. As a result, spreading this gospel to society and converting the state to this ideal constituted their evangelical mission. If they successfully Christianized Americans, then the world would follow. With a proper social gospel state, they reasoned, the United States could offer a new framework for global order, an international system in which powerful nations cared for those who were powerless. While in Ohio in 1915, Wilson stood before the FCC and expanded upon his earlier message to Columbus businessmen, asserting, "America is great in the world, not as she is a successful government merely, but as she is the successful embodiment of a great ideal of unselfish citizenship. That is what makes the world feel America draw it like a lodestone."[9] Knowing his audience well, Wilson drew upon the FCC's commitment to social reform and gave their evangelical mission new import by making it relevant to U.S. diplomats and their international audiences.[10] He made the social gospel a matter of U.S. foreign relations.

This interpretation of Christian mission, especially its relevance to a life of civil service, pervaded Wilson's career. Southern evangelicalism and social Christianity shaped Wilson's conception of democracy. For Wilson, democracy was a form of government based in a Calvinist notion of God's order that regulated citizens according to social divisions he understood to be natural and inherently good, particularly whites' racial superiority and patriarchy. He also regarded democracy as a national way of life, an ideal society reflecting the ethos of the social gospel and, therefore, worth spreading around the world. Successful evangelization of this democracy unified America's domestic politics and foreign policy with the telos of humanity. Seen in light of this context, Wilson's intention to advance democracy reflected the aspirations of a specific ideological tradition with a habit of conflating its interests with universal truths. As someone "steeped" in this culture, he applied his *particular* democratic vision to the Great War while describing his vision as satisfying the *universal* good.[11]

Wilson encountered opposition from many sides when competing notions of Christianity, democracy, nationalism, and internationalism met at the Paris Peace Conference and in the U.S. Senate. He and many American Protestants expected one portion of the treaty, the Covenant of the League of Nations, to be the culmination of their social gospel endeavors; instead, the public debate erupting from this document and the ideas it contained solidified an otherwise shifting American religious landscape. It resulted in a great war of the white Protestant establishment concerning the place of American evangelical activism, whether the locus of religious exercise pertained to the church alone or also to the state. In other words, from what ideological location should Christians conduct their evangelical mission—beyond the parameters of the church (and therefore through mainstream culture and its institutions) or within the immediate jurisdiction of the church (and therefore removed from mainstream culture and institutions)? This question was not new to evangelicals. Throughout the nineteenth century, American evangelicals parsed the boundaries of a biblical injunction to be in the world, but not of it. The formation of an international organization composed of member nations—and the U.S. president's instrumental role in creating it—recast this evangelical concern to affect the role of the United States in the world.

Wilson's liberal internationalism must be understood as a part of this American religious history. It was a product of his cultural context, a historical moment in which concerns about religion's influence on society permeated social, political, and legal activism. In 1919, Wilson and his international vision became fodder for debates about what it meant to be Christian and American and how American citizens should reconcile the two. His Christian identity, his religiosity, and the veracity of his ideologies were questioned; they were also exalted. These conversations, however, were not exclusively intraevangelical ones but a larger national, and at times global, discourse about world order. Democrats and Republicans no less than fundamentalists and modernists turned to Wilson in the 1920s as evidence for the truth behind their political claims. Throughout the twentieth century, representations of Wilson and "Wilsonian" internationalism continued to shape what it meant to be American and what resources would be marshaled for the production of American identity to audiences at home and abroad. The man and his mission became powerful symbols for defining and redefining the boundaries of nationalism for a new era in international relations.

Wilson, Wilsons, Wilsonians

Understanding how a southern Presbyterian boy grew to represent liberal internationalism requires an exploration of his religious identity, the Reconstruction-era context in which it was forged, and its reformulation in the twentieth century. In what follows, Wilson provides a lens through which to understand how American religion and foreign relations were coconstituted between the Civil War and World War II. Wilson's approach to internationalism was an expression of his religious identity, which, because of its intimate relationship to the state, helped to transform American religion and politics in the twentieth century. Wilson's religious identity, and the shifting cultural sands it was built upon, allowed him to transition from the Old South to the progressive North. It is also the reason he represents seemingly contradictory policy positions like liberal internationalism and domestic segregation. By reconstructing the cultural context Wilson knew, historians can gain insight into the twentieth century's "Wilsonian moment" and understand more fully how U.S. foreign relations were remade in his image.[12]

Each chapter seeks to understand religion in relationship to American national identity in regional, national, and global contexts. Chapter 1 provides foundational information for Wilson's religious self-description. Historians rightly situate Wilson's ideological development within southern Presbyterianism, but rarely do they acknowledge how Presbyterianism, a religious institution with its own body of thought, changed between 1856 and 1924. This chapter locates Presbyterianism within white southern evangelical culture and the significant changes that shaped its development in the long nineteenth century. Rather than approach religion, race, gender, and politics as separate portions of Wilson's conceptual framework, this chapter presents Wilson as an intersectional figure whose place within society and self-understanding resulted from multiple forms of privilege. From his family's support of the Confederacy to his tenure at Princeton, Wilson valued a social order that expected educated white male leaders to serve "the least" among them. Those who espoused this conception of society reinforced social divisions even as they sought to penetrate them with a Christian ethic of service.

With this background, Chapter 2 turns to the 1912 presidential campaign as a reflection of the informal white Protestant moral establishment of the early twentieth century. Through the election, Wilson constructed his private and public self as a part of his location in this culture. Wilson's sense of calling to public service did not result in a private religious experience in his home or at church but rather a public performance of religious devotion through civic office. Chapter 3 continues this theme by demonstrating how Wilson's administration and social Christians found common cause in the Great War. Wilson's insistence that the United States "served" other nations and sought to "make the world safe for democracy"—even by force—was central to a social gospel message that conceived of democracy and Christianity as intertwined means to achieving the kingdom of God on earth. From outside this particular, and peculiarly American, social gospel outlook, Wilson's internationalism can appear logically inconsistent. But when his specific interpretations of "equality," "service," and "democracy" come in to view, Wilson's approach toward internationalism crystalizes as the culmination of a specific white middle-class American Protestant movement.

Chapter 4 further explores the relationship Wilson imagined between Christianity and internationalism by discussing the limits of his conceptions of a Christianized world order. When much of the world expected Wilson to make a grand statement about the importance of God in world affairs, he made no effort to include "God," "Providence," or any other formal articulation about the state of religion in the Treaty of Versailles. Wilson's approach to foreign policy, much like his approach to domestic concerns, prioritized the establishment of an enduring moral structure for governance over sectarian particularities or temporary political concerns. Religion, in Paris in 1919, was but one among many diplomatic concerns and received no special favor from Wilson.

Wilson's performance at the Paris Peace Conference disappointed most Americans, including some of his most ardent evangelical supporters. In this context, Chapter 5 turns to the fights over the League of Nations. On the Senate floor and at public forums around the country, Wilson's opponents criticized the Covenant of the League of Nations according to their own theological justifications for world order, national sovereignty, and American exceptionalism. This chapter illustrates how senators' ideas about religion, which were both naturalized in American culture and expedient to their political agenda, shaped their foreign policy. Both Republican and Democratic senators characterized Wilson's internationalism through their own ideological convictions about God's order, nationalism, and millennial expectation, creating a parallel fight over proper interpretation of American religion. As white Protestants debated the terms of American Christianity through the League of Nations fights, "evangelical" became a Christian identity in transition, one forged in relation to other Protestants and the current historical moment.

This bitter Protestant division during the postwar period had consequences for American identity and its global context. The ostensible end to World War I revealed the intensity of white Protestants' competing biblical narratives. Chapter 6, therefore, examines the rejection of Wilson's internationalism, Wilson's death, and the legacy of Wilsonianism. Channeling their "modernist impulse," the white liberal Protestants who faithfully supported Wilson rallied behind the symbol of the fallen president to renarrate their national and international hopes. Political leaders who served in the Wilson administration, like Newton Baker and Franklin Delano Roosevelt, turned public discourse toward a new postwar Americanism that looked beyond the nation's borders and valued religion generally. Wilson's internationalism received a makeover that reformulated Wilson's Presbyterianism as "Judeo-Christian" to reflect the new "trifaith" consensus in American culture.[13] Wilsonians forged new alliances with Catholics and Jews to challenge the new normalcy of white evangelicalism in the 1920s and 1930s. Their efforts to redefine Wilson's vision for a new age had less to do with providing a clearer perspective on the Great War than negotiating the current state of religious difference in the United States.

When scholars describe Wilsonian internationalism as "idealism," they are not using a neutral analytical category but rather a term fraught with conceptual challenges. At times, idealism is a foil to realism, a preference for what the world ought to be rather than what it is. This certainly played a part in Wilson's approach to foreign affairs: Wilson wanted to make the world anew. Naming his vision as idealistic, however, carries with it a history of public discourse about the legitimacy of certain ideas and civic endeavors. Wilson and Wilsonian internationalism illustrate how the rubric for judging such legitimacy has changed over time. At the beginning of Wilson's presidency, his credibility was rooted in Christian statesmanship. By the end of it, as informally established white Protestant mores had shifted, Americans contested the Christian basis for his statesmanship. Grounding Wilson's internationalist vision in idealism, rather than exploring the religious roots of his ideology, has allowed both his supporters and detractors to distance themselves from each other.

Wilson in Context

This book did not begin with an intense admiration for President Woodrow Wilson. Nor did it originate from disdain. In fact, it did not start with a president at all. I had originally planned to investigate a liberal Protestant social reform movement that wanted to turn the world upside down. In the final two decades of the nineteenth century, a collection of ministers across the United States hoped to reorder the world to reflect their own beliefs. They published books and novels, formed nonsectarian social reform organizations, and raised money to fund these efforts. The heart of their enterprise rested upon rededicating local, state, and federal governments to caring for the general welfare of the people through social services and regulatory standards. They also sought to spread their American-born vision to other nations, a mission to construct a more perfect world that would be the true embodiment of Christianity. This largely white, university-educated group of Protestants initially were proud to call themselves idealists and Christians. A few decades into their efforts, however, they—and others—began to use the former but not the latter to describe their movement.

Both this group and the era in which they lived are highly contested by scholars. Historians and religious studies scholars have used various names for these reformers: social Christians, social gospelers, liberal evangelicals, modernists, ecumenists, and public Protestants, to name a few. Signifiers for groups, eras, or ideas are not stable categories that can be applied consistently across time periods; instead, they are variables that change over time. This includes concepts and values that have defined American identity, such as democracy, internationalism, isolationism, idealism, freedom, and equality. Scholars and their subjects may evoke the same terminology, but they often employ those terms in different ways for a variety of reasons. Recognizing and naming these differences is an important detail in the craft of historical research. It is the first step in translating the past to the present. This book, then, is about how these historical figures and the historians who write about them conceive of both this group and this era. In other words, it is as much about the past as it is about the historical process that made these terms seem natural in narratives of American history.

To study religion is to study people and their classifications, especially those marking differences such as human and nonhuman, natural and unnatural, moral and immoral. Whereas the study of theology concerns the nature and character of the divine, my considerations of religion here are anthropological because religion is not an agent in and of itself. It is often considered to be a private, individual identity or experience, but the signifiers and exercises associated with it only make sense in a social context. As a result, religion, in this work, is a socially constructed category of human activity that changes over time, a product of human social engagement expressed in discourse and signified through material resources. Christianity, then, is not a fixed entity in history but part of a process of defining and redefining that occurs over time by different people and institutions, including those who identify as

Christians. To talk about American evangelicals, for example, is to rely upon a consensus in development, an idea and identity with a past. In this work, American evangelicalism is not a singular entity but a set of representations by and for those who call themselves American and evangelical. These identities are articulated and lived by a number of different constituencies who possess overlapping characteristics but do not necessarily agree on all parts of their shared identity.

Woodrow Wilson provides a window into this historical moment because the way his contemporaries and later historians characterized him reveals the fascinating arc of historical change. With both pride and derision, Americans from the 1910s to the 1940s, and even well beyond, have called Wilson a Christian and an idealist. Their claims were often motivated by an interest in asserting a specific conception of U.S. religion and politics. In this work, I am interested in the public functions of Wilson's Christian identity because it gives insight into how the Wilsonian moment reshaped historical narratives of U.S. foreign relations and American religions. I offer a history of the swift change in public discourse from Wilson's Christian statesmanship to Wilsonian idealism. This work contributes to historiographies of American religion and foreign relations by reexamining the cultural context Wilson knew and by recognizing the curated boundaries between religion and politics, liberal and conservative, and, in this instance, idealist and evangelical.

Seen in this light, this book is also an interpretation of the relationship between American religions and U.S. foreign relations in the twentieth century based on the life and career of Woodrow Wilson. If foreign policy is a representation of the nation to the world, then domestic fights about national identity are crucial to its history.[14] Descriptions of American culture require wrestling with the place and power of religion to its historical development. American Protestants and their constructions of legitimate and illegitimate expressions of religion and politics are central to the story of how Americans conceived of their purpose in world affairs. Wilsonian internationalism is one example of how a formulation of America in the world resulted from the coconstitution of religion and politics in a global context.

1

From Reconstruction to Regeneration

Woodrow Wilson was a deeply religious man. Men who do not understand the religious spirit need not even try to understand him.

—EDWIN ALDERMAN[1]

Between me and the other world there is ever an unasked question: unasked by some through feelings of delicacy; by others through the difficulty of rightly framing it. All, nevertheless, flutter round it. . . . To the real question, How does it feel to be a problem? I answer seldom a word.

—W. E. B. DU BOIS[2]

Thomas Woodrow Wilson grew up with the Civil War and matured alongside Reconstruction. Born in 1856 in the slaveholding South, "Tommy" experienced a momentous shift in American life firsthand. One month before his fourth birthday, he witnessed a man visit his childhood home to tell his father, Reverend Joseph Wilson, the presidential election results. Abraham Lincoln had been elected president, and they expected war to follow.[3] From his bedroom window in Augusta, Georgia, Tommy watched trains bring men and munitions to aid Confederate rebels. After the Battle of Chickamauga in 1863, the church where his father preached became the hospital where his mother, Janet (Woodrow) Wilson, cared for wounded soldiers. The grounds of the church where he often played baseball with his friends became a prison for Union soldiers. After the North secured its victory, Tommy looked on from the steps of the manse as Union soldiers escorted the president of the Confederate States of America in chains to prison. The South, especially the churches shaping its regional identity, held the Wilson family together, supplied their livelihood, and determined their sense of what it meant to be American. This war between brother soldiers and their nations haunted the American culture they knew well after union was restored.

As he developed in the shadow of the war, Tommy chose to be called Woodrow. Time and age led Woodrow to craft his own identity in light of past sectional strife. Tommy, the young rebel, likely never imagined that one day he would be president of the United States—let alone think of himself as being compared favorably to Lincoln. Thomas Woodrow Wilson's life seems to be filled with contradictions like these. The historical record is scattered with evidence that does not seem to add up. Although "Tommy" was born into a prominent southern Presbyterian home supportive of the Confederacy and slavery, "Woodrow" would be known as a champion of self-determination and equality among nations. This son of a Confederate chaplain devoted his career to promoting the need to serve humanity and renewing the nation's democracy; however, his civil service also established precedents for segregating government offices, restricting access to public institutions, and limiting democratic participation among African Americans, women, and immigrants. And yet, throughout his life, whether as a Confederate sympathizer or as president of the United States, he used the same scripture as his guide. Making sense of how these aspects of his life were consistent, rather than contradictions, is key to understanding Wilson and the American culture he knew.

Southern Evangelicalism and Its Discontents

Reverend Joseph Wilson and his wife, Jessie, instilled in their children the values of discipline and decorum typical of white middle-class Presbyterians in the South.[4] They attended church twice a week; they prayed together at their family dinner table; they ate meals prepared by an African American domestic worker;[5] and they enjoyed parlor entertainment after their meals, often singing hymns alongside a melodeon. They lived neither in poverty nor complete privilege; the Wilsons' home contained the "comfort and simplicity" of southern Victorian décor.[6] As one family friend recalled, a visitor could walk through their home and find the walls and the library contained both "sacred and secular" objects.[7] This was not surprising for a southern manse. Rather than detract from the importance of Christianity, this mix of interests demonstrated the family's investment in a well-educated Christian life filled with a variety of experiences.[8]

As was the case for other white southern evangelical families, patriarchy was the gravitational force that held the Wilsons' private and public lives together. Their home internalized and modeled the larger order they believed to be natural for society. Reverend Wilson was a public figure for the Presbyterian Church, but the home served as the center of his family's Christian identity. His leadership at home provided one of his first lessons to his children in understanding God's will and order for the universe. Intending to imitate Christ's relationship to the church, the southern patriarch aimed to embody God's sovereignty and the social hierarchies flowing from it. By his leadership in the home and in public life, he taught his children how to understand race, class, and gender as a part of God's design. Because the Wilsons believed white men had a pivotal role to play in private and public life, Reverend Wilson gave special attention to his son.

As members of a Calvinist tradition, the Wilsons considered education key to learning and living their interpretation of Christian theology. When a young Tommy experienced difficulty learning how to read, for example, his father tailored his lessons to account for his son's needs rather than merely accept this circumstance. Recognizing God's design did not preclude human action to improve upon one's condition. Rather than dwell on Tommy's weakness, Reverend Wilson focused his son's studies on the art of debate and oration, using biblical hermeneutics as his guide. Tommy improved his reading skills while further developing his existing strengths. Reverend Wilson, as a highly respected southern minister, ensured that his son would not only know his church doctrine but would also overcome his shortcomings through a disciplined work ethic. This form of instruction served several purposes, as father taught son that studying and reciting their beliefs went hand in hand with putting those beliefs into practice. Through both circumstance and design, Reverend Wilson applied the truths he knew from church to his children's lives at home.

For the Wilsons, the purpose of Tommy's education was not merely to increase his knowledge but to embody God's will for the edification of the entire family. Reverend Wilson's lessons, then, became an opportunity to further cultivate proper male leadership. Together, father and son developed shared interests as the patriarch modeled acceptable forms of piety and play. Both developed an affinity for reading, enjoying especially the work of Walter Scott. A popular writer among white southerners, Scott validated white male authority and the social life of the Old South.[9] Their mutual fondness for creative prose led them to challenge each other with verbal contests, usually with puns.[10] Playfulness taught Tommy the boundaries of work and leisure and what his father considered the proper balance of the two. The reverence and constructive play found in the Wilsons' home could also be found in other white Calvinist homes in the nineteenth-century South. By his parents' faith and purposeful instruction, every aspect of young Tommy's life could serve as a lesson for constructing his Christian character.

As the family patriarch, Reverend Wilson loomed large in his son's life. Looking back on his childhood as an adult, Wilson recalled: "[My father] was the best instructor, the most inspiring companion, I venture to say, that a youngster ever had."[11] While he admired his father, he kept their relationship in mind, never forgetting his place in the family hierarchy. Inside the walls of a church, he could only think of himself as Reverend Wilson's son.[12] Even though Tommy would eventually hold the highest political office in the nation, he remained humbled at the thought of his father. Standing before his own presbytery as president of the United States, he confessed, "I only wish that I could claim some of the vital connection with the church which he could claim—because those of us who stand outside of the active ministrations of the church, so to say, get an illegitimate usury from it. We do not seem to add a great deal to its capital, but we do live on its investments."[13] Reverend Wilson played such a large role in shaping his son's understanding of Christianity that Tommy grew to be a man who believed he only lived off of the dividends of his father's investments.

As Reverend Wilson received ministerial appointments in the postbellum South, the Wilson family moved from Virginia to Georgia in 1860, Georgia to South Carolina in 1870, and South Carolina to North Carolina in 1874. Along the way, Wilson's mother ensured the stability of the family's Christian home. Despite the prominence of Reverend Wilson in both historians' accounts and Wilson's own memories, it was Jessie who taught her children formal Presbyterian doctrine through the catechism. Decades later, Tommy and his wife, Ellen, followed the same practice. Ellen, like her mother-in-law, instilled formal Presbyterian doctrine in her children as well. For both generations of Wilsons, the home—rather than the church—served as the basis of a Christian education. Reverend Wilson insisted upon this practice because he believed "if they couldn't give their own children religious instruction at home, [then] Sunday School wouldn't help much."[14] Together, husband and wife poured the foundation for their children's understanding of scripture, a precursor to the moral structure that would be erected by the church.

The Wilson family's emphasis on hearth and home was part of their larger commitment to a Calvinist notion of divine order. For the Wilsons, first the home and, second, life beyond its walls confirmed God's sovereignty. Norms for racial, religious, class, and gender hierarchies reflected what they believed to be the proper order of the cosmos. The Wilsons, like other white southern evangelicals, affirmed the institution of slavery as evidence of God's design. After examining scripture, Reverend Wilson determined slavery not only had roots in biblical history but also advanced Christianity. He insisted that the institution was "a first and important step in ascertaining the will of God."[15] In his eyes, men who disapproved of slavery were "shortsighted"; those who declared it "unworthy of the countenance of Christianity" were "wicked." When masters cared for their slaves as Christ did the church, Reverend Wilson believed, slavery revealed supernatural truths about God and humanity. Since slaves and slave masters confirmed God's order, he instructed his congregants to see any threat to the institution as a threat to God's will. Furthermore, he saw no reason to fear divine punishment for upholding slavery and slaveholders because the Bible was "silent" on direct prohibitions against it.

According to his sermon "Mutual Relation of Masters and Slaves," Reverend Wilson believed slavery pleased God by "saving a lower race from the destruction of heathenism" and, when "under divine management," it could "refine, exalt, and enrich its superior race."[16] Reverend Wilson's position reflected a typical Calvinist understanding of society: all people can be equal before God while not necessarily equals to each other economically, politically, or socially. Patriarchs, for instance, naturally existed above their spouse, children, and property because they held a duty to protect those under their care. To Reverend Wilson, society inherently included superior and inferior races as well as classes of people. The Wilsons believed upholding this social order not only improved the lives of slaves but also, and perhaps more importantly, edified white masters as they performed their biblical duty to care for the least among them. Many white southern Christians agreed. The Wilsons, together with their church and surrounding community, taught their children in word and deed that white male leadership was at the heart of God's design.

The Wilson family's insistence on a divine order based on white supremacy made a lasting impression on Tommy. Along with other young white men in the Reconstruction South, Tommy tried to make sense of his place in American culture following the Civil War. In both his private and public papers, he reconsidered the lessons his parents taught him in light of the South's defeat. Rather than assert the "natural," biblical differences between races, he insisted upon social differences as a matter of practicality. In an unpublished essay, "The Politics and the Industries of the New South," Tommy argued that white southerners had to remain unified because they were faced with an opposing unified voting bloc in franchised freedmen. "Never to suffer themselves to be ruled by another race in every respect so unlike themselves," he claimed, white southerners took the most "intelligible" course. As a law school graduate, Tommy did not consider this position as a matter of racial animosity but sound reasoning. He claimed he did not object to the color of nonwhite skin. Tommy insisted instead that these social hierarchies were a matter of "intelligence" and "design" when he felt threatened by African American men being included within the body politic.

As he reinterpreted his regional past, Tommy began to reconstruct his own identity. He published several essays on whiteness, blackness, and the place of the South in American culture. As he did, he wrote under pseudonyms and changed his pen names several times between his first classes at Davidson College in North Carolina and completion of his graduate degree at Johns Hopkins University. In one such essay, he clarified his reasons for resisting the enfranchisement of freedmen: "We object to their votes because their *minds* are dark, [because] they are ignorant, uneducated, and incompetent to

FIGURE 1.1. Woodrow Wilson with his wife, Ellen, and three daughters circa 1912. Courtesy of the Library of Congress, Prints and Photographs Division, LC-USZ62-96670.

form an enlightened opinion on any of the public questions which they may be called on to decide at the polls."[17] Maintaining divisions between whiteness and blackness, he attempted to shift the focus of difference from race to education. Wilson, like others attempting to reconstruct a republic built upon a white Protestant nationalism, tried to soften his rhetoric but continued to reinforce the importance of white men's minds and bodies.[18]

Wilson's worldview was complemented—if not bolstered—by his first wife, Ellen. Also the child of a Presbyterian minister, Ellen (Axon) Wilson cherished the South and ensured that her children knew their white southern evangelical roots. When she was pregnant with the first of her three children, Ellen moved away from her husband, who was teaching at Bryn Mawr College, to return to Georgia. In spite of the potential risks of traveling by herself, she insisted on the move because she did not want her child born a Northerner. Ellen's staunch support of the South as culturally superior to the North continued after the birth of her children. Their daughter Eleanor remembered being "hustled off to school at Raleigh, North Carolina" because her mother "did not want me to talk like a 'Yankee.'" As the children of northern transplants following Reconstruction, Eleanor and her sisters had to learn—just as their nineteenth-century evangelical grandparents did—how to speak "southern."[19] The Wilsons must have considered the decision successful, as Eleanor wrote in her memoir: "I went, determined to acquire an accent like [my mother's], and in a few weeks was more southern than any southerner— speaking what father called 'educated n-----.'"[20] Eleanor was proud that her education inoculated her from being a complete Northerner, allowing her to continue her parents' cultural heritage. Wilson casually dismantled his daughter's sense of accomplishment, however, reminding her that regardless of appearances, her southern identity was adopted, a learned and therefore unnatural performance. Although they lived in the North, the Wilsons' daughters constructed their own southern identity by focusing on what could be shared between the two regions: evangelicalism and white supremacy.[21]

Historians' attempts to place Wilson in relationship to racism in America is confusing at best. Some historians contend that Wilson held "advanced" views for a southerner of his time.[22] Since Wilson wrote optimistically about human progress and spoke eloquently about the advancement of democracy, this reasoning suggests, he cannot be fully associated with the culture of the "Old" antebellum South or groups like the Ku Klux Klan.[23] Other historians admit that as president, Wilson supported racist policies, but those actions were inconsistent with his Christian piety or devotion to democratic expansion.[24] The existing documentation makes abundantly clear that Wilson opposed enfranchising freedmen because he saw such enfranchisement as the main source of the New South's problems. Likewise, Wilson did not recognize a contradiction between his membership in the Presbyterian Church and his belief in the superiority of white "Anglo-Saxons." As he learned from his parents and as he taught his own daughters, upholding racial hierarchies and preserving patriarchy maintained God's order. To the Wilsons, this social order preserved in legal codes and social mores ensured that all in America— full citizens, freedmen, and their dependents—followed God's will.

Wilson did not, however, merely mirror his parents' worldview for the rest of his life. While Reverend Wilson and Jessie were certainly influential in shaping their son's identity, they did not share the same ideologies. After all, he did not grow up in his father's South. "Tommy" became "Woodrow" as the "Old" South became the "New" South. Tommy's world was oriented around his father's church and the battles of the Civil War near their manse in the South; Woodrow enjoyed the privilege of studying law and political science at multiple universities in the North. When the South struggled with the social, economic, and political consequences of the war and Reconstruction, Woodrow wrote essays about it from Princeton, New Jersey. Describing Reverend Wilson's worldview tells us what Wilson might have learned as a boy, but it does not necessarily tell us what Wilson believed as an adult man. Both father and son agreed that life on earth reflected a divine order, but seismic shifts in American culture separated these men's notion of what constituted God's *proper* order. Each fervently sought to follow God's will, but their means to do so diverged as American evangelicalism changed following the Civil War.

New South, New Wilson

As Reconstruction ended, Woodrow Wilson did not lament the Lost Cause. His college notes and diary entries point instead to a young man trying to move beyond sectional strife. In a draft of a speech entitled "The Union," Wilson emphasized what he thought drew all Americans together: the U.S. Constitution and its principle of liberty. According to Wilson, liberty, the "fundamental principle" of the union, is "preserved only by perfect accord between the states." True patriots, those who bridge divisions, stand in stark contrast to "the fanatical partisans who enrage the people by their frantic writings of the bloody shirt under the specious pretense of zeal for the Constitution." Rather than choose North or South, Wilson grounded his argument in the living document that governed the United States. Unity, not sectionalism, was the expression of his generation. He pleaded with both sides to meet in the middle and embrace the inevitable march of progress possible under a shared banner of "liberty and union, now and forever, one and inseparable."[25] Rather than fan sectional flames, as a previous generation did, the son of a Confederate chaplain sought to strengthen the ties that bound the North and South, especially those connections that transcended party agendas. Wilson appealed to his brethren, white men in both the North and South, to work toward a common good.[26] As with many white men coming of age during Reconstruction, he insisted that the South needed the help of the North if it were to progress. The New South could not induce its own rebirth because the South's social problems belonged to the entire nation.

As he expressed his desire for national unity, Wilson struggled with his own place in American culture. He self-consciously worried whether his northern education would poison his southern roots. As newlyweds, Wilson and Ellen tried to make sense of these changes to American identity through their love letters. Ellen, for instance, teased her husband that his education was "northernizing" him. When Wilson admitted how much the accusation hurt him, Ellen backpedaled, astutely crafting a new identity for her husband to embody:

> Of course you are not a "Southerner" either in the old sense; you are an American citizen—of Southern birth. I *do* believe you love the South, darling—that she hasn't a truer son, that you will be, and are, infinitely

better, more helpful son to her than any of those who cling so desperately
to the past and the old prejudices. I believe you are her *greatest* son in this
generation and also the one who will have the greatest claim on her gratitude. But you *are* free from "provincialisms" of *any* sort—that expresses the
whole state of the case. Oh, I am so glad that you do not have any of those
prejudices! What a clog they would be at once to your usefulness and your
own success in life.[27]

Ellen and Woodrow were well aware of their tenuous identities as southerners living above the Mason-Dixon Line. They no longer belonged to a South
committed to states' rights nor did they fit comfortably in a North that did
not organize society by the divine principles they followed. They had to create
their own place in American life.

The Wilsons found their saving grace in their religious identity. Raised in
southern Presbyterian churches with well-respected ministers as their fathers,
Ellen and Woodrow never questioned their family traditions. Despite their
parents' influence, however, the Wilsons' Presbyterianism did not belong
solely to the South. It allowed them to transition seamlessly to elite northern institutions, such as Princeton University. Their assumptions about the
importance of paternal leadership, white superiority, and a government reinforcing the two as pillars of American culture fit comfortably in both the New
South and progressive North. The Wilsons' white elite Protestantism allowed
them to transcend any residual sectionalism. It also provided the continuity necessary to preserve their status in American society regardless of where
they lived. Their public Christian identity, and not church or home life alone,
oriented their world.

The Wilsons remained devoted to a single religious affiliation wherever
they lived, yet the cultural ground upon which they stood shifted. Even
as they strove to be a traditional Presbyterian family, Presbyterianism—
like all other religious affiliations—experienced its own changes after the
Civil War. The new norms were made painfully clear to both the Wilson
family and Presbyterian churches throughout the United States when one
of their own unintentionally challenged tradition. In 1884, Wilson's uncle,
Reverend James Woodrow, discussed the theory of evolution in an address
to Columbia Theological Seminary's alumni. After examining the most
recent scientific research and interpreting scripture, Reverend Woodrow
suggested that evolution may explain the process of Creation. This speech
served as the culmination of his work as the Perkins Professor of Natural Science at Columbia Theological Seminary. After twenty years of service in this position, Reverend Woodrow's reputation came under fire.
The controversy ignited through this speech represents one of the many

transformations of American Protestantism during the late nineteenth century in microcosm.

Like his brother-in-law Joseph Wilson, Reverend Woodrow saw no contradiction between studying religion and science. As far as he was concerned, both the visible, natural world and the invisible, spiritual world contributed to understanding God's will. As a believer in the inerrancy of the scripture, he did not consider his position to be a challenge to Christianity; yet, by postulating such a claim, Reverend Woodrow found himself accused of heresy by his peers in the Presbyterian Church. Charged with detracting from the veracity of scripture, Reverend Woodrow spent the end of the nineteenth century caught in a multiyear debate within regional synods and, eventually, the Presbyterian General Assembly. He became the public face of Presbyterian heresy despite his careful preparation for what he anticipated to be, at most, a position that would incite discussion about the process of Creation.

Ironically, Reverend Woodrow had attempted to avoid controversy by sending a draft of his speech to his brother-in-law. Reverend Wilson replied in advance of the speech, assuring his brother-in-law that he had no reason to fear an opposition: "It is a noble statement of the true state of the facts, and that outs [sic] just where the blade ought to fall. That good will come of it I cannot doubt—at least to the extent of stopping the mouths of whispers and fomenters of trouble." Reverend Wilson predicted that after Reverend Woodrow's forthcoming address "there will be none to peep, except such as are hopelessly malignant, or dreadfully ignorant, or fools. There could not be a more masterly exhibition of truth upon a recondite subject than this address contains. If any one shall find heresy in it, then shall I claim to be written down a heretic."[28] Both Reverend Wilson and Reverend Woodrow identified as strict biblicists, yet neither considered scientific theories, like evolution, heretical. Reverend Woodrow's intellectual pursuits in the mid-nineteenth century earned him a position at Columbia Theological Seminary in order to pursue the precise intellectual inquiry that would lead to his "heresy" in the late nineteenth century.

The Wilson family was blindsided by a cultural shift among American Protestants. A number of factors contributed to the transformation of orthodoxy for Presbyterians as well as other denominations. Through the rise of book culture, spiritualism, and psychology, American Protestants expanded their notion of authoritative texts and experiences. Accordingly, many broadened the rubric of their faith to include reading novels, participating in séances, playing sports, consuming the products of modern industry, and engaging in empirical study.[29] Evangelicals in particular played with the boundaries of their own orthodoxy even as they defended the importance of a line between sin and piety. The normative standard of Protestant behavior was not quarantined around a particular creed or church but instead was experimentally and actively tested.[30] With these new sources of authority also came new modes of interpretation. Throughout the nineteenth century, Protestants increasingly embraced historical-critical interpretations of the Bible, valued individual rationalism alongside or in place of scripture alone as the basis of theological authority, depended upon plain-spoken, common-sense statements of faith and adapted the Gospel message to include agendas for social and theological reform.[31] This process—and an adherence to the inherent value of processes—constituted a "liberal" Protestantism in the Gilded Age and Progressive Era.

Reverend Woodrow's heresy trial, then, was but one in a series of formal and informal trials that occurred across Protestant denominations. Reverend Woodrow was not attempting to distance himself from his evangelical tradition. He had expected his address to be a mere rearticulation of orthodoxy based on new knowledge. Many of his peers, however, considered it an untoward innovation that detracted from the tradition they knew. Without intending to innovate, Reverend Woodrow contributed to doctrinal changes that reoriented what it meant to hold an orthodox position in the Presbyterian Church. Indeed, both Reverend Wilson and his detractors considered themselves to represent the traditional Presbyterian position. Both supplied well-reasoned arguments. Reverend Woodrow's willingness to interpret scripture alongside science was commonplace before the Civil War but had become heretical after Reconstruction. Despite these conflicts, the Wilson and Woodrow families remained members of the Presbyterian Church for their entire lives; however, who the Presbyterian Church—and other Protestant denominations—considered members and what was considered orthodox changed considerably in the same period.

In much the same way that regional sectionalism mattered less after Reconstruction, denominational sectarianism carried much less weight among white American Protestants in the latter decades of the nineteenth century. Protestants across denominations bonded over their shared positions on social, political, and economic issues more than their theological doctrines. Whether or not one attended a Methodist or Baptist church on Sundays revealed less about one's Christianity than the books one read and the ways one spent his or her leisure time. The issue that mattered to most white evangelicals was the degree to which one chose to be "of" the world—whether one participated fully in white "mainstream" secular culture or remained isolated in white evangelical circles for work, education, and entertainment.

Reconstructing the Good Society

As an undergraduate and graduate student, Wilson wrote a series of articles for the *North Carolina Presbyterian* that serve as the best window into his religious identity at the time. Wilson considered the questions plaguing American evangelicals following Reconstruction: What is the proper balance between one's private and public expression of Christianity? What role do individual Christians play in the advancement of Christianity? To what extent should Christianity adapt to modern changes in social, political, and economic life or remain steadfast in light of change? Wilson answered these questions in six essays that form the basis of historians' understanding of his Christian identity. Tenuously and, as a result, unevenly, he moved away from the faith of his father. Even as he attempted to apply the principles he learned as a boy, the context in which he lived remade those principles anew.

Rather than settle debates about his theology, Wilson's public essays about his religion point to a young man deciding what Christianity meant to him at a time when the boundaries between liberal and conservative orthodoxies were in flux. Historians and contemporary religious thinkers alike have defined this distinction in American Christianity in a variety of ways. Catherine Brekus and other historians of American religion encourage conceptualizing American "Christianities" as a method for recognizing the complex variations among Christian identities.[32] Historian Martin Marty has used the terms "private" and "public" to separate Protestants according to their preferred locus of religious expression.[33] Many other scholars of American religion attend to divisions by referring to liberal or conservative theologies, denoting the relative embrace or rejection of institutional authority, modernity, or secularism. Neither set of terms quite fits figures like Wilson who lived through a time period in which adherents redefined tradition and their relationship to it. The cultural shifts following Reconstruction did not create strict divisions along any singular cultural marker.

Regardless of the terminology used, the Wilson family—spanning three generations from Reverend Joseph Wilson to Woodrow Wilson's youngest daughter Eleanor—purposefully engaged with the world, or secular, public life, as a necessary component of their religious identity. Based on the example of two patriarchs—Reverend Wilson and Reverend Woodrow—multiple generations of the Wilson family openly read secular scholarship alongside scripture, and they attempted to apply their interpretation of the gospel message to the time and place in which they lived. In much the same way that he crossed sectional divides, Wilson negotiated sectarian divides by focusing on what united white American Protestants. Following in his uncle's steps, Wilson sought to carry tradition forward in light of new circumstances; he wanted to adapt tradition to modern life, neither rejecting nor fully embracing history. Although he relied upon the progressive Christian discourse of the time, Wilson continued to emphasize paternal leadership and white superiority as necessary for proper social order. As guidelines naturalized in American culture, these two principles—and men like Wilson who benefited from them—belonged to neither the North nor the South, liberal nor conservative ideologies.

Using the pen name "Twiwood" in his first published essay, "Work-Day Religion," Wilson cautioned fellow Christians against being too complacent in their ritual practice.[34] Supported by his father's editorial position and his mother's editing skills, Wilson expressed frustration with Christians who confined their religion to certain spheres of life. "Christian character," he asserted, "is perfected only by that work-day religion—a religion pervading every act—which is carried with us into every walk of life and made our one stay and hope."[35] Wilson contended that one's Christianity is not experienced on a limited basis, such as a momentous conversion, but rather must be cultivated day by day, through everyday discipline in all walks of life. Closing with 2 Thessalonians 3:13, "be not weary in well doing," Wilson drew upon his childhood lessons to encourage readers to develop their Christian character continually throughout daily life.[36] In the process, he began to articulate what he perceived to be authentic, or "true," forms of Christianity.

Wilson advanced an early example of a message social gospel theologian Washington Gladden would popularize ten years later in *Applied Christianity*.[37] Gladden, a Congregationalist minister, exhorted Christians to refashion their understanding of the Gospel away from the salvation of individual souls and toward "social salvation." With social salvation, society as a whole, rather than individuals alone, reaps divine rewards and punishments. These "social" Christians came to believe that biblical principles applied to individuals *and* society. They believed that society could be saved, and that salvation would occur through selfless individual service to others. In his essays, Wilson asserted that Christianity did not belong within the church alone but should be expressed publicly and in service to others. Those public performances of Christianity were to be modeled after the ethics of Jesus: "The most humble and insignificant services of the household and the business office, should be attended to with the feeling that we are serving God in the conscientious discharge of them . . . [because] we are moulding [*sic*] ourselves more and more after the perfect image of Christ."[38] In this view, Wilson followed the growing trend in which Christians relocated the locus of their faith from cultivating church membership in insular Christian communities to employing their ideologies outside the church building.

For Wilson, this model for Christianity was a natural progression of the Christian thought and practice he learned in his parents' home. It made sense to him because he had watched his father model God's divine order through paternal care for his family, his community, and his country. Growing up in the South, service meant caring for those inferior to you—a position that assumed his own elitism and maintained social hierarchies based on white male leadership. At the same time, Wilson participated in the growing trend that rejected a strict divide between church activities and other aspects of public life. Whether one viewed this position as sacralizing secular life or secularizing sacred space depends on how one defined the boundaries of religion and public life.

In his published essays, Wilson demonstrated how he purposefully, albeit selectively, constructed some boundaries and not others. Though he flattened the differences between private and public life, Wilson drew the line at substituting experience for scripture. In his religious essay "The Bible," Wilson proclaimed, "The radical error among modern christians [sic] is neglect of the Word of God." Of particular concern for Wilson was the growing tendency for Christians "to seek for religious information and instruction" from sources outside of scripture, especially "lesser streams of knowledge."[39] This fear was widespread. As historians Candy Gunther Brown and John Lardas Modern have shown, evangelicals developed a thriving print culture through the early to mid-nineteenth century. Their self-made boundaries between the sacred and secular blurred in the process.[40] Wilson enjoyed participating in this print culture, but he also remained uneasy about its potential to displace the Bible's importance to Americans. Like thousands of other evangelicals, Wilson welcomed the overwhelming presence of evangelicalism in American culture, but he also sought to maintain its purity. Wilson was comfortable enjoying popular literature so long as it did not detract from following God's will, a line in the sands of secularism difficult to explain and more difficult to locate.

Even as he actively participated in it, Wilson criticized these "modernist" trends as they developed within American Protestantism.[41] He grew particularly frustrated with coreligionists who abandoned tradition in favor of materialistic, individualistic, and overly sympathetic sentiments. In his essay "The Positive in Religion," Wilson lamented the "growing tendency" to shy away from "the harsh tenets and severe doctrines of our fathers" and replace them with "more loving principles and milder teachings."[42] Men who resist the popular urge "to put our own interpretations upon the teachings of the Bible, and simply to follow the dictates each of his own conscience," Wilson asserted, are not subscribing to "'harsh' Christianity" but maintaining the proper image of

Christ who was both "lovely and gentle" and an enforcer of God's law.[43] Refusing to accept the premise that obedience and punishment might be aspects in opposition to a God of love, Wilson upheld an older Presbyterian view of the Gospel.[44] As a Calvinist, Wilson did not question the righteousness of God's sovereignty over humanity; yet he was increasingly enticed by modernity and the individual's authority in interpreting scripture. Wilson's essays encapsulated the developing antagonisms within American evangelicalism at the end of the nineteenth century: to what extent can Christianity be adapted to the modern world without losing sight of biblical revelation?

Although he never mentioned his position directly, Wilson's writings at Princeton provide insight into his eschatology.[45] Wilson, like many liberal-trending Protestants of his time, did not understand the biblical millennium as an event transcending human agency. Rather than wait, as a premillennialist, for the conditions necessary to bring about the millennium (because humans do not possess the agency necessary to sway God's will), postmillennialists preferred to create the conditions necessary for Christ's return (believing, in contrast, that human action could induce God's plan for the universe).[46] For instance, in a short essay titled "Christ's Army," Wilson described humanity (with unusual flare) as "divided into two great armies. The field of battle is the world." On this battlefield stood God's chosen people, led by Christ and "immediately behind the great Captain of Salvation come the veteran regiments of the soldiers of the cross with steady tread, their feet shod with the preparation of the Gospel of Peace, girt about with truth, their breast-plates of righteousness glittering beneath the bright rays of their Master's love, each one grasping the sword of the Spirit."[47] This cosmic picture led Wilson to assert both the need for pious Christians to battle for the Lord in their daily lives and the assurance of victory in such battles through Christ's return. More deeply, in this depiction of a supernatural battle in which believers serve as soldiers for God, Wilson presumed that humans actively contributed to God's will.

His placement in American Christianity, as a result, cannot fall along a strict linear spectrum of liberal and conservative. His position on eschatology, for example, resists a conservative label because he valued human progress and perfectability. At the same time, though, identifying him as a liberal does not usually encompass his expectations for biblical prophesies to occur in time. In this phase of his life, Wilson expressed his Christian identity along a matrix of progressive, socially minded liberal Protestantism and a more individual, piety-minded orthodoxy. With his pulse on the emergent modernism of American Protestantism, Wilson wrote about the need to adapt the Gospel message, individual character, and the church to reflect changes to modern life. Coupled with his family's acceptance of biblical criticism and a broad, continual education, his opinions in these essays constitute the most basic tenets of liberal Protestantism at the end of the nineteenth century: a self-conscious and continuous adaption of one's Christianity to contemporary life. Coming from a southern Presbyterian family, however, Wilson moderated these adaptations by grounding them firmly in traditional Calvinist concepts. This tactic was favored among Calvinist religious leaders who supported social Christianity, such as Gladden and Walter Rauschenbusch. Given southern Presbyterians' traditional reliance upon a Calvinist interpretation of scripture, it is not surprising that Wilson would also anchor innovations in what he considered tried-and-true orthodoxy.

In spite of appearing traditional, Wilson, like all social Christians, directed his religious identity toward public service. He participated in a movement that relied upon Christians engaging with the state to reform laws pertaining to public life. In his "A Christian Statesman" essay, Wilson reminded his readers that "in the Bible a saving faith in Christ is represented as an ornament and help to the business man; an unfailing aid to the soldier who is fighting in a just cause . . . and above all, as the first requisite for a statesman, upon whom rests so heavy a responsibility, both to God and man."[48] Wilson's ideal civil servant, like a Christian worker in any other field, must first pass a test of proper Christian living. Once elected, Wilson mused, a Christian Statesman would not fall prey to partisanship because he would fear divine judgment.[49] Above all else, Wilson concluded, "let his faith be in Christ his Savior, let his truth be truth which is in accordance with the Bible's standard, and let his whole conversation and life be such as becomes a Christian, and, therefore, a gentleman."[50] Christianity, in other words, informs proper statecraft. Wilson refashioned the southern evangelical model of his boyhood home into a modern Christianity specifically designed for civil servants who, through their position in office, would both model proper conduct and fortify their own piety.

As Wilson mused on Christianity in America, Reconstruction's end was beginning. Immigration began to have a noticeable effect on the nation's population. Laborers, African Americans, immigrants, and socially conscious middle-class white Americans decried the abuses of laissez-faire capitalism. Americans across social, political, and religious spectrums expressed their ideal goals for society. White social Christians set their sights on remaking America in their image, knowing that their ideal might never be achieved but insisting that they must work toward a more perfect world anyway. Over the next five decades, utopian Christian novels written by Edward Bellamy, Charles Sheldon, and Bruce Barton (as well as many others) flew off the shelves as Americans imagined their ideals made manifest. Their efforts varied as temperance pledges, Sabbath observance laws, and "uplift" agencies contributed to a new wave of progressive reform.[51] Wilson, too, was awash in the sea of Christian social reform.

Religion and the State

By the 1880s, after he had graduated from Princeton, Wilson stopped writing about Christianity specifically; instead, he began to concentrate on synthesizing American history and democracy. It would be a mistake to view Wilson's essays on Christian living only as religious writings. Since Wilson did not think of religion as separate from public life, it would be more appropriate to consider these essays as a part of his conception of society and the public good. Wilson supported the separation of church and state, but his ideas of separating his religion and his politics were another matter entirely. Like the education he received at home, his essays were not about knowing or saying the proper words but about constructing and nurturing one's sense of self in society. Wilson's public record on Christianity was part of the development of his Christian identity and also a part of his more general consideration of paternal service, whiteness, and what it meant to be American. By writing, he participated in a larger public discourse rooted in reshaping American culture. Wilson's increasingly liberal approach to Protestantism, particularly his emphasis on individual interpretive authority, postmillennial activism, and the need to adapt Christianity to modern life, related to the development of his political ideals.

This synthesis began when Wilson was a graduate student in political science at Johns Hopkins University. Among his professors were Herbert Baxter Adams, who founded John Hopkins' School of History and Political Science, and Richard Ely, head of the Department of Political Economy. Between 1885 (the year of his conferral) and the turn of the century, Wilson was his most prolific. He published *Congressional Government*, which also served as his dissertation, *The Study of Administration*, *The State: Elements of Historical and Practical Politics*, *An Old Master and Other Political Essays*, *George Washington*, and the five-volume *A History of the American People*.[52] Even though his subject matter concerned history, politics, and the state, Wilson's thought in this period should not be considered distinct from his earlier publications. Both areas of study relied upon an assumed natural order for society prioritizing white paternal authority in service to inferior others.

As a second-year law student at the University of Virginia, Wilson wrote to the editor of his local paper expressing discontent with an article that praised

Archbishop [later Cardinal] James Gibbons of Baltimore and Bishop Keane of Richmond. Again using a pen name, Wilson objected to the article, which referred to "the two Romish orators [as] models of the truest methods of public speech." In so doing, Wilson contended, the newspaper "incidentally decries the written sermons which are weekly the means of the instruction of thousands from nearly all the Protestant pulpits in the land." "With candid ignorance," he continued, the newspaper then showcased Archbishop Gibbons as (in the words of the original article) "a striking picture of the progress of *Christianity* from its inception until now." Such an interpretation, Wilson alleged, rendered unrecognizable the distinction "between a true history of Christianity and a history of Romish organization" when "any Protestant reader—nay, any intelligent reader" would know the difference.[53]

At first blush this letter seems like an outlier in Wilson's long history of conciliatory speech to an array of religious groups. Once he became president of the United States, Wilson encouraged unity among a variety of religious bodies, urging them to minimize their theological differences. Despite anti-Catholic protests, for instance, he continued to employ Joseph Tumulty, a Catholic who served as his personal secretary and tacit chief of staff.[54] Wilson was even the first president to visit the Vatican while in office. His "Anti-Sham" letter to the editor, then, seems out of character. When Wilson's religious concerns are quarantined from his political interests, it is difficult to see these aspects of Wilson's intellectual development as integrated.[55] Focusing on the end of Wilson's letter, the source of his frustration becomes clearer:

> In giving unqualified endorsement to the views of the Romish prelates, he is helping on the aggressive advances of an organization whose cardinal tenets are openly antagonistic to the principles of free government—an organization which, whenever and wherever it dares, prefers and enforces obedience to its own laws rather than to those of the state—an organization whose avowed object it is to gain ascendancy over all civil authority.

Wilson's problem with the Vatican and Catholic priests had little to do with theological doctrine, the nature of the priesthood, or questions of transubstantiation; on the contrary, Wilson considered Catholicism problematic because he perceived it to support and champion civil governments and systems of power that Wilson found abhorrent.[56]

Approaching religion and politics as separable aspects of one's identity was a common strategy utilized in support of anti-Catholic public policies throughout American history. In a culture dominated by white Protestants, enforcing a boundary between religion and politics often meant limiting Catholicism, or other forms of religion deemed illegitimate, in public life.[57]

According to Wilson, Catholicism and those who supported its public expression threatened the public's *civil* life, not one's individual religious identity. From his parents' instruction through to his graduate training at Johns Hopkins University, Wilson learned that civil governments based their authority on a covenant with their citizens. The people granted their consent to be governed in exchange for the establishment and cultivation of the public good.[58] From this point of view, Protestants feared Catholicism not as a theological competitor but rather as a threat to the foundation of American life—individual liberty upholding the public good. As far as Wilson was concerned, widespread acceptance of Catholic clergy as models for public participation meant condoning an institution that could not encourage American democratic institutions.

White Protestants like Wilson considered this fear warranted. If local newspaper reports commemorating a bishop as a model citizen were any indication, then the public had become more tolerant of everyday Catholic acts. If Catholics increased their presence in everyday public life, the logic went, unsuspecting Protestants would be subtly overwhelmed by a civic cancer.[59] Wilson's letter, for example, closes by admitting, "Probably the editor of the *Star* does not *think,* and every one should be warned against the influence of those who speak without sober forethought."[60] Failure to think, or the inability to think clearly, was precisely the danger the Catholic Church presented to American citizens and their cultivation of a liberal state—at least according to white Protestants like Wilson. From within the American culture Wilson knew, the tightly woven interconnections between religion and politics could not be unraveled. As a product of an elite, educated white Protestant moral establishment, Wilson had little incentive to challenge this cultural authority.

Wilson repeated his point in a similar, second letter. He wrote a response to an editorial that he mistakenly interpreted as a paid advertisement on behalf of religious toleration.[61] Writing again under a pen name, he objected to the newspaper allowing ads to support the Roman Catholic Church because "its strength is used to exalt its power above the civil power, and its influence to unfit its adherents for intelligent or patriotic citizenship." Wilson's letter to the editor speaks both to his views about religious pluralism and to his developing views of the purpose of American democracy. For Wilson, public life could not thrive unless the state was the only sovereign temporal power in citizens' lives. This political supposition was influenced by his own Protestant conception of proper religion, leading him to assume Catholicism to be outside the bounds of "true" religion. Overwhelmingly, many white Protestants like Wilson believed Catholics could not comfortably belong to American public life. This assumption did not apply to church or theological preferences alone but also to his ideas of citizenship. His conception of what it meant to be American only allowed for a Protestant notion of political authority.[62]

Wilson was not unique in his attitudes toward Catholicism. Anti-Catholic discourse was central to the development of both mainstream white Protestantism and American democracy in the nineteenth and early twentieth centuries.[63] His Protestant conception of the state was informed by his upbringing and by classes he took at Princeton University. In Professor Lyman H. Atwater's lectures on civil government, for instance, discussions of papal infallibility, adherence to the Sabbath, and other ostensibly theological issues belonged within expositions of proper government. When Atwater asked Wilson's class if America is a Christian nation, he offered an answer that first required an exposition of human sin, religion, and "true" Christianity. He began by explaining the errors of papal infallibility, a doctrine he considered false because the human mind is fallible. The majority of Americans living "a moral and Christian life," then, did not provide a suitable reason to classify the United States as a Christian nation according to Atwater. Instead, the United States is "a Christian nation in contrast to being a heathen or pagan or atheistic nation" because Protestantism "has moulded our national life[,] institutions [, and] laws."[64] As Wilson learned from his professor, understanding the nature and function of a state requires first understanding the human condition. To understand the human condition, Wilson learned, one must embrace Protestantism as the truest expression of religion and as the moral establishment in American culture, albeit an informal one.[65]

Wilson's lessons as a university student reflected what his teachers considered necessary to cultivate the public good: an understanding of and respect for the individual, civil authority, and public participation that developed through Protestant intellectual life. He had no reason to doubt this view as it confirmed his childhood lessons from his family, and the Supreme Court upheld similar ideas a few years later through cases like *Church of the Holy Trinity v. the United States* (1892). While it may be difficult to imagine a son of the South fitting comfortably in the North, religious institutions in the Reconstruction Era supplied the context necessary to repair the sectional differences that shaped Wilson's childhood. White Protestant notions of patriarchy, service, and statecraft gave Wilson the tools necessary to be both a southern evangelical Democrat and a northern progressive social reformer.

In Service to the Nation

Twenty-four years after he graduated, Wilson became president of his alma mater, Princeton University. In his inaugural address, Wilson wove together the varied strands that united his identity. He promised to build upon the heritage of faith and learning established by the founding fathers of both the university and the nation. The tradition they began, Wilson explained, spanned the "boundaries of thought and action" by relying on "the spirit of religion." That spirit, he declared, gave a man's education "permanent validity" because it included a moral component.[66] Religion informed the best kind of education, the kind that ensured the stability of the common good. For Wilson, it was not any religion, but specifically Protestant Christianity, that "lifted highest" because it freed the mind in ways that could uniquely form the basis of a continually changing yet fortified culture.[67] He knew this because, in his estimation, the United States was the world's best example of such a culture.

Institutions like Princeton produced the most necessary resource to maintain a Protestant moral establishment in America: men ready to serve their country. "Princeton has stood for the nation's service, to produce men and patriots," he declared. Those men were especially patriotic because they were equipped—naturally by God but also through a disciplined ethic of education—to serve others. With an education that drew upon and reinforced a white paternal social order, Wilson explained, "we are here not merely to release the faculties of men for their own use, but also to quicken their social understanding, instruct their consciences, and give them the catholic vision of those who know their just relations to their fellow men."[68] Wilson pledged Princeton to the service of the nation by supplying white men, strengthened by a Protestant ideal of paternal service, who could transform American democracy and move the nation closer to its own ideal:

> It is serving the nation to give men the enlightenments of a general training; it is serving the nation to equip fit men for thorough scientific investigation and for the tasks of exact scholarship, for science and scholarship carry the truth forward from generation to generation and give the certain touch of knowledge to the processes of life.[69]

The first step did not begin with books or buildings but by inculcating students with a disciplined ethic of investing themselves in the progress of society. Progress was not defined as dismantling barriers between social distinctions like race, class, or gender but rather through aligning those distinctions under proper Christian leadership. As the head of Princeton University, Wilson believed he could contribute to the progress of the nation by instilling the Christian values he knew in young elite white men who would likely serve in the nation's most respected offices. He would, however, fulfill this role before his students.

Christianization of America in the World

The State is a universal phenomenon, democracy is a universal truth, and Christianity, its followers believe, is the universal religion.

— REVEREND SAMUEL BATTEN[1]

In the summer of 1912, Ellen Wilson informed a family friend that she expected the Democratic Party to nominate her husband for president. As Democrats rallied around their candidate, Ellen confessed she was "so desperately tired of the whole subject already."[2] Wilson's career was not a responsibility for him alone but one shared with his entire family. Ellen and her daughters had supported Wilson as president of Princeton University and, since 1910, as governor of New Jersey. The nationwide campaign for president had not yet begun, yet they were weary of the spotlight. In the next few months, the Wilson family drew their strength from the thought that they could play an instrumental role in curing what ailed society. Ellen found the perseverance necessary to carry on because it seemed clear her family could be useful to the nation—and possibly even the world. "If God wants to use him so," she told her friend in closing, "He will make straight the path."[3] When Wilson received the Democratic Party's nomination in July, it only confirmed for Ellen that he possessed a God-given responsibility to serve society.

In the next four months, Wilson faced two previous presidents and a popular socialist activist in the race for the presidency. Despite being relatively unknown compared to the other candidates, Wilson showed no signs of timidity on the national stage. Nor did he reveal any sign of anxiety to his family, assuming he felt any anxiety at all. The evening of Election Day, Wilson read literature to his wife and daughters after their family meal, just as he did most other days. His youngest daughter, Eleanor, however, could not contain her emotions as they waited to hear the results. As her sisters listened to their father read out loud, she paced around the house. Together, they all heard Princeton's Nassau Hall bell begin to ring. As it rang "like a thing possessed," the Wilson family knew it meant they would soon be the First Family.[4] With a new path now clear, Ellen's exhaustion had to be repurposed.

As well-wishers crowded on the porch and marched down the street sing-ing Princeton's alma mater, "Old Nassau," Eleanor saw her parents take each other by the hand. Rather than look at each other with joy, the president-elect "looked serious and grave" before he turned to face the crowd. Standing on top of a chair, surrounded by burning torches, Wilson gave his first speech as president-elect. Eleanor witnessed the scene from a second-story window with "a sense of awe, almost of terror." She did not recognize the man before her. She later explained, "He was no longer the man with whom we had lived in warm sweet intimacy—he was no longer my father."[5] She looked upon a man who was "utterly, utterly unfamiliar" because "these people, strangers, had chosen him to be their leader, [and] now claimed him. He belonged to them. I had no part in it. I felt deserted and alone." Momentarily regretting the loss of her father to national politics, Eleanor felt a brief respite when he began to speak. "Tears of relief welled into my eyes," she recalled, because it was the same voice that read and sang to her as a child.[6]

As far as Eleanor was concerned, her father had passed from their loving, private life into another realm—the public and treacherous world of national politics. She suddenly felt as if he was no longer the father of Margaret, Jessie, or Little Nelle; he was no longer Ellen's husband or Reverend Joseph Wilson's son; he was something else entirely. Woodrow Wilson was now the president of the United States. By March of the following year, Wilson's days would be filled with official matters of state. His statements, both inside the White House and outside of it, would represent the United States of America. His every utterance would be interpreted as a matter of public record. As long as he held the nation's highest office, his actions would be judged as a reflection of the U.S. federal government and the American people.

Little Nelle's fears about her father's transformation from private citizen to public servant make explicit a longstanding assumption about politicians: their private life is wholly distinct from their public identity. This under-standing of private and public as separate—and separable—parallels discus-sions of religion and politics. Distinctions between religion and politics, like those of public and private life, are deeply engrained in American culture, yet they are not fixed locations. Little Nelle, Wilson, and contemporary scholars often consider public figures to be set apart from the person they are outside of their office and inside their home. Both sets of distinctions are flexible rep-resentations that change over time and within different contexts. An individ-ual's attempt to separate privately held religious beliefs from a public political action is not an event but rather an ongoing process intended to construct and maintain his or her identity. An individual's public political and religious affiliations—and the relationship between the two—are not final results but a means of identification that is continually constituted and reconstituted in relationship to social circumstances.

Identifying religion as private and politics as public misrepresents the Wilson family's vision for a life of civil service. For Wilson, his religious affiliation called him to political office. Indeed, the paternal service Wilson learned through southern evangelicalism and liberal Protestant social reform animated his career. And yet the Wilson family's view was only one possible interpretation of how religion could shape Wilson's actions as a candidate for public office. From journalists to theologians, members of the American public attempted to locate a line between Wilson's religion and his politics. These kinds of assessments, from the early twentieth century and well beyond it, form competing *representations* of Wilson, many of which present religion and politics as predetermined settings in American culture. Each description, however, demonstrates how Eleanor, Wilson, and American voters actively constructed these cultural concepts. That they so frequently disagreed points to one of the most notable aspects of American culture in the early twentieth century: American Protestants openly sought to redefine the proper boundaries of social life through state-based reform.

Religion in Progressive Politics

In the waning years of the nineteenth century, white Protestants feared that religion—as they knew it—was losing ground as the center of American life. In many ways it was. By the turn of the century, the body politic did not look the same as it once did. Millions of Catholic and Jewish immigrants altered what had once been an overwhelmingly white, Anglo-American, Protestant cultural landscape. African American voters, and in some states women voters as well, disrupted the monopoly white male citizens previously held in elections. Josiah Strong, a Congregationalist minister and an early social gospel advocate, lamented these changes in *Our Country: Its Possible Future and Its Present Crisis*. Using the 1890 census as his guide, Strong described what he saw as the current perils facing the nation, specifically naming immigration, Romanism, Mormonism, intemperance, wealth, and urbanization. In his telling, these perils threatened to displace white Anglo-American Protestants from the heart of American culture. In response, Strong argued, white Protestants needed to renew their missionary and political activity, both at home and abroad.

In Strong's estimation, the future of the world depended upon Anglo-Saxons who, as a race, drew their strength from white English-speaking peoples. He encouraged white middle-class Americans to recognize the urgent need for their service to others. Strong's plea made a telling conflation: what was good for him was good for the nation and even the world; what threatened him threatened all. This anxiety about the nation losing its strength caused white Protestants to create informal alliances across denominational lines. Despite continued parochial and partisan differences among Protestant denominations, they could generally agree that American culture needed reform. Through networks of power and privilege, white middle- and upper-class Protestants assumed the role of cultural custodians, protecting and maintaining an American culture they valued.[7] This was not, however, a particularly inclusive endeavor. White Protestants excluded a variety of other groups interested in reform even as they developed ecumenical faith-based institutions and espoused a nonsectarian message. Distrust of Catholics, Jews, African Americans, and Mormons formed the subtext of many of their efforts to cure society's ills. This set the tone and, at times, legal parameters on what constituted proper American identity.[8] Protestant reformers forged legal precedents, state and federal legislation, and changes to public education that valued religious and racial difference so long as it maintained white Protestant moral and cultural order.

The 1912 presidential election demonstrated the power of this white Protestant consensus through a series of public spectacles. No event drew greater attention than Theodore Roosevelt's defection from the Republican Party. While the world was not "standing at Armageddon" as Roosevelt declared, this election relied upon voters placing political parties within a particular Christian context. Biblical figures and imagery, along with extrabiblical rhetoric, defined campaign events. When Roosevelt announced his candidacy with the newly formed Progressive Party, gospel hymns with war-themed rhetoric permeated the event. The Democratic Party, in contrast, promoted Wilson as a living example of the biblical parable of the Good Samaritan. Even Socialist Party candidate Eugene V. Debs relied upon biblical figures, like Moses and Jesus, to communicate the principles of socialism more effectively to voters. Meanwhile, William Howard Taft, the incumbent and Republican Party candidate, offered a comparatively lackluster message urging voters to avoid "the promise of a millennium" offered by his competitors. Together, the presidential candidates demonstrated the extent to which white, nonsectarian, socially progressive Protestants had established themselves as mainstream American culture.[9]

This four-candidate race and the open discrimination of African American voters poignantly revealed deep divisions within American life.

Throughout the campaign each candidate reinforced a dominant white Protestant culture Strong hoped to maintain. Public rallies and their printed accounts cultivated a political culture that relied upon religious rhetoric to garner voters' support and to sell newspapers. Democrats, Republicans, Progressives, and Socialists drew upon white Protestant social networks and their nonsectarian discourse to shape their candidate's call for reform. The new norm for presidential candidates required an emotional but not overly sentimental description of one's beliefs and values; a knowledge of general biblical lessons without reliance upon specific creeds or scripture; a broadly learned but not elitist intellectualism; a heartfelt motivation for reform but not revolution; and a concern for social problems that balanced individual responsibility and social obligations. Deviance from this acceptable persona garnered unwelcome attention from reporters and political cartoonists who were anxious to tell these stories. Religious affiliation and rhetoric emphasizing faith and progress, then, were several aspects of each candidate's presidential image that political parties calibrated to maximize their appeal.

Wilson experienced this ethos informally and subtly as the public analyzed the Democratic ticket. For instance, once Wilson received his party's nomination, the *New York Times* noted that Wilson and his running mate, Thomas Marshall, were both Presbyterians. The *New York Times* teased both men for being "of the purest blue stocking variety" and "of the Simon-Pure sort" who could recite their catechism. Wilson and Marshall's religious persuasion—as members of a specific denomination with a defined doctrine—was curiously outdated, even for the Progressive Era. The *New York Times* innocuously parodied these sectarian candidates, reporting tongue in cheek that they were "predestined" to win because their "calling and election are almost sure."[10] Presbyterianism—and the assumptions that others could apply to it—could supply a stamp of approval for Wilson's moral character but could not, by itself, attest to Wilson's alignment with the popular religious sentiments of the era. Even though Wilson belonged to a historically evangelical denomination, his Presbyterianism drew attention as a form of partisanship evangelicals tended to avoid. In a cultural climate that valued nonsectarian, plainspoken religious sentiments more than parochial and doctrinal stalwarts, Wilson's faith was initially mocked.

Progressive Party candidate Teddy Roosevelt fared better in capturing newspaper headlines and an evangelical following. One month after Roosevelt had formally cut his ties with Republicans—and on the same day Democrats announced Wilson as their nominee—he accepted Progressives' nomination with a "Confession of Faith." Roosevelt affirmed the new party's foundation

FIGURE 2.1. Theodore Roosevelt attempts to baptize the GOP in "Teddyism" while Taft, Barnes, Lodge, Penrose, Crane, Root, and others intervene. From Udo Keppler, "Salvation Is Free, But It Doesn't Appeal to Him," *Puck* 72, no. 1849 (August 7, 1912), centerfold. Courtesy of the Library of Congress, Prints and Photographs Division, LC-DIG-ppmsca-27865.

upon "eternal principles of righteousness," and its members shared an "endless crusade against wrong":

> To you who strive in a spirit of brotherhood for the betterment of our nation, to you who gird yourselves for this great new fight in the never-ending warfare for the good of humankind I say in closing: We stand at Armageddon and we battle for the Lord.[11]

At the same event, Roosevelt's supporters sang "Battle Hymn of the Republic," "His Truth Is Marching On," and "Onward Christian Soldiers"[12] as a testament to their faith in his message. African American delegate H. O. Maxim led other "Crusaders" in prayer with Psalm 23, a recitation beloved by a variety of denominations.[13] Both the content and structure of Progressive events resembled nonsectarian, nondenominational evangelical revivals.

Roosevelt's biblical imagery and Progressives' devotion to his cause heightened the party's enthusiasm to a fever pitch. Roosevelt seemed to proclaim the reality of Revelation and the imminence of Armageddon.[14] As he did, Roosevelt relied upon an ambiguous theological discourse that avoided specific biblical references and doctrinal creeds. Roosevelt's popularity, especially the favor he curried from the loyalty of liberal Protestants, points to the profound changes that were occurring in American culture during the early twentieth century. Roosevelt's general, nonsectarian Protestantism exuded cultural legitimacy not simply as an acceptable expression of religion in politics but also as the proper form of Christian thought and behavior in American life. Roosevelt's language was identifiably Protestant, yet his theological underpinnings were vague; his presentations were acceptably heartfelt and appropriately emotional for his audience. He was recognizable as a Protestant without being overtly doctrinal or parochial. American Protestants welcomed particular forms of emotional performance in public; Roosevelt and his "bully pulpit" remained the best production to date.

Taft, in contrast, struggled to embody a broadly appealing form of American Christianity. Even though Taft and his supporters tried to stake the incumbent's character in Christian piety, he was overshadowed by both Wilson and Roosevelt. Rather than his faith signaling his good character (as with Wilson) or his constituents' faith pairing well with his rhetoric (as with Roosevelt), Taft had to defend his faith against detractors who claimed he was not truly Christian. Just one year earlier, Taft, a Unitarian, was asked multiple times to denounce his religious tradition and clarify his beliefs against the "libel" of associating with Unitarians.[15] Taft, however, refused to betray Unitarianism and its history as an American tradition. Rather than draw attention to the commonalities he shared with other Christians, Taft asserted his sectarian identity as an important component of his career. He described his denomination as a fitting faith for the nation's capital because Washington, DC, is "a centre for liberal religious thought and education," a place where "a Church typifying broad, liberal, tolerant Christianity" should be at home.[16] This strategy did not sit well with American Christians who preferred parochial differences to remain hidden or charmingly outdated.

Taft relied upon clergy members to defend the legitimacy of his liberal Protestant tradition. Dr. John Wesley Hill, for example, minimized the differences between Unitarianism and other denominations to make his case for Taft's faith. He explained to All Souls Church that President Taft, like many American Christians, supported the notion of a "brotherhood of man" and "fatherhood of God."[17] In other words, Taft believed that humanity was ultimately connected under God's order despite outward differences—a theological position that Roosevelt, Wilson, and most reform-minded Protestants also held. Vouching for the president, Hill insisted that Taft belonged to the less radical "Channing School" of Unitarianism.[18] By referring to Taft as a Channing-Unitarian, Hill contended that he was not so liberal as to reject the divinity of Jesus, as other Unitarians might. This was an important indication that Taft was neither too liberal nor too elite in his education and, therefore, closer to a nonsectarian Protestantism than his affiliation might first suggest.

Hill asserted Taft embodied the principles and practices that all Christians emulate.[19] The attempt backfired, however, because drawing attention to Taft's Unitarianism implied that Taft was out of touch with other American Protestants and, therefore, unfit for office. No matter how much Taft tried to prove that his denominational affiliation supplied him with the necessary piety to rightly perform the duties of president, the public rejected the claim. Americans seemed to value religion in public life so long as it diverted attention away from sectarianism.

The dominant movement behind this nonsectarian Protestant ethos was social Christianity.[20] Rather than a denomination or a single institution, social Christianity encompassed a variety of historical Protestant denominations, parachurch organizations, and liberal theological persuasions.[21] At the heart of this movement was the belief that Christianity is a religion based on social as well as individual salvation, an idea that society as well as individuals could— and should—be saved through the Gospel message. Social Christians believed that individual salvation would be realized in heaven after life, but "social salvation" would be experienced in this lifetime on earth. It would occur through the perfection or Christianization of temporal affairs. Social Christians expected this process to begin, first by recognizing large-scale problems within society, and second, by working to correct or alleviate the systematic injustices that contribute to, or even create, problems for society as a whole.

Self-proclaimed social Christians' definitions of social injustice varied widely. Social ills included an overlapping set of concerns, such as poverty, concentrated wealth, child labor, prostitution, drunkenness, public sanitation, and other injustices that violated their sense of minimal social standards. Some considered race to be a social problem, by which most meant the practice of racial discrimination and not necessarily the existence of race as a category for individual identity. When considered at all, there was little consensus among social Christians, especially with regard to African Americans' experiences of racial prejudice.[22] Social Christians did not agree on whether or not racial difference upheld or eroded the public good. After all, the underlying motivation for reform relied upon appeals like Strong's that assumed the world urgently needed the leadership of one race above all others. Implicit in their concern for society, however, was sympathy for the "downtrodden" and the ways that the present social order affected individuals. Witnessing the rise of laissez-faire capitalism, robber barons, and dangerous working conditions, these socially conscious Christians became increasingly convinced that society—not individuals—was at fault for what they found undesirable in American life, namely drunkenness, extreme disparities in wealth, and an unclean urban life.[23]

Social Christians "applied" the Gospel message to their reform efforts, a process that they referred to as "applied Christianity." Social Christians, however, exerted this impulse unevenly. On the radical end, Christian socialists sought to revolutionize the social and economic order and correct structural problems; on the other end of the spectrum, conservative social Christians concentrated on philanthropy and conversion-oriented faith-based institutional efforts like denominational publications and church-affiliated soup kitchens or orphanages to alleviate specific conditions, like homelessness. The broad swath in between belonged to Christian reformers who turned to state-based civic institutions at all levels of government either as individual social activists or through nonsectarian Protestant volunteer organizations. Their peers to the right accused them of leaving the church for society; their peers to the left accused them of not being revolutionary enough, by working within the system. These state-based social Christians included governing institutions in their conception of Christian mission not as a site in need of reform but as the necessary means through which reform occurred.

By the second decade of the twentieth century, these social Christians had garnered enough support that they no longer found themselves a minority movement. Social Christian ideas dominated reform discourse across a variety of public organizations. In 1912, the Federal Council of Churches of Christ in America (FCC) codified the nonsectarian social Christian message in "A Social Service Catechism." Coauthored by Samuel Z. Batten, Walter Rauschenbusch, Jacob Riis, Graham Taylor, Harry F. Ward, and Charles S. Macfarland, the catechism represented a new orthodoxy within American Protestantism. With the largest coalition of Protestant churches funding its publication, the catechism marked the widespread acceptance of the social gospel as a fundamental component of middle-class Protestant piety and evangelical mission efforts. It cut across denominational boundaries and existed without an institutional home. It was a doctrine especially written for a nonsectarian audience.

Modeled after the "Social Service Catechism" Batten wrote for the Northern Baptist Convention, the catechism begins by defining social service as "the social application of Christian principles" or "that form of effort for man's betterment which seeks to uplift and transform his associated and community life."[24] The "fundamental idea," according to the catechism, is "the kingdom of God, which in the Christian conception of things may mean much more than a human society, but can never mean anything less."[25] In other words, social Christians may associate the kingdom of God with otherworldly supernatural affairs, but they did not do so at the expense of worldly, temporal concerns. As the culmination of three decades of social Christian thought and practice, the catechism explained social service as Christian actions that "relieve distress and need," "discover the causes and conditions" of social problems, and "remove bad cause and conditions." Rather than creating new institutions, the catechism exhorted Christians to use, cooperate with, and marshal existing organizations—"the church, the family, the school, [and] the state—with Christian social service."[26]

Like many social Christian works, the catechism did not provide clearly defined terms or neatly outlined procedures. The authors took a more moderate approach by working inside the status quo rather than overturning it. The publication of the catechism instead marked a newly held Protestant consensus that Christians must actively participate in public life to actualize—through human action—the ideal society, or the kingdom of God on earth. Devotees maintained their denominational affiliations and their formal theological tenants, but their public practice focused on social and political activism aimed at improving society. American Christians continued to disagree about proper interpretations of the Bible, the purpose of Christianity in society, and the source(s) of authority and universal truth. They debated immigration and citizenship, the nature of democracy, and the strengths and weaknesses of capitalism. And yet American Protestants found common ground in the commitment to serve others, a practice that united them all. Social and political activism intersected with religious practice because reforming society was the centerpiece to this shared vision for proper Christian living.

Influential Democrats, especially William Jennings Bryan, recognized that Wilson offered a unique alternative to the other candidates. All candidates preached a message of working toward a brotherhood of mankind, a reformed society that benefitted all while correcting social problems. Wilson appeared as a blessing hidden among the reeds of the Democratic Party because he could do so while building a consensus across partisan divisions. As a southerner, Wilson's commitment to Democrats ran deep. Growing up alongside Reconstruction efforts, he held a longstanding grudge against the Republican Party yet not all Republican policies. As governor of New Jersey, Wilson supported unions and laborers, building a reputation for standing up to established economic trusts and defending the "common man" against the forces of industrialization. His tenure at Princeton demonstrated that he deserved the title of "reformer." With a record of publications and speeches on the importance of service and education, Wilson belonged to a coterie of university men who envisioned education as a wellspring for democracy. He believed the next generation of leaders—young white Protestant men of social privilege—could change the world by contributing their skills, talents, and privileges in service to others. The latest knowledge from the emergent "social sciences" would allow these men to diagnose and treat a variety of social problems. Wilson insisted proper education, with Christian instruction and piety at its core, could regenerate society to form a more perfect union.[27]

Juxtaposed against the rough-and-tumble masculinity of Roosevelt, Wilson could appear weak, bookish, or even less of a man. Democrats attempted to counteract this negative perception by projecting an alternative masculinity. Wilson supporters, for instance, depicted a man who was no stranger to rolling up his sleeves and tackling problems. Far from the out-of-touch professor-turned-politician his opponents painted him to be, Democrats presented Wilson as the candidate who could rescue the nation from the very men who allowed economic problems to take root in American social life. Democrats pictured Wilson as the reformer who stood up for the principles that could make the nation better. As the embodiment of Victorian manhood, Wilson could defend and protect the nation better than its two previous presidents. Wilson was the "man for the job" because he balanced fatherly protection, masculine pride, and Christlike compassion for those less

FIGURE 2.2. Woodrow Wilson, the Good Samaritan, offers the "Consumer" a drink of "Tariff Reform" and applies "Direct Relief" to his wounds. "Roosevelt" and "Taft" walk by without helping. Courtesy of the Library of Congress, Prints and Photographs Division, LC-DIG-ppmsca-27883. From Udo J. Keppler, "The Good Samaritan," *Harper's Weekly* 72, no. 1858 (October 9, 1912), centerfold.

fortunate. *Harper's Weekly* displayed this gendered campaign in color in an array of political cartoons, including one titled "The Good Samaritan." Wilson, the cartoon depicted, recognized the needs of others and acted on their behalf, while the other candidates passed by those in need.[28]

The gendered performances among the presidential candidates not only distinguished men of different political parties but also pointed to an underlying tension among American Protestants: how to bring men back into the fold. Muscular Christianity, a movement parallel to social Christianity, encouraged and developed Christian notions of health and manliness. Aimed particularly (though not exclusively) at men, muscular Christianity urged the cultivation of strong bodies, through both sport and diet, as a vital part of one's piety.[29] Although historians typically cite Roosevelt as the epitome of Progressive Era masculinity, Wilson also represented an important feature of this broader Protestant culture. He applied his healthy Christian body to activities that improved society. This muscular Christian message fit well with the culture of southern masculinity and honor that Wilson knew so well: true gentlemen protected the defenseless and voiceless.

Whether one was a muscular Christian or a social Christian or both, American Protestants looked to Jesus as the moral-ethical ideal of service to others. The Men and Religion Forward Movement, for example, explained that Jesus "worked along both lines of service" because, on the one hand, Jesus "sought to change society by transforming individuals . . . to preserve and illuminate and alter the community" and, on the other, "He strove to establish a new social order of love in which men would be moulded [sic] from birth into sons and daughters of the Most High."[30] Individual and social salvation, then, were not opposing interests but intertwined evangelical missions.[31] Commanded by God, they believed that each Christian must devote his or her life to improving the lives of others.[32] The ethic of service, rather than a specific service endeavor, defined the various impulses social Christians fostered. These efforts, despite being inspired by a particular interpretation of Christian practice, did not necessarily involve religious institutions. Some social Christians found churches limited their ability to serve.[33] In other words, social Christian men needed to apply their Christianity in the streets, in their place of business, and in elected office.

Without mentioning his denominational affiliation or religious practices directly—and keeping his specific theological views private—Wilson conveyed his desire to engage in social service. By expressing ostensibly universal truths, Wilson secured a loyal social Christian following despite the publicity of his denominational affiliation. In doing so, Wilson commanded the social Christian milieu in ways that his opponents could not. This frustrated social Christians who expected Roosevelt to be their natural candidate as the clearly identifiable "progressive." Social gospel minister and novelist Charles Sheldon, for instance, begged fellow minister Lyman Abbott for insight about Roosevelt's stance on temperance. After months of campaigns, Sheldon still could not tell where Roosevelt stood on the social issue.[34] Wilson, in contrast, successfully used his denominational affiliation to demonstrate nonsectarian commitments to public reform. Even Raymond Robins, leader of the Men and Religion Forward Movement and a friend of Roosevelt, admitted that Wilson was "the best nomination for President since I have known public life."[35] The majority of Americans agreed.

Not satisfied with merely electing the right candidate, the FCC sought a guarantee that the president-elect understood his mission in office. Writing to Wilson shortly after his inauguration, the FCC executive board reminded the president that its members voted for a public servant who acted in accord with their social Christian ends. Based on his campaign performances, the council expected this president to follow through on the precepts already outlined in their Social Service Catechism: namely, actively working to construct the kingdom of God on earth. The council informed the president that they, too, would be planning an agenda for the next four years, suggesting that together they could make their shared hope a reality.[36] Three weeks later the president personally replied to Charles Macfarland, the FCC's secretary, acknowledging their shared interests.[37] Their correspondence began an important relationship that spanned two presidential terms and one world war to help reshape American Protestant life in the twentieth century.

Christian Piety and Progress

On the eve of his inauguration, the president-elect received a letter from Felixina Shepherd Baker, Reverend James Woodrow's wife. Aunt Felie sent her best wishes to her nephew, Tommy: "May our Heavenly Father's richest blessings rest upon you. May He protect you from all harm, and may He guide and direct you in all things."[38] These blessings from family members, friends, and numerous citizens arrived by letter and telegraph as Wilson stepped into the nation's highest political office. Even he confessed his supplications to a confidante: "God give me a clear head, good counsellors, and a pure heart."[39] Moving to the 1600 block of Pennsylvania Avenue would not interrupt his family's traditions, but Wilson's presidential papers and private correspondence suggest that religion in his White House was not a profound interior experience. As during his campaign, religion for Wilson was a practical, pragmatic affair that promoted American civic life. It shaped his approach to public policy primarily by regulating his conception of civic duty and public life.

Wilson was not in any sense a religious "seeker." He remained a committed Presbyterian his entire life, never wavering from this self-identification. His name not only appears in church records, but he found value in attending services. Wilson maintained regular church attendance throughout his tenure as president, including while aboard the *George Washington* when he traveled to the Paris Peace Conference. Upon his relocation to Washington, DC, in 1913, Wilson dutifully wrote Reverend James Taylor to request to join the Central Presbyterian Church. Taylor assured the president that he and his family were welcome additions, offering to assign the First Family a pew, even though it was not customary, "so that you may feel perfectly at home in our church."[40] As Taylor hoped, Wilson came to adore Central Presbyterian. He later referred to it as a "dear old-fashioned church such as I used to go to when I was a boy," a sentiment of extreme pride.[41]

Knowing that Wilson attended church gives insights into his Sunday schedule but not necessarily about the significance of those services to his life. In many ways, Central Presbyterian Church provided an escape for Wilson by temporarily removing the president from the demands of national politics. Previous presidents had attended First Presbyterian Church, a house of worship so close to the capitol building that it became known as the "Little White Church under the Hill."[42] Central Presbyterian, however, offered Wilson an opportunity to escape from Congress at least once a week.[43] Geographically and culturally, Central Presbyterian was a different place from First. It was the only southern Presbyterian church in Washington, DC. Even its walls reminded Wilson of boyhood memories, assuring him that he was surrounded by "simple and genuine people" who appeared "indifferent" to Washington's politics.

Wilson did not always attend church to listen to sermons or, even, fellowship among likeminded believers. The letters he wrote to friends and family indicate that he primarily attended for the reprieve it offered from political life.[44] In other words, church provided Wilson with a refuge from the state. Maintaining the Sabbath, then, may have fulfilled religious ritual, but it also provided relief from the demands of office. Wilson confided to his close friend Mary Allen Hulbert that on Sundays he slept until ten o'clock, attended church, wrote letters to family and friends, and took "a little drive in the motor" with friend and personal physician Cary Grayson.[45] This made the Sabbath special, not as a supernatural and holy day but rather as a day set apart for the temporary estrangement from matters of state. He explained the "delightful renewal" he experienced when he could talk to likeminded people, "to those whom I love and respect, whom I understand and who understand me—without explanations of any kind!"[46] Since no explanations were needed on this day, Wilson could "indulge" in "uncharitable reflections on a Sunday," recognizing that he "ought not" but he felt comfortable enough to do so anyway.[47] He could divulge, for example, how he was "trying to handle an impossible president of Mexico"[48] without worrying about repercussions from journalists or other politicians. Private citizens could opine as they saw fit; public leaders could not, except on the Sabbath when public life came to a halt.

In much the same way that he distinguished between Sundays and Mondays, Wilson recognized a difference between his personal opinion as a private citizen and his statements as a public figure. In his first term, Wilson carefully distinguished between his private and public self. For instance, when speaking to the Manhattan Club, Wilson hesitated before answering an audience member's question on military preparedness. A private citizen may be "free to speak his own thoughts and to risk his own opinions in this matter," but he could not. Instead, he spoke "as the trustee and guardian of a nation's rights, charged with the duty of speaking for that nation in matters involving her sovereignty." For Wilson, this distinction between private citizen and public agent was necessary precisely because he held a "solemn obligation" to protect American citizens and maintain "our sacred heritage."[49] Providence bestowed a civic obligation on him, voters had evaluated him worthy, and the public recorded his performance in the annals of history.

As a result, Wilson often felt bound, as a prisoner, to his title and office. For his first Fourth of July weekend as president and the fiftieth anniversary of the battle of Gettysburg, Wilson's family traveled to Cornish, New Hampshire, while he stayed in the White House. Without his family, Wilson lamented the travails of life as president when the office and the person have a difference of opinion.[50] Despite his desire to vacation with his family, he knew he must fulfill the expectations of the nation and stay in the White House during a national holiday. Yet he was torn, writing to Hulbert: "All day long I have been fighting against the weakness and silliness of feeling sorry for myself. I feel more than ever like a prisoner, like a sort of special slave, beguiled by the respect and deference of those about me, but in fact durance vile and splendid."[51] Lacking the sensitivity or, perhaps, the awareness to recognize the less-than-subtle difference between slavery and elected office, Wilson crassly expressed the feeling of a privileged identity divided.

To Wilson, as president, the Fourth represented more than just a family holiday. He knew if he abandoned the White House on this important anniversary of the Civil War, Americans would notice and wonder if his loyalties remained with the South. Even though "old men both in blue and in gray are to be there," Wilson recognized that holding public office required doing what was best for the nation and not himself. Not wanting to disappoint the nation or confuse—dare even lose—his supporters, he did what the office demanded. "Again I clapped my heels together, saluted, and prepared to obey orders, not give them," he explained, adding sardonically at the end of his letter, "Ah, but it's grand being President and running the Government. Advise all your friends to try it."[52] Life in office further reinforced the service ethos Wilson first learned in his southern evangelical home and developed later through social Christian mission.

Wilson carefully crafted his public image as he adjusted to life in the White House. He self-consciously attended to his public persona. Wilson did not quarantine his religious life or his views on Christianity from these considerations but instead calibrated them to maintain the boundaries between church and state that nonsectarian Protestants preferred. When S. Townsend Weaver, a Methodist pastor in Washington, wrote Wilson to inquire about his views on the Sabbath, Wilson first insisted that he valued its observance.[53] Then he elaborated on why he encouraged it: "I am not the least interested in the observance of the Sabbath as a political question. I am deeply interested in it as a social question and as touching the religion and spiritual welfare of the people, not only of this city, but of the whole country."[54] Wilson and others considered maintaining the Sabbath day, in this respect, a wellspring for bolstering a greater public good. If citizens observed the Sabbath, then society reflected moral virtue. Supporting it meant concerning oneself with improving all of society rather than individual self-edification. To support the observance of the Sabbath for political reasons would be a disingenuous form of piety; political support of the Sabbath would be a matter of personal gain. Upholding the Sabbath for social reasons was a more authentic form of religious practice for nonsectarian Protestants because it had society's best interests at heart.

In this vein, religion was not a journey for individuals working toward their salvation nor did it pertain to specific denominations and their membership rolls. Wilson considered the purpose of attending church or adhering to religious institutions and their doctrines to be a civic endeavor, strengthening social bonds over and above any single entity. As far as Dr. Grayson could tell, Wilson viewed Christianity as "socially necessary" because it nurtured a more perfect society. In this respect, the church was necessary because it fostered "a union of individuals seeking not only their own salvation but seeking to follow God through service to mankind."[55] Wilson valued the Presbyterian Church, but the purpose of his Christian practice was not confined to it. This

attitude resonated with Christians across denominational affiliations who
shared a sense that they too followed God's will by serving others.

Those living by this ethos insisted that religious activity should not be contained within the walls of the church.[56] Observing the Sabbath, for instance,
mattered less as a marker of one's piety, because Christian ritual and the performance of it occurred in the home or at work as much as—and at times
even more than—in a church pew. Wilson and others were not bound to a
strict division between church and state, religion and politics, or the religious
and the secular because they actively constructed the new norms that shaped
those concepts.[57] The social implications of one's actions, or the contributions
toward upholding or improving the public good, marked the boundaries of
white American Protestantism. As social Christians' interpretation of proper
Christian living became the established norm for mainstream America, their
agenda for reform—and the assumptions that made it "good" for society—
became increasingly identified with the markers of progress.

Social Christians like Wilson articulated a separation between their political and social motivations while simultaneously espousing a specific denominational affiliation. This practice exemplified the shifting norms for religion
and politics in the early twentieth century. The appropriateness of religious
activism in public space was determined not so much by the absence of religious motivations as by others being able to discern that one had the appropriate civic intent. "Good" religion maintained the normative separation of
public and private action, while "bad" religion violated those norms. These
boundaries were useful to elite white Protestants because they created the
conditions necessary for their social Christianity to thrive.

To Serve God and Man

Even though Wilson belonged to a Presbyterian church and maintained the
Sabbath, he did not experience the fulfillment of God's will while in a house
of worship. His piety and devotion came to fruition instead in the White
House, a civic building dedicated to preserving American nationalism.
Wilson publicly acknowledged the relationship between his civic duties and
religious conscience when he completed one of the major accomplishments
of his first year in office, reforming the protective tariff. The Revenue Act of
1913, or Underwood Tariff Act, reduced the protective tariff to almost half
of the rates set previously in 1909 and introduced a graduated income tax.
Standing in the Oval Office, President Wilson attempted to express his "very
peculiar pleasure" in securing this piece of legislation to approximately fifty
witnesses.[58] Seven months into his first term of office, Wilson proclaimed,

On the Way to the Promised Land.

"And thou shalt smite the rock, and there shall come water out of it, that the people may drink."
—Exodus XVII. 6.

FIGURE 2.3. In "On the Way to the Promised Land," Woodrow Wilson as Moses strikes his staff on the rock of "Campaign Pledges" on the mountain of "Practical Politics" to cause "Currency Reforms" and "Tariff Reform" to flow to businessmen and laborers. From Udo Keppler, "On the Way to the Promised Land," *Puck* 74, no. 1924 (January 14, 1914), centerfold. Courtesy of the Library of Congress, Prints and Photographs Division, LC-DIG-ppmsca-28016.

with noticeable emotion, "We shall go the rest of the journey and sleep at the journey's end like men with a quiet conscience, knowing that we have served our fellow men and have, thereby, tried to serve God."[59] Tax law, of all places, validated Wilson's ethic of Christian service and secured his place in the social gospel reform movement.

Wilson's statement expressed formally what his supporters had suspected throughout the presidential campaign—that Wilson believed he was serving God when he served the American people. In no uncertain terms, Wilson revealed the connection he saw between his faith and his political activism. Wilson understood his policy agenda as a means through which to apply Christian principles to the modern age. By improving the social standing of "the rank and file of the people," Wilson believed he not only created good public policy but he was, first and foremost, following the will of God. Social Christians agreed. This was a matter of restoring honor to national politics and the Democratic Party. As the leader of both, Wilson felt an obligation to "redeem its name and serve the people of the United States."[60] Wilson, who was rarely straightforward, associated his political office—as president and leader of the Democratic Party—with a postmillennial obligation to regenerate society through service to those less fortunate.

Wilson's contemporaries recognized his use of Christian service discourse and saw it as a sign of more changes to come. Christian missionary Charles Ernest Scott, for example, wrote to the president from China to heartily approve of Wilson's action on tariff reform. In the process, Scott offered a unique perspective on American domestic politics. As "a Christian man in a heathen land," Scott explained, he thought Americans "are *hungry* for a President to summon them to heights of *moral* endeavor; hungry to follow a President of vision, who is thoroughly religious with religion applied to life like 'Father Abraham,' whom *the people answered.*" Scott believed this desire to be universally present across all demographics. Even the Republican-dominated Massachusetts, he insisted, wanted a president who gave them a higher calling.[61] Wilson could be that type of president, earning respect from unlikely places, because he set high standards for morality in public life.

Wilson respected the opinions of missionaries like Scott because he wished he could be as useful as they were in advancing Christianity. He envied missionaries because they got their hands dirty, put their lives at risk, and sacrificed their own desires for humanity.[62] Wilson wished he could too. He saw the potential for serving others in his own position but regretted the lack of urgency and devotion present in the work of a minister or a missionary. Within the next two years, however, world events would lead him to change his opinion about the potential of his own role in transforming the world. He would make himself the servant in chief, projecting social Christian ideals on a national level in order to provide a global example of the kingdom of God on earth.

Wilson's insecurities put him in a curious relationship with social Christianity. In moments of self-reflection, he did not believe he contributed to humanity in the same way that clergy members did. Yet Wilson consistently insisted that Christians needed to contribute to the public good in their everyday lives. Individual acts of service, Wilson believed, provided the means necessary to solve social problems. This presents historians with an apparent contradiction, as Wilson encouraged other Christians to do what he could not give himself credit for doing. Having proclaimed in 1913 that he served God and Americans by shepherding legislation, in 1915 he asserted to the FCC that "legislation cannot save society. Legislation cannot even rectify society."[63] Wilson had not so much reversed himself as acknowledged that legislation alone was not enough. Social Christian leaders and legislation at the federal level required appropriate mobilization on the state and local level.

Even in moments of ostensible inconsistency, Wilson reflected the predominant social Christian and nonsectarian impulses of his age. Laws, Wilson explained to the FCC, *reflect* society's current moral fiber; therefore, laws alone cannot be expected to change social norms or to transform the inner attitudes of individuals. When laws precede social transformation or try to initiate cultural rebirth, Wilson reasoned, "most people will not understand it and, if they do understand, they will resent it, and whether they understand it and resent it or not, they will not obey it."[64] Wilson's assertion to FCC members was a correction to the order of operations rather than an objection to the ultimate goal. He cautioned the FCC that their means—using legislation to fulfill millennial expectation—could not produce their desired ends unless they also balanced their efforts with changing the broader culture. Both he and the FCC's members agreed that regenerating society was, as Wilson declared, "the business, primarily, it seems to me, of the Christian."[65]

Wilson's speech to the FCC expressed a sentiment central to social gospel theology. For example, in Walter Rauschenbusch's *Christianity and the Social Crisis*, the social gospel theologian argued, "Any permanent and useful advance in legislation is dependent on the previous creation of moral conviction and custom . . . If the law advances faster than the average moral sense, it becomes inoperative and harmful." Published the same year as the presidential election, *Christianity and the Social Crisis* outlined the role religion should play in society. Like Wilson, Rauschenbusch cautioned against legislating morality; instead, he advocated educational and religious institutions, that is social rather than political entities, as the arbiters of change: "The real advance, therefore, will have to come through those social forces which create and train the sense of right. The religious and education forces in their totality are the real power that runs the cart uphill; the State can merely push a billet of wood under the wheels to keep it from rolling down again."[66] Wilson, Rauschenbusch, and other social Christians agreed that first Christians had to establish a culture that could create the legislation they wanted to see.[67] Attempting the process in reverse would produce both bad legislation and an unnatural order of social change.

These notions of church and the state were complementary instruments for achieving the ultimate goal of the social gospel, the establishment of the kingdom of God on earth. As Rauschenbusch explained succinctly, "The State is the representative of things as they are; the Church is the representative of things as they ought to be."[68] He expected the two to exist in tension, at times even conflict, but progressing together nonetheless. As Rauschenbusch saw it, the relationship between these two entities had been corrupted over time. Christianity—by which Rauschenbusch meant historically, but not exclusively, the Roman Catholic Church—had made itself "the end" object, existing "for her own sake" rather than "a working organization to create the Christian life in individuals and the kingdom of God in human society."[69] The Church's "influence on the State was often a disturbing and disastrous one," Rauschenbusch asserted, when "the Church fought for her own political interests and not for the cause of the people."[70]

Far from the antistatist evangelicals of the late twentieth century, evangelists of the social gospel believed church and state needed to work together for Christian ends. According to Rauschenbusch, the state—its laws and administrative functions—ideally maintained justice.[71] So long as churches competed with the state as the mechanism for moral enforcement, or as Christians avoided civic service, Rauschenbusch argued, the state could not perform its "sacred" function of justice. He explained, "If men conceive of political duties as a high religious service to man and God, the State can be a powerful agent in the bettering of human life."[72] The church, he argued, had the power to rectify the broken relationship between religion and politics by working through the state to regenerate souls and restore society. If the state is anti-Christian or immoral, then in his estimation the church was ultimately responsible.

Any change to public life, social Christians agreed, needed to emerge democratically from laypeople rather than through the dictates of clergy or politicians. Once individual Christians embraced the social gospel they could elect like-minded politicians, then, over time, society could become the kingdom of God on earth. Instantiations of individual and collective transformations would demonstrate not only the real, material force of Christianity in the world but also its ultimate truth. Wilson explained, "The proof of Christianity is written in the biography of the saints, and by the saints I do not mean the technical saints—those whom the church or the world has picked out to label saints, for they are not very numerable—but the people whose lives, whose individual lives, have been transformed by Christianity."[73] Revealing his Calvinist roots, Wilson pointed to individual lay Christians as the "real" evidence of Christianity's claim to "right" religion. Individual Christians applying Christianity in their daily lives was the closest thing to proof of Christian truth.[74]

Wilson, like other elite or middle-class nonsectarian Protestant reformers, wanted to change society from within the existing social structure, not revolutionize or destroy current social hierarchies. His career as a politician reflects this commitment to social salvation. Indeed, Wilson believed, "we hold our Christianity as a private, individual matter, if we think of it at all. Our idea is that we will save ourselves, whereas, in my conception, Christianity was just as much intended to save society as to save the individual."[75] He even considered social salvation, at times, more important than individual salvation because "society creates the atmospheric conditions under which all moral lives are lived, and the atmosphere is more important than the attitude of the individual."[76] Wilson's performance of civic duties was not exclusively a matter of politics or government but a sustained effort to Christianize the culture in which he lived. If he and other social Christians Christianized the United States as they intended, then they assumed Americanizing the world would follow.

A Christianized America in the World

Christian endeavors like Wilson's were commonplace in the early twentieth century. Nonsectarian organizations sought to reform urban life and public education to reflect the moral standards they wished to see in public life. As American Christians expanded their notion of society, missionary societies extended these efforts beyond the borders of the United States. When Wilson reflected on world history and current events, he concluded "that transformation is to be found all over the Christian world and is multiplied and repeated as Christianity gains fresh territory in the heathen world."[77] The gospel message of service to others, he believed, changed the lives of nonbelievers and false believers alike because it alone raised standards of civilization and moral character wherever it was introduced.[78] According to Wilson, no other force commanded as much discipline, self-sacrifice, and unselfishness as Christianity.

Christians belonged to a tradition that upheld "the principles of self-sacrifice and devotion." Christians who truly embodied those values would also fully devote themselves to their nation and the business of the world. According to Wilson, the only thing that came close to the transformative power of Christianity was patriotism. Through service to one's country, as with Christianity, "men will go into the fire of battle and freely give their lives for something greater than themselves."[79] Wilson did not need to legislate or enforce laws that were intended to regenerate society to demonstrate his faith to voters following the social gospel. They could—and did—expect Wilson to be the type of president who had already experienced a transformation and acted accordingly.

Nonsectarian white middle-class Protestants believed this effortlessly, not least of all because Wilson proclaimed it to the churches he visited. At the Maryland Annual Conference of the Methodist Protestant Church, for example, Wilson admitted that, while life as a president may seem "engaged in the things that were temporary and ephemeral," he understood it "had to do with the interests of the human race and with human souls."[80] The U.S. government, like the Christian church, was in the business of matters transcendent, universal, and eternal. Wilson declared beneath those in civil service "lie the eternal principles of justice and of righteousness, which, in my conviction, at any rate, we do not derive from ourselves, but from the same source from which a great church derives its inspiration and authority."[81] While maintaining nonsectarian language, Wilson firmly stood upon a Protestant foundation. The government, under his administration, could be trusted to be acting in accord with Protestant churches like those the Methodist audience would have attended.

Wilson was not speaking in abstract metaphors or idealistic prose. He spoke at a time "when a great cloud of trouble hangs and broods over the greater part of the world." The unique conditions in Europe confirmed that the war was a "contest for some eternal principle of right" that would, at some unnamed future point in time, "enlighten our judgment" if "we can all hold our spirits in readiness to accept the truth when it dawns on us and is revealed to us in the outcome of this titanic struggle."[82] Wilson expected the war in Europe to provide revelation to those wise enough to recognize the message. In order to discern the best course of action, he did not turn to Central Presbyterian Church or scripture for guidance but rather the Oval Office and his own policy agenda to lead the way to an ideal state on earth.

3

Blessed Are the Peacemakers

The greatest problem which faces the world at the present time is not as to whether the Western civilization will conquer the world—that is settled. Its victory is inevitable. The real problem is whether Christianity will conquer civilization.

—SHAILER MATHEWS[1]

In the summer of 1914 the Wilson family's world changed dramatically. European empires had spent the summer months succumbing to war.[2] On June 28, Serbian rebels assassinated the heir to the Austro-Hungarian empire, Archduke Franz Ferdinand, and his wife. One month later, Austria-Hungary declared war on Serbia. By the end of July, Russia, bound by previous diplomatic agreements to protect Serbia, mobilized its armed forces against Austria-Hungary. On August 1, Germany announced its unconditional support of Austria-Hungary and declared war on Russia, causing France to follow through on its agreement to protect Russia. Days later Germany declared war on France and invaded Belgium, leading Great Britain to enter the war. President Wilson, however, was not consumed with these foreign affairs. On August 3, Dr. Grayson informed the Wilson family that the First Lady's death was imminent. In ill health for years, Ellen Wilson was dying from Bright's disease. As the world watched Europe devolve into what would be known as the Great War, the president witnessed his wife slowly lose her life.[3]

Ellen provided a model for her husband to follow years later. She did not let her own condition obscure her sense of duty to serve others. From her deathbed, she inquired about the status of legislation she helped to bring to politicians' attention. On August 6, just days after Great Britain declared war on Germany and the same day that Austria-Hungary declared war on Russia, Congress passed the Alley Dwelling Act of 1914. Ellen, who had been shocked at some of the living conditions in the capital, lobbied for a bill that set minimum standards for housing structures in alleyways. "Mrs. Wilson's Bill" eliminated makeshift shanty structures in alleys, many of which were in predominately African American neighborhoods. This bill did not, however, call for new housing to replace the unlawful ones. When the act went into effect, as many as twelve thousand Washington, DC, residents could no longer live in their homes.[4] With her daughters and her husband at her side, Ellen died as one of the first First Ladies to personally and publicly influence legislation.

Ellen's death hung like a shadow over the president. He wrote to his confidante Mary Ann Hulbert, confessing, "God has stricken me almost beyond what I can bear."[5] Those who worked closely with the president could not avoid his palpable grief. Three months after Ellen's death, Colonel Edward M. House documented what the president confessed to him privately: "He said he was broken in spirit by Mrs. Wilson's death, and was not fit to be President because he did not think straight any longer."[6] Aware of his own state of mind, Wilson admitted to Hulbert that he had not, until now, understood what it meant to have a broken heart. When this happens to someone, he explained, "it just means that he lives by the compulsion of necessity and duty only," leaving him "dead in heart and body."[7] By the second week of August in 1914, Wilson clung to his civic duties because he felt as if they were all he had left.

Wilson described this historic summer in much the same way Thomas Paine described the American Revolution. These were "days that are to try men's souls."[8] It certainly was for him. Between his wife's death and the war, Wilson's private grief became intertwined with public distress. In both his private correspondence and his public statements, Wilson grew less concerned with distinguishing between his roles as private citizen and public servant. He spoke with greater confidence as the embodiment of the nation, welcoming any distraction from his own thoughts. As the war and his grief persisted, Wilson's emphasis on service shifted from an individual serving others to the United States serving the world. In this time of uncertainty, Wilson more pointedly asserted the importance of America's role in global affairs. As the extent of the war became clearer in August 1914, the prospect of determining the postwar peace captured his attention more than military battles. He considered this war an opportunity for the United States to demonstrate its willingness to serve the world through Christian internationalism. Whether the United States was a neutral or belligerent nation, Wilson intended to usher all nations to a new era of human history. Witnessing the president's grief and civil service, Dr. Grayson later explained the Great War as "the public climax of Woodrow Wilson's Christianity."[9]

A Moral Empire

As hostilities intensified in Europe, Wilson insisted upon Americans' neutrality. He did so not as a principled stance against war but as a pragmatic strategy in foreign affairs. If Americans were to hold any significant role in the war, he reasoned, it would be as outsiders to the conflict. This privileged position would afford the United States—and he as the president—greater authority during this time of global uncertainty. Speaking to the Columbus, Ohio, Chamber of Commerce in 1915, Wilson drew attention to this special status for Americans in the world. He challenged local businessmen to leverage their unique position by considering commerce and trade as endeavors taken on behalf of the nation. Individual acts of service to the nation, such as international business partnerships, would build a living testament to the United States for the world to witness.[10] According to Wilson's logic, if American businessmen demonstrated a "spirit of service and achievement" in their capitalist ventures, they would cultivate a global component to American statecraft. Business partners would be like friends sharing a mutually beneficial relationship that could build up a "common kinship of all mankind."[11] This "American spirit," Wilson predicted, "will have its conquest far and wide."

Wilson clarified that he did not mean "conquest" in the traditional military sense. America's triumph would be peaceful because its rise to power would be the result of a "mediating influence" across the world. Rather than take control by force, Americans would come to power through the will of the world. Neutrality was key to fostering this influence because it imbued the United States with an objectivity that European nations lacked. Distance from Europe and European models of governance would give the United States credibility as an arbiter for ultimate international peace. Wilson's vision, however, required cooperation among the federal government, private industry, and American citizens. Once the interests of the state, corporations, and individual citizens were aligned in a common cause, Americans could successfully intervene in world affairs. The resulting cultural intervention, or "spiritual mediation," would reshape the norms and expectations of international society. The world could be transformed through American intervention, in Wilson's estimation, so long as Americans invested themselves in service on behalf of others. Private industry, the state, and religious institutions were all necessary pieces of Wilson's global vision.

Speaking at the annual meeting of the Federal Council of Churches while in Columbus, Ohio, Wilson proclaimed that Americans were uniquely capable of exacting this influence in the world because God bestowed an exceptional purpose on Americans and their nation. For Wilson, the United States had a special mission "to show men the paths of liberty and of mutual serviceability, to lift the common man out of the [current] paths, out of the slough of discouragement and even despair; set his feet upon firm ground."[12] With this civic mission statement, Wilson adeptly echoed several biblical messages without specifically naming any one. His national mission reflected Proverbs 2:20–21, "So you will walk in the way of the good and keep to the paths of the righteous. For the upright will inhabit the land, and those with integrity will remain in it," as well as Psalm 26:12, "But as for me, I shall walk in my integrity; redeem me, and be gracious to me. My foot stands on level ground; in the great assembly I will bless the Lord." He also alluded to Isaiah 26:7, "The path of the righteous is level; you make level the way of the righteous," and Isaiah 42:16, regarding God's chosen people, "I will turn the darkness before them into light, the rough places into level ground." Even though Wilson and his audience were well versed in biblical exegesis, they both benefited from Wilson's ambiguous biblical allusions. His purposefully imprecise language allowed the audience to focus on a shared general dependence on scripture when biblical hermeneutics may have drawn attention to competing interpretations.

Wilson's plainspoken association of American culture and biblical ideas resonated with the nonsectarian atmosphere of the FCC. The FCC had built its own mission around a white middle-class social gospel, an interpretation of the New Testament emphasizing an ethic of service modeled after Jesus and an eschatology of social salvation realized through an ideal state on earth. Understanding his audience well, Wilson declared the United States was a successful nation because it was the "embodiment of a great ideal of unselfish citizenship."[13] Speaking the FCC's language of service, Wilson gave credit where the FCC was sure credit was due—Christians who modeled their lives on Jesus's moral example of service to those in need. FCC general secretary Charles Macfarland considered Wilson's speech a "great help" to their endeavors, one that Wilson could never fully know.[14] The feeling was mutual. The president, sitting and speaking side by side with these church leaders, infused their message and initiatives with greater public significance. At the same time, the FCC reinforced Wilson's political clout by lending the support of the largest ecumenical network of Protestant churches. The FCC, as a faith-based organization, and Wilson, as the figurehead for the state, both espoused a message of the importance of service to hold society together. It seemed entirely natural to Macfarland, then, when he offered the FCC's "moral and spiritual help" to the president as hostilities increased in Europe.[15] Preparing to travel to Europe on his own goodwill mission, Macfarland hoped to foster cooperation across transnational Christian networks.[16] Since Wilson acted in service to the FCC, he was willing to return the favor alongside or even through the office of the presidency.

Despite the nation's official neutrality, many American Christians felt connected to the plight of their European brethren.[17] They were invested in the war as a matter of transnational, global, and, at times, supernatural significance.[18] American Christians, like their European counterparts, made sense of the war through biblical interpretation, often describing hostilities through biblical allegory and Christian history. They cast their enemies in terms of good and evil, justified the use of violence as holy or as a crusade, and relied upon apocalyptic rhetoric to explain the import of current events.[19] Europe's war did not incite a crisis of conscience for white middle-class proponents of the social gospel. Their support of U.S. neutrality was not a moral stance toward war, but a strategic position in a time of war. The outbreak of hostilities merely confirmed their sense of urgency to reform society and transform the world through social salvation. In this light, "preparedness" efforts did not contradict neutrality because both were efforts to establish the kingdom of God on earth.

Few Americans needed to be convinced that violence could be a force for good in the world.[20] The Civil War and the Spanish American War loomed over many Americans as a reminder that some wars are necessary to save souls and protect national interests and integrity. While some vocal Americans wanted to stand on the side of peace and pacifism, their declarations often depended upon a statement regarding *this* war and not *all* wars.[21] For example, Washington Gladden, a Congregational minister and theologian of the social gospel, used the war as evidence of what he believed to be the current crisis within Christianity. War was not the result of the presence of evil in the world but rather the expected result when fellow Christians failed to apply the gospel message to society.[22] Gladden was a pacifist who did not condone armed conflict; yet he considered Europe's war to be a consequence of Christians refusing to recognize the need to "save" society as well as individuals' souls. Accepting this message as the truer interpretation of the New Testament, social Christians, even pacifists like Gladden, discerned this war as an *opportunity* for American Christians to help create a more perfect world. He exhorted fellow Christians to recognize this war as part of the continuous battle to establish the eschaton of a perfected society, what social Christians called "the kingdom of God on earth."

From this perspective, Christians could be implicated in the progress and peril of social trends. Wars, such as the Crusades, the Thirty Years' War, and the present conflict, could be part of a march toward progress, eventually leading to the millennium, if Christians responded appropriately. With Wilson echoing social gospel figures like Gladden, the FCC made the most of the moment. As early as 1915, Protestant missionary and educator Sidney Gulick and the FCC Commission on Peace and Arbitration called upon its members to recognize the war as a Christian crusade for a new age. The immediate war might have been in Europe, but the United States was one of the many battlefields of a larger Christian mission.[23] Gulick, as a result, hoped to rally

American Christians under the banner of a "war against war."[24] With a hundred thousand pastors in the organization's membership, he expected a swift mobilization effort in which "ballots shall be our bullets. Legislatures must be captured. Golden Rule laws must be enacted by national and state legislatures."[25] Private and public resources worked together for a common cause of electing men who legislated shared Christian ideals. The motivation and mobilization may have been faith based, but the goal remained influencing the state through Christian statecraft. The business of the FCC and its members focused on making America a Christianized nation, an example for the world to follow.

In this mobilization effort, the state and its institutions, as well as individuals, had to apply the gospel message to its conduct. Just as "true" Christians followed in Jesus's footsteps, social Christians reasoned, "true" Christian *nations* should emulate Jesus through their laws and policies. White middle-class social Christians built their approach to domestic and international politics around the assumption that great individuals and nations must place the needs of others over their own self-interest.[26] This assumption that individuals *and* nations could both imitate Jesus would prove to be fodder for critics of social Christianity, especially in the postwar period. In equal measure from the left and the right, social Christians would be accused of misunderstanding Christianity and statecraft. During the war, however, numerous policymakers joined social Christians in conflating their expectations for individuals and nations.

Rather than invest in faith-based community initiatives, social Christians pursued state-based reforms. Specific laws contributed to a larger eschatological vision of bringing the state under the influence of evangelical mission efforts. As early as 1909, Gladden appealed to the American Board of Commissioners for Foreign Missions to dedicate their evangelical efforts toward building the nation rather than the church. Since Christians have focused exclusively on the spiritual aspects of their millennial hopes, he explained, "it is difficult for us to realize that it was to a political rather than an ecclesiastical organization that all these promises are addressed."[27] In other words, the key to realizing the kingdom of God on earth was the conversion, or Christianizing, of the nation-state, and not converting individuals or increasing the membership of any church. Europe's war presented an opportunity for these social Christians to fulfill their Christian mission of "saving" global society by restoring what they considered the fulfillment of the New Testament and the Protestant Reformation.

White middle-class social Christians looked to the United States with millennial expectation as *the* nation that could be converted into the ideal society on earth, a global conversion experience. To social Christians, this responsibility fell to the United States above all other nations because of its exceptional genesis in world history as "the child of religious liberty."[28] This idea has its own history and legendary status in popular American culture.[29] The myth of religious freedom was so central to social Christian narratives of millennial progress that they saw the fate of American democracy and the fate of Christianity as intertwined.[30] They held a teleological commitment to advancing America's democracy in order to fulfill their evangelical mission.

The same year that Wilson predicted America's "peaceful conquest," Macfarland published his own expectation of America's "moral conquest" in *Christian Service and the Modern World.* In a time when the world was in need, many reformers stepped back from their agitation efforts to aid European counterparts or rededicate energy to humanitarian aid. Social Christians like Macfarland, however, were not among those reformers. He exhorted Christians to recognize the exceptional nature of America and its eventual global triumph.[31] To be a light to the world, he explained, partisans must work together to reach consensus, justice must come from those in power aiding those without power, and all must feel compelled to contribute to the whole. The violence and horror of the war did not cause social Christians to reconsider their message and retreat from publishing pamphlets or lobbying for new legislation. Instead, they capitalized on the moment.

The war and Wilson motivated the FCC to declare what it considered the "true" Christian message. If the New Testament was based upon the idea that there was no difference between Jew or Gentile, circumcised and uncircumcised, social Christians reasoned, then "God knows nothing about races or nations."[32] When each nation can see beyond their own nationalism to "shake off the hypnotism of statecraft and diplomacy, and witness the brotherhood of the world," then humanity can experience social salvation.[33] Macfarland and the FCC viewed the war as a catalyst for establishing this brotherhood, embracing the chance to give the world a new kind of education. Children would learn "the principles of a world-wide brotherhood that breaks down every social and political barrier that has been created by the failing vision of man."[34] They would then learn their social gospel. Dislocating cultural distinctions like race, ethnicity, nationalism, and sectarianism was a necessary first step before the FCC, or Wilson, could reorient social life around their own transcendent Christian ideal.[35]

This impulse to establish a global brotherhood took on a new meaning during the war, but it had begun decades earlier. Congregational minister and *Outlook* editor Lyman Abbott, for instance, articulated this central tenet to social Christianity in 1901. In *The Rights of Man,* he explained that the purpose of the Gospel was to establish a brotherhood "founded neither on consanguinity, nor race, nor congeniality in character, nor agreement in opinion." Temporal social distinctions, like race, ethnicity, or nationality, ultimately did not matter, he argued, because "whether they are Caucasian, Indian, Chinaman, or African, whether wise or foolish, cultivated or uncultivated, good or bad, therefore all men are brethren; they are brethren because one is their Father which is in heaven."[36] Gender and sexuality went unmentioned in Abbott's exposition, remaining remarkably authoritative through their unmarked presence. This sort of social order, known as a brotherhood of man under a fatherhood of God, was not only an abstract religious principle but also a political ideal.

For Abbott, the New Testament provided the ideal blueprint for the nation-state. Jesus supplied the moral and political philosophies necessary for democracy by folding politics under the purview of his ministry.[37] He gave an example for all Christians to follow, through "revival and reconstruction," uniting humanity together under God and reconstituting society in God's kingdom. Abbott liked to point out that Jesus taught his disciples to pray "Thy Kingdom come thy will be done in *earth* as it is in heaven," as a sign that being Christian was not a choice between living for this world or a world to come.[38] With this emphasis on "earth" alongside "heaven," Abbott understood Jesus's ministry as emphasizing the need for a human effort to establish a perfected *state* on earth. With this understanding of Jesus and the Gospel message, Abbott considered government—particularly democratic forms of government—"a profound religious faith."[39] From his perspective, the establishment, maintenance, and advancement of democracy was intimately connected to Christianity.

By dedicating one's life to it, the individual Christian fulfilled his or her evangelical mission and reflected biblical truth. This Christian democracy, however, departed from Enlightenment-inspired political thought. Abbott's Christian notion of democracy did *not* attempt to make all men equals in society. Abbott stated his position quite plainly, arguing, "Jesus Christ never taught, by even remote implication, the natural equality of men; on the contrary, he recognized explicitly that some men are greater than others." *Biblical* equality instead was based on the notion that "he that is greatest among you shall be your servant." In his view of the Gospels, Abbott explained, Jesus did not remove social inequalities but gave them new purpose.[40] For a nation to be properly Christian, then, it must do the same. Since all "brothers" are not equal, he reasoned, this biblical democracy did not make all citizens equals. Abbott followed this interpretation of Christianity by adhering to a social order in which superior citizens served inferior ones.

In many ways, the United States seemed to be the best expression of this Christian approach to democracy. Americans upheld a national story and a global tradition that had encouraged a legal framework for slavery, among other social and cultural inequalities, like class and gender. In Abbott's view of American democracy, these structural, social, and political inequalities made the United States a great nation. His discourse of Christian service relied upon a theology that preferred white Anglo-American Protestant men as the naturally superior "brother" who served all others under the Father-hood of God; it simultaneously insisted upon equality, freedom, and democracy as the ultimate goals of humanity; and it encouraged the former as the means to realizing the latter. This kind of society presumed that some citizens would be strong and others weak. It required certain citizens to be their brother's keeper. Social Christians like Abbott asserted it was the ideal form of democracy and, as a result, a fulfillment of Christian eschatology.[41] An ethos of service based on the strong caring for the weak provided the foundation upon which this ideal Christian democracy could be built. It provided the social cohesion necessary for a form of racial and international unity intended to discriminate.

Tropes of redemption and rebirth saturated American popular culture at the turn of the twentieth century.[42] Elite white social Christians began imploring fellow Christians to reconsider the nature and purpose of Christianity after Reconstruction, and their mobilization efforts continued through the Great War. In this period, the social gospel reached the height of its popularity.[43] The Great War did not introduce these concepts to American Christians, but it did offer the possibility of extending American Protestant influence beyond U.S. borders and into international law. Social Christians' hope of establishing the kingdom of God on earth proved more resilient, not more fragile, as Europe divided between Allied and Central Powers. News accounts about the war confirmed what social Christians already believed to be true: global Christianity in its current form was failing, and the United States had to revive it for the sake of the world.[44] They reaffirmed their faith and nationalism together as they attempted to Christianize the state. They considered a Christianized America, a powerful nation serving in the world according to the moral principles of Jesus, as the best means for fulfilling the ultimate goal of the church.

War in Peace

After five months of mourning the loss of the First Lady, the president still found no pleasures in life, yet he remained certain of God's design. On a Sunday afternoon car ride in January 1915, Wilson debated the veracity of the morning's sermon with White House guests. They considered the minister's response to the statement "God was behind everything and working out his own plan." Without hesitation, Wilson argued the affirmative. "*My* life would not be worth living," he asserted, "if it were not for the driving purpose of religion, for *faith*, pure and simple. I have seen all my life the arguments against it without ever having been moved by them." Amazed at his certainty, his guests pressed further, convinced he must have had "a religious Sturm and Drang period." "No, never for a moment have I had one doubt about my religious beliefs," he professed. "There are people who *believe* only so far as they *understand*," but he considered those people "presumptuous" as they used "their understanding as the standard of the universe."[45] He insisted he was not one of those people. He believed beyond, or perhaps even in spite of, what he understood.

By March 1915, Wilson was certain of more than his faith alone. At first sight of Edith Bolling Galt, the president was sure he was in love. Galt, an affluent and independent widow living in Washington, DC, shared Virginia roots with Wilson. She, much like his daughters and late wife, found the president charming and was captivated by his quick wit and storytelling.[46] Their courtship was relatively quick—five months after Ellen's death and one year before the next general election—but it invigorated them both. They married in December 1915, eight months after they first met, in a private ceremony in Edith's townhome. A combination of her respect for the Oval Office and an insistence upon their privacy led Edith to dismiss any attempt to have a ceremony at the White House. True to their nonsectarian Protestantism, the happy couple held a dual service, with an Episcopalian and Presbyterian minister to represent each of their denominations. There is no indication Wilson attempted to persuade Edith to change her denominational affiliation, though it is unlikely she would even have considered. He was completely smitten with his new helpmate: "Her unconscious interpretation of faith and duty make all the way clear; her power to comprehend makes work and thought alike easier and more near to what it seeks."[47]

With Edith now at his side, Wilson faced the world with renewed vigor. In June 1916, Senator Ollie James, chairman of the Democratic Party Convention, formally notified President Wilson of his nomination for reelection to the presidency. On behalf of the party, he called Wilson "for service to America and mankind" and named eighteen acts illustrating Wilson's demonstration of this duty thus far: "A service that has given justice to all men upon free and equal terms; a service that has restored taxation to its historical and constitutional function"; and, finally, "a service whose victories for the freedom of the seas, the rights of neutral life, the protection of American citizens

FIGURE 3.1. Woodrow Wilson at Shadow Lawn, where he was notified of his nomination as the Demo-cratic Party's presidential candidate for the 1916 election. Courtesy of the Library of Congress, Prints and Photograph Division, George Grantham Bain Collection, LC-B2-3966-8.

and American rights stands resplendent in the world's international law and in the earth's diplomacy."[48] The crowd listened quietly until James declared, "I can hear the Master say to Wilson, 'Blessed are the peacemakers, for they shall be called the children of God.'"[49] The crowd then roared. Wilson's great-est service to Americans was not sending their sons into battle in defense of the nation. He kept the United States out of war while also making the world recognize the right—and the might—of America in the world.

To celebrate, a band played "My Country 'Tis of Thee," quickly followed by "The Star-Spangled Banner." Yet no one could hear the music. The del-egates cheered for twenty-one continuous minutes, drowning out all other sounds.[50] James returned to his praise of Wilson, including him in the "trin-ity" of American heroes, along with George Washington and Abraham Lin-coln. He reiterated the image "of Christ on the battlefield giving to Woodrow Wilson the reward of the peacemaker" and insisting that, regardless of party lines, all should agree he represented every American citizen.[51] The implica-tion was clear, as the *New York Times* reported: a vote for Wilson was a vote in favor of "the hand that might write the peace treaty of the world."[52] Even in 1916, while the United States was a neutral nation witnessing Europe's con-flict, the potential role for Wilson and the United States in the world was coming into focus. Democrats galvanized American expectations of Wilson leading the world to the peace that was bound to follow war.

When Wilson accepted his party's nomination, he emphasized the basis of his policy on neutrality. "To stand aloof from the politics of Europe" was one reason he explained, but not the only one. Since the United States was not party to any of the treaties that tethered European nations to one another, Americans had no obligation to fight. At the same time, however, Americans had a duty "to prevent, if it were possible, the indefinite extension of the fires of hate and desolation kindled by that terrible conflict." Rather than fuel the flames of war, Wilson believed the United States should remain neutral "to serve mankind by reserving our strength and our resources for the anxious and difficult days of restoration and healing which must follow, when peace will have to build its house anew."[53] Wilson maintained neutrality through the 1916 election not because he wanted to avoid foreign entanglements entirely; he insisted upon neutrality as a strategy for gaining a lucrative position for determining the outcomes of the war. For the time being, war was not an efficient use of U.S. resources. The popular refrain of the campaign, "he kept us out of war," implied a moral opposition to fighting, but Wilson conceived of neutrality as a means of *peacemaking*, not pacifism.

In January 1917, after a majority of the nation reelected him by one of the smallest margins in U.S. history, Wilson reiterated the importance of a postwar peace through his "Peace without Victory" speech. Interested in the permanency of the future postwar peace, Wilson declared his commitment to establishing a treaty based on the equality of rights:

> Right must be based upon the common strength, not upon the individual strength, of the nations upon whose concert peace will depend. Equality of territory or of resources there of course cannot be; nor any other sort of equality not gained in the ordinary peaceful and legitimate development of the peoples themselves. But no one asks or expects anything more than an equality of rights. Mankind is looking now for freedom of life, not for equipoises of power.[54]

Similar to his approach to American society, Wilson did not call for the end of hierarchical power relations among nations. Instead, he asked his audience to recognize that all nations, like all individuals, possessed the same inherent rights: "That every people should be left free to determine its own polity, its own way of development—unhindered, unthreatened, unafraid, the little along with the great and powerful." Following the tradition of social Christians before him, Wilson conflated his particular, and peculiarly, white American Protestant view of equality with a universally applicable truth. The distance between his specific religious ideologies and universal truisms was lost on Wilson as he associated them with "American" values. The majority of the nation, however slim, stood behind him on election day, equating American political ideals with the greater good of humanity.

Social Christian ministers reveled in the president's declaration. George Herron, chair of applied Christianity at Grinnell College, praised the president for understanding what social Christians had been asserting for decades. Writing to coreligionists in Europe, Herron insisted that Wilson was pivotal to the social Christian cause because "he divinely schemes to bring it about that America . . . shall become as a colossal apostle, shepherding the world into the kingdom of God."[55] Written after Wilson's reelection, this essay and others were compiled for American readers as *Woodrow Wilson and the World's Peace*, a volume of essays speculating on the president's ultimate design. Based on the "Peace without Victory" speech, Herron predicted Wilson would be mocked as utopian by critics and claimed as pacifist by peace organizations, just like other social Christians. He felt he had a common cause in Wilson's vision. By focusing on peace settlements instead of preparing for war, Herron discerned, Wilson understood that the Great War was to be won in a peaceful conquest of hearts and minds. He determined the Senate had "*become as God's burning altar*" with Wilson's words "*encircling the world as a divine visitation*."[56] He fully expected Capitol Hill to be the site for the Christianization of the world, where social salvation would be actualized.

Not everyone shared Herron's enthusiasm. The "Peace without Victory" speech gave congressmen and public figures like Theodore Roosevelt opportunities to criticize the president for avoiding military preparedness and attempting to broker peace negotiations prematurely. Wilson's speech only reinforced Roosevelt's critique that the commander in chief was putting the cart before the horse. All those tensions subsided, though, when Wilson appeared before Congress on April 2, 1917, to deliver his War Address. Reading a message he crafted in seclusion earlier in the day, Wilson received the hearty approval of Congress. After three years of neutrality, the president urged Congress to support American military intervention in Europe. Wilson assured Congress, the American public, and the world that "we have no selfish ends to serve. We desire no conquest, no dominion. We seek no indemnities for ourselves, no material compensation for the sacrifices we shall freely make. We are but one of the champions of the rights of mankind."[57] Wilson explained that the United States could no longer remain neutral when "autocratic governments backed by organized force" prevent peoples from being free and the world from being peaceful. Wilson asked Congress to declare war not because the United States wanted to fight but because "the world must be made safe for democracy." With this declaration and widespread support from the public, Wilson directed the nation toward war and a new vision for international engagement.

Wilson closed his speech by reiterating the reason why the United States was called to enter this war—to fight "for democracy, for the right of those who submit to authority to have a voice in their own governments, for the rights and liberties of small nations, for a universal dominion of right by such a concert of free peoples as shall bring peace and safety to all nations and make the world itself at last free." Americans were willing to sacrifice themselves for others to have the freedoms that they enjoyed. To this final thought he added, "God helping her [the United States], she can do no other."[58] Echoing the words of Martin Luther, Wilson viewed the United States as compelled to wield the sword of the spirit with a clear conscience. Wilson's message called Christians to serve in this war not merely by calling upon God but rather by emphasizing democracy, the consent of the governed, and protecting small nations. For social Christians in particular, these were the markers of a perfected state. Advancing American democracy abroad was the fulfillment of their sense of Christian mission more so than any public appeal for God's guidance. Without explicitly invoking doctrine, Wilson articulated a war message that reflected Americans' general interest in serving those in need while also drawing upon a specific social gospel ethic.

Congress responded in good faith. The Senate debated and approved the war measure within two days, on April 4. On April 6, after two more days of debate, the house conducted its roll call. After hours of passionate speeches from pacifists and a poignant declaration against war from the first congresswoman, Jeanette Rankin, the house also declared war. On Good Friday 1917, the United States formally entered the Great War. In the course of the next month, the president received correspondence from Allied nations overjoyed with Congress's decision. British ambassador Sir Cecil Arthur Spring Rice enclosed portions of Isaiah 62 in his letter of support: "The spirit of the Lord God is upon me: because the Lord hath anointed me to preach good tidings unto the meek: he hath sent me to bind up the brokenhearted: to proclaim liberty to the captives: to proclaim the acceptable year of the Lord, and the day of vengeance of our God: to comfort all that mourn." Similarly, Robert Seymour Bridges, the British poet laureate, penned a poem "To the United States of America" following America's entry in the Great War. Calling upon his "Brothers in Blood," Bridges expressed a shared international cause as "we pledged to win the Rights of Man" and "transform the earth" through a "League of Peace," which he believed to be Wilson's "high call to work the world's salvation."[59]

Wilson's rhetoric of service and world peace appealed broadly to most Americans, but it had a special appeal to white nonsectarian middle-class Protestants who indeed had "the world's salvation" in mind. The FCC led Protestant mobilization efforts by organizing a conference in Washington, DC, to coordinate its own strategy for the war.[60] With representatives from the Home Missions Council, The Foreign Missions Conference of North America, The Federation of Women's Boards of Foreign Missions of the United States, The Council of Women for Home Missions, The International Committee of the Young Men's Christian Association, The National Board of the Young Women's Christian Association, The American Bible Society, and the World Alliance for Promoting International Friendship Through Churches, as well as the more than one hundred thousand clergy members who belonged to the FCC, the meeting demonstrated American Protestantism's overwhelming support for the president.

In word and deed, social Christian organizations and their members contributed to the war effort to lay the groundwork for a postwar peace created in their own image. Considering American democracy to be "the expression of Christianity," the FCC mobilized its members to "continuously create in the people the determination that this war shall end in nothing less than a constructive peace that may be the beginning of a world democracy."[61] More ardent ministers, like Rev. Austen K. DeBlois of the First Baptist Church in Boston, declared the Great War to be "America's Holy War," "a grand campaign for righteousness" in which "America seeks to rebuild the moral order of the world."[62] The FCC, YMCA, and thousands of liberal Protestant ministers waited with expectation to see if the president could, as they hoped, establish a new world order. The hope and burden of their millennial expectations rested upon Wilson's shoulders.

Support for the war appeared broad and overwhelming among religious Americans, regardless of their institutional affiliations. Jewish Americans coordinated war efforts under the Jewish Welfare Board and other affiliated societies.[63] Similarly, Catholic churches organized under the National Catholic War Council, with Cardinal James Gibbons leading the war effort "to the end that the great and holy cause of liberty may triumph."[64] Taking note, the Wilson administration enlisted the help of faith-based organizations in creating and distributing propaganda materials, recruiting soldiers, and raising money for the war effort.[65] FCC ministers, for example, asked their male adherents to pledge their bodies to the nation; they asked mothers to report the number of young men living in their neighborhood to make sure no one of age would be missed.[66] The Wilson administration relied upon religious institutions and religiously affiliated organizations to increase revenue for the war through wildly successful "Liberty Bond Sundays." The level of cooperation Protestant churches gave to the federal government during the war led one historian to declare that the separation of church and state became a "pleasant fiction" during the war.[67] For social gospel evangelists, however, separation was never a reality nor a goal.

As had been the case for previous wars, many churches supported U.S. entry into the Great War even before President Wilson asked Congress to make this declaration of war. The president's actions reflected the wartime perspective many white Protestant ministers had advocated since 1914. Wilson, in other words, followed the example of prominent American Protestant ministers. Evangelist Billy Sunday, for example, encouraged revivalists to hate German militants as an outward expression of their patriotism and religious devotion. Sunday, a proponent of "muscular" Christianity, did not allow any middle ground on the war issue: "In these days all are patriots or traitors, to your country and the cause of Jesus Christ."[68] Sunday, who delivered a sermon at a New York City revival just days after Congress had declared war, did not need to make major adjustments to his standard revival sermon once the United States joined the war effort. The title, "God's Grenadiers," and the militant imagery remained unchanged. His primary revision was adding an announcement giving directions to the nearest enlistment agency, one just across the street from the revival.[69]

Wilson's endorsement of military action found favor not only from the Baseball Evangelist but also from Theodore Roosevelt. Since 1915, Roosevelt had openly critiqued President Wilson for neglecting to prepare the nation for war when Americans' safety on the sea first became compromised. After a German U-boat sank the *Lusitania*, Roosevelt decried Americans who continued to resist U.S. entry to the war. He accused pacifists of not being real men, of lacking patriotism, and of being unchristian in their response to acts of aggression. This trinity of failures led Roosevelt to attempt to smoke out the "foes" of what he began to call "100-percent Americanism." Roosevelt identified two types of citizens who corroded the United States from within. First, he named "the professional pacifist" who belonged to a peace movement "financed by certain big capitalists." Without a doubt, Roosevelt singled out Andrew Carnegie and his Church Peace Union (CPU), an organization the well-known philanthropist began a year earlier with a personal donation of two million dollars. Second, Roosevelt drew attention to the "parlor pacifist, the white-handed or sissy type of pacifist"—almost certainly a reference to William Jennings Bryan, who had resigned his position as secretary of state as a result of Wilson's decision to begin preparing the military for war.[70] According to Roosevelt, these "peace at any costs" pacifists eroded "the virile virtues" of civilization by betraying their country and all of humanity.[71] A proper American man, Roosevelt claimed, would support military prepara- tion and stand ready to fight for his nation. Failure to do so turned a man away from his duty to country, a type of betrayal so great that it violated God's order for the world.

Roosevelt objected not so much to *peace* per se but to the *type of* peace that Carnegie and Bryan advocated. In the wake of the Spanish-American War, many Americans—including Carnegie and FCC ministers—second- guessed their encouragement of the use of violence to "civilize" the Phil- ippines. Carnegie believed the United States had crossed the line between serving the needs of others through military strength and gaining territory by conquest. He directly confronted Christian supporters of the war, chal- lenging ministers to live up to the "truisms" that "all founders of religions" upheld, namely the Golden Rule.[72] After a decade of activism, when Ameri- cans clamored for preparedness, the nonpartisan, nonsectarian CPU contin- ued to insist that *all* war is barbaric and that churches should lead the call to eradicate it as a justifiable means to any political end.

Roosevelt vehemently rejected this perspective. For Roosevelt, righteous- ness—or better still, a righteous justice—towered above mere peace. Not all peace proposals were created equally; only those in which "right" defeated "wrong" were worthwhile. Roosevelt's distinctions divided otherwise like- minded progressives. Peace and antiwar advocate Jane Addams, who had campaigned for the Progressive Party in 1912, admitted that "peace was for- ever a bone of contention" between her and Roosevelt.[73] The two had plenty of friendly debates over the topic; in Addams's words, their disagreements were "never acrimonious" but "sometimes hilarious," as Roosevelt was fond of pointing out "that it was he who had received the Nobel Peace Prize and that he had therefore been internationally recognized as the American authority on the subject."[74] Although Addams would earn her own Nobel Peace Prize in 1931, public opinion rested with Roosevelt in 1917.

An overwhelming number of Americans considered themselves members of the peace movement in the United States, but this movement was far from monolithic. It included divergent positions from Roosevelt and Sunday, who both accepted violence as a potentially necessary means for peace, to Addams and Carnegie, who each considered all forms of violence as unnecessary and uncivilized. As a result, by 1917, the most popular peace organization was one that encompassed both of these positions. The League to Enforce Peace (LEP), with former U.S. president William Howard Taft as its first president, brought together pacifism and preparedness as equally possible means for achieving a *lasting* peace.[75] The LEP counted among its members diverse public figures who tended to disagree about how best to achieve world peace, such as Abbott Lawrence Lowell, Rabbi Stephen Wise, James Cardinal Gibbons, and Washington Gladden. The LEP was nevertheless able to create a consensus among these competing peace efforts because, from its inception in 1915, it proposed a "league of nations" as a feasible organization that could ensure stability in international affairs.[76]

Peace in War

General support for peace and a broad support for an international body that governed, or at least monitored, global affairs gave the impression that Americans were united in their expectations about the postwar world. All Americans—many pacifists included—seemed to "enlist" in the cause of war after April 1917 because they were optimistic about the good America could contribute to the Allies. The so-called crusading American spirit and vocal sentiments of its inevitable triumph effectively silenced Americans who belonged to historically pacifist denominations or transnational faith communities with ties to the Central Powers. Baptist minister and social gospel theologian Walter Rauschenbusch, for example, refused to endorse U.S. intervention, much to the ire of his colleagues at Rochester Theological Seminary. Germany was his parents' country of origin and the fount from which his own social gospel theology grew. As much as President Wilson and others said they held the German government, and not the German people, responsible for the Great War, Rauschenbusch refused to condone actions that increased the suffering of German citizens. Before April 1917, he publicly condemned the idea of preparedness on biblical grounds. Self-interest consumed modern life, he argued, from individual salvation, which he considered an inherently selfish form of piety, to preparedness, a military strategy that exalted one's own nation above all others. After April 1917, Rauschenbusch followed his colleagues' advice, censoring his beliefs for the sake of the public reputation of his employer and the German immigrants he shepherded through the pulpit.[77] After all, he could at least agree that individuals and nations—especially Americans and the United States—should commit themselves to Christian acts of service that placed the needs of society above individual desires. This was the ideological basis for his book, *A Theology for the Social Gospel*, published the same year the United States entered the war.

Like Rauschenbusch, most Americans responded favorably to the obligation to serve even if they objected to *the* Great War or *a* war generally. Wilson, for the sake of both expediency and ideology, focused on this duty. He rooted his controversial endorsement of conscription within this sense of civic responsibility, what he referred to as "a universal obligation to serve."[78] Wilson assumed all male citizens had an equal stake in preserving the nation even though all did not benefit equally from citizenship. On national registration day on June 5, 1917, when all men between the ages of twenty-one and thirty-one were required to register for military duty, Wilson reiterated the importance of the Selective Service Act. While attending a reunion of confederate veterans in Washington, DC, Wilson proclaimed that young men around America were registering, as the former confederate soldiers did, "as evidence of this great idea, that in a democracy the duty to serve and the privilege to serve falls upon all alike."[79] For Wilson, proper masculinity would be reflected in the man who registered, because "deeper than the volunteer spirit is the spirit of obligation."[80] Wilson insisted that this spirit rests deep in men's souls and, with tragic irony, proclaimed all men should be "ready to be summoned to the duty of supporting the great government under which we live."[81]

When Wilson called upon able-bodied men to sacrifice themselves, a religious and legal compulsion motivated him and other American men.[82] Even though historically pacifist denominations, like the Society of Friends, did not waver in their abhorrence of war, they too contributed to their country and the war effort.[83] Wilson's insistence upon service brought disparate portions of American society together, in part because civic responsibility provided public recognition for citizens outside of the mainstream white Anglo-American Protestant norm. Supporting Wilson's war aims afforded a type of civic privilege not enjoyed by all Americans. For instance, many Catholic churches, some of which had German-immigrant parishioners, supported America's involvement in the war to demonstrate their loyalty to America and put to rest Protestant stereotypes alleging Catholics could only pledge allegiance to the Vatican. Catholic mobilization efforts were not driven by the millennialism expressed by their Protestant counterparts, but parishoners were nonetheless motivated by the president's call to serve. Priests and laypeople alike displayed their patriotism by enlisting and participating in war bond drives to demonstrate their loyalty to the nation and their expectation of equal treatment following the war.

Similarly, African Americans pledged their support for the war effort at the encouragement of black churches and civil rights leaders as a part of the continued movement to gain equal civil rights. African American clergy urged their congregants to participate and exhorted the president to take note. John Milton Waldron, pastor of Shiloh Baptist Church in Washington, DC, wrote to the president after Congress declared war to request that the president consider making a public statement about race relations now that the country was at war. African Americans were "enthusiastic" and "earnest" in their support of Wilson, the Democratic Party, and the United States, Waldron explained, but assurance of their equal and fair treatment during the war would be welcome.[84] Waldron invited the president to make a public statement of support in person at his church. He wanted to serve his country and work alongside the president "in the King's business," but he knew African American soldiers would need some sort of guarantee of protection if they were to be treated fairly in their service to the nation.[85]

Wilson gave African Americans plenty of reasons to ask directly, as Waldron did, if Wilson would support them as much as they would support—and had supported—him. By 1917, Wilson had demonstrated to African Americans that the "new freedom" he campaigned on in 1912 did not extend to all. In his first term, President Wilson reversed the integration policies in civil service offices, returning them to segregated workspaces. He created an official color line in federal government positions where previous administrations had not (and in some cases had actively worked to integrate).[86] Having lost the support of African American leaders like W. E. B. Du Bois and received harsh criticism from William Trotter (who, at one point, was escorted out of the White House for decrying the president's hypocrisy in person), Wilson no longer stood on sure footing when it came to African American voters.

Perhaps because of this shaky standing, or perhaps because he had the power to do so, Wilson replied to Waldron in a brief message: "Your letter was the first notice I had that many of the members of the colored race were not enthusiastic in their support of the Government in this crisis."[87] Wilson neither accepted nor declined the invitation to speak at Shiloh Baptist; yet he made the stakes clear. Potential critiques of the president could be perceived as, at best, an unpatriotic refusal to support the country and, at worst, treason. Waldron, however, understood the tenuousness of race relations better than the president. He and other African American men knew that the war brought their masculinity, citizenship, religious devotion, and claim to an American identity under fire. It also meant that World War I presented an opportunity to challenge racial stereotypes by upholding gender, religious, and civic obligations.[88]

Three months after this exchange, race riots began to break out across the United States. Considering the riots a state and local matter, Wilson remained silent on the issue through most of the summer of 1917. By August, however, martial law was declared in Houston after African American soldiers and a white mob, including both local white police officers and armed white civilians, fought in the streets. Despite Du Bois's proclamation, "If this is our country, this is our war," white citizens did not agree that African Americans stood on equal ground. Even though he issued a public condemnation of the tragic events, Wilson was among those who considered African American soldiers in the wrong, alleging in a private meeting that they "want the whole sidewalk."[89] For Wilson, maintaining order at home, especially a social hierarchy based upon "natural" divisions within society, was necessary for maintaining democracy. For race reform activists, the order that Wilson enforced undermined the pronouncements he made about the American spirit and its exceptional role in the world. As a result, African American soldiers became, for white and black Americans alike, a powerful symbol upon which the ability of the United States to spread democracy turned.[90]

To twentieth-century eyes, the incongruity between Wilson's commitment to advancing democracy abroad and restraining it at home seems to be, as one historian put it, a "failure of moral conscience."[91] Wilson's Presbyterian childhood taught him that all people were equal in the eyes of God, but it also taught him that God created both masters and slaves who were equal in their sin, salvation, and access to God's grace but not equals in society on earth. To the Wilson family, social stratification based on distinctions of race, class, and gender was not counter to the spirit of democracy but rather an integral part of it by providential design. His effort to spread democracy, then, was an enterprise qualified by a particular *type* of democracy, born in America and made more perfect through the "civilizing" force of his Christianity. The disparity between Wilson's notion of democracy and the state of social equality in the United States was obvious to those who did not benefit from his vision. After the passage of the Espionage Act of 1917 and Sedition Act in 1918, African Americans, along with labor, women's suffrage, and peace activists, found themselves in an increasingly dangerous position, as their dissent could be prosecuted. Many experienced the consequences of these laws, either formally through fines and prison sentences or informally through public derision and even mob violence.

With the legal and social stakes high, expressing dissent exacted a handsome price. Those who objected to war as a matter of conscience, however, struggled to remain quiet.[92] When ardent pacifists spoke out, they became exposed targets. They faced potential legal consequences for denouncing a president during a time of war and social consequences for violating social norms many Americans believed to be a natural, religious duty to support their country. In October 1917, for example, news spread that three California ministers—Robert Whitaker, Floyd Hardin, and Harold Storey—were planning to host a meeting for fellow Christian pacifists in Pasadena, California. Famed evangelist Billy Sunday publicly rebuked the men, saying, "The Christian Pacifists ought to be treated as Frank Little was treated at Butte. Let the coroner attend to the rest of the job."[93] Little, a union organizer and member of the Industrial Workers of the World, was lynched a month earlier after expressing his disdain for the war effort. He died in Butte, Montana, at the hands of vigilantes while attempting to organize a miners' strike. A few days after Sunday's statement, the Christian pacifists he compared to Little were "mobbed and hounded," arrested by police as they recited Psalm 23.[94]

According to the National Civil Liberties Bureau, which took up the Christian pacifists' cause, the Home Guards of Pasadena, who served under the direction of the governor, forcibly removed the ministers from the private residence in which they met. Outside the home a crowd of women, children, and civilian men cheered. Once the removal of participants was complete, onlookers sang "My Country 'Tis of Thee."[95] Charged with unlawful assembly, refusing to disperse, and disturbing the peace, these pacifist Christian ministers found no friends among a jury of nine women and three men. Judge White made clear the kind of crimes these men committed, explaining in his ruling, "Duty to country is a duty of conscience, a duty to God. For country exists by natural divine right. . . . The religion of patriotism was not sufficiently considered by you three defendants, and yet it is this religion which gives to country its majesty and to patriotism its sacredness and force." To make an example out of this case, he added that Pasadena would not "harbor" disloyal citizens "who preach antagonism to the president of the United States in his holy desire to protect our people from the brutality of a nation that has not been equaled since the crucifixion of Christ, the Saviour of mankind."[96] The American public charged these pacifists, and other dissenters like them, on several counts: posing as a religious group while "teaching no dogma of faith," disturbing the perceived natural order of God and country (indeed, God *then* nationalism), and disabusing themselves of loyalty to their commander in chief. Sincerely held individual beliefs held no legal authority over religion in America.

Given the potential consequences, many other pacifists kept their protests to themselves. Dissent still persisted, but in limited forms as citizens were arrested, assaulted, or lynched for their views. The National Civil Liberties Union attempted to draw attention to the plight of religious groups challenging the war and the president, alleging "the problem of the Christian pacifists is the measure of her [the nation's] faith in democracy as well as of her belief in freedom of religion."[97] In this environment, where there was a greater incentive to support the war, it is difficult to recognize significant distinctions within the war effort. All supporters were not full champions for the cause. Complicating the categorizations, those who agreed with or benefited from Wilson's war aims often conflated their own ambitions for universal truths. Wilson too was guilty of this rhetorical sleight of hand. Grayson later explained, "He was not a reformer in the usual sense of the word, but he was the champion of humanity. He was not an extreme enthusiast about any legislation designed to make the individual better. He conceived that this was the work of the Holy Spirit."[98] Wilson and his elite white social Christian coterie believed this war could usher in a new world order fashioned after what he believed to be true and universal Christian principles. No one seemed to have the power to disagree.

4

New World Order

The stage is set, the destiny disclosed. It has come about by no plan of our conceiving, but by the hand of God who led us into this way. We cannot turn back. We can only go forward, with lifted eyes and freshened spirit, to follow the vision. It was of this that we dreamed at our birth. America shall in truth show the way. The light streams upon the path ahead, and nowhere else.

—WOODROW WILSON[1]

When the United States Congress declared war in April 1917, Edith Benham breathed a sigh of relief. Benham, as the White House social secretary, was responsible for maintaining the president's—and therefore the nation's—neutrality at all White House events. Serving at the pleasure of the president, she had to carefully place ambassadors and other international representatives around a dinner table without exacerbating tensions between nations. More often than not, she had to plan state affairs in such a way that representatives from conflicting nations never occupied the same room at the same time.[2] That was, of course, when state social affairs could be conducted at all. With the rest of the world at war, it was not appropriate for the White House to flaunt frivolity. Neutrality was a complicated business for heads of state, corporate interests, and social secretaries alike. With the official declaration of war, Benham's responsibilities came into clearer view, seating arrangements fell into place, and dinners could be planned without the fear of undue international conflict. More importantly for Benham, those around Washington looked forward to social events again.[3] War, ironically, meant the capital's socialites could once again enjoy life.

Benham was not the only person who felt a clearer focus as a result of the United States' entry into the war. From former presidents Theodore Roosevelt and William Howard Taft to the clergy of the FCC, many elite white Christians believed that the United States could better serve the world as a nation at war rather than as a neutral one. Armed and fighting, American soldiers could demonstrate the "true" spirit of Christian service and, eventually, the redeeming promise of American democracy.[4] President Wilson similarly embraced the war as an opportunity to advance a Christianized democracy in which the powerful cared for the powerless across the world. Wilson revealed his saturation in the social gospel movement through the practicalities of peace negotiations.

For Wilson, U.S. engagement with belligerent nations, during both neutrality and war, followed a single purpose—to ensure the kind of postwar peace that improved global civilization. The best civilizing force in the world, in his estimation, was the social Christian ethic of service based on Jesus's ministry and exemplified through U.S. democracy. Wilson's conviction inspired him to assert the value of "small" nations as equal to that of "great" nations and the duty of those superior nations to care for the inferior ones. As a necessary first step toward both of these goals, he insisted upon the importance of national sovereignty, especially for each nation's people to determine their own government. In public speeches and diplomatic correspondence, he also emphasized the need for free trade and open seas and to make international agreements in public view as an extension of his core vision. People all over the world—from leaders across Europe to citizens in Armenia, Japan, and Russia—recognized that Wilson based his statesmanship on his interpretation of Christianity. As a result, the archbishop of Canterbury, Pope Benedict XV, and lay Christians around the world appealed to Wilson to strike the appropriate Christian tone at the Paris Peace Conference.

Wilson's reputation as a Christian statesman was widespread, but, in many ways, it was misunderstood. His insistence upon establishing a league of nations, along with his design for it, developed from his teleological understanding of scripture and U.S. history. U.S. leadership in assembling a grand partnership of nations, especially one replacing European imperialism and colonialism, fulfilled Wilson's notion of America's purpose in the world. His foreign policy, much like his domestic agenda, prioritized the establishment of a nonsectarian moral structure for governance over forging partisan alliances or fully addressing temporary territorial concerns. He considered his approach to the League of Nations as religious and Christian, but not necessarily for the reasons observers expected. Wilson was unrelenting in this overarching mission, which put him at odds with other Christian internationalists who wanted him to include "God" within the Covenant of the League of Nations. To their dismay, he concentrated on the word made flesh, rather than the word alone.

The World Made New

In his approach to both neutrality and to war, Wilson kept peace in mind. Even though the means changed from 1914 to 1917, Wilson consistently described the United States as in service to the world, a champion of mankind.

He openly referred to the United States as the most likely candidate to usher the world to peace, with he as its chief negotiator. From the beginning of the Great War, Wilson regarded the United States as a special participant because its purpose transcended the interests of any one nation. Drawing upon white Protestant moralisms, he based his version of American exceptionalism upon a teleological interpretation of U.S. and world history in which the U.S. government, formed by the consent of the people, served as the culmination of Christian progress. In this way, Wilson believed, American democracy stood as a testament to God's order and represented the progressive unfolding of God's will. It was not perfect, but citizens could adapt and improve it over time. Democracy in the United States, then, continually developed through the will of the people, a will he firmly believed flowed naturally from the wellspring of providential design. Under this logic, American democracy thrived precisely because it transformed gradually as a result of its citizens' moral development, a process accelerated through Christian mission to move the nation closer to social salvation. Wilson continually affirmed this position at public appearances around the United States, in speeches to Congress, and in private correspondence with world leaders.

The president's tendency to articulate the United States' role over and above other nations in this way caused tensions with the Allies once the United States formally entered the war. England and France, in particular, wanted an ally in their fight against Germany rather than an international partner that sought to remake the world. The Allies desperately needed reinforcements, both able-bodied men and munitions, and they remained concerned with both practicalities. While the arrival of U.S. troops and supplies certainly fulfilled these needs, U.S. involvement also shifted the Allies' war objectives. When Wilson asked Congress to declare war, he did not contradict his earlier pronouncements about the role of the United States in the war. He maintained the principle concepts outlined in January 1917 through his "Peace without Victory" speech. The *purpose* of U.S. involvement remained the same—to ensure a permanent peace built upon a global order that valued the "consent of the governed" and "supported a partnership of democratic nations." What a formal declaration of war did change was the import of Wilson's vision. These statements became more than the platitudes of an isolated national leader. By April, they were legitimated war objectives shaping the terms for peace.[5]

While Wilson considered his proposed peace an ideal goal for all peoples, he had a particular vision in mind. His universalizing and often ambiguous discourse allowed Christians to reach consensus on the notion of peace without completely agreeing on any one interpretation. For example, Pope

Benedict XV shared the president's interest in a "peace without victory." He implored belligerent nations to settle the conflict according to the status quo prior to the war and to commit to future disarmament and arbitration.[6] Benedict saw an opportunity to establish a Christian basis for peace in Wilson's message.[7] Their conceptions of satisfying a "Christian" peace differed considerably. Benedict, and lay Catholics around the world, wanted the Roman Catholic Church to arbitrate peace negotiations as a neutral party who could imbue any potential treaties with religious significance. Historically, the Church had experience in such a position and, with the world at war, Benedict considered this a moment to potentially restore the Holy See's role in world affairs. The Church, however, also had a recent history of existing outside of international negotiations, and many European states found no reason to break this trend.

While Benedict offered a plausible interpretation of a "peace without victory," this was not the one Wilson sought. The Pope and the president were two world leaders shaped by Christianity. They shared several policy positions, such as seeking a reduction in arms and a restructuring of international engagement; however, Wilson considered their political agency to derive from significantly different sources of authority. After some debate within the administration, Wilson responded to the Pope's proposal for a Christian peace, succinctly stating, "Our response must be based upon the stern facts and upon nothing else."[8] The United States, he said, would seek "not a mere cessation of arms . . . [but] a stable and enduring peace," which required "saving the free peoples of the world from the menace and the actual power of a vast military establishment controlled by an irresponsible government" that had planned to "dominate the world."[9] The peace that Wilson wanted would endure by stamping out autocratic governments limiting the liberty of their citizens and, therefore, citizens everywhere. Wilson counted Catholicism—but not individual Catholics—as one of those authoritative structures that limited individual liberty. He would not allow Benedict to occupy a seat at the table of peace negotiations as if he were equal to or greater than national leaders. Reconstituting world order, to Wilson's mind, was a job for a secular political leader and not for clergy, especially those representing the Roman Catholic Church. While Benedict and Wilson shared a common interest in establishing a lasting peace that destroyed the roots that led to the present conflict, their interpretations of Christianity and political philosophy pointed to different solutions.

From the outset of war through U.S. entrance into it, Wilson concentrated on the United States orchestrating a specific kind of postwar peace. Fighting to establish a peace without victory did not imply that there would not be victors; instead, he meant that the outcome must benefit the common good regardless of which side had the upper hand. Territorial distribution and the fate of colonized people were, of course, a concern, but only so far as they related to what Wilson considered the global good. This kind of nonpunitive resolution, for Wilson, could be measured by the *intent* of postwar settlement and evaluated according to the purpose of territorial acquisition after the war. When he called for a "peace without victory," Wilson did not object to redrawing the world map per se. He did advocate for ending the war in such a way that land was not redistributed for a victorious nation's aggrandizement. Past wars, he believed, had perpetuated a global order in which national power triumphed over other sovereigns. This violated his sense of God's order because great power required the kind of leadership in which the strong cared for the weak rather than preyed upon them. He believed a new world order was needed precisely because European empires had habituated a flawed—and failing—style of global governance. To Wilson, establishing a permanent peace would require a new world system that did not require nations to enlarge their power at the expense of others. Changing global governance, rather than redistributing land alone, would be the only means to stability in Wilson's eyes because it could end Europe's longstanding example of imperialism.

Wilson thought his vision applied to all peoples, but he did not trust just anyone to aid in its development. In November 1917, Wilson asked Edward M. House, his most trusted advisor, to arrange a "group of men" to help draft the U.S. position for peace negotiations. House assembled a team of experts who not only gathered information and analyzed data but also crafted drafts for the content and language of policies. The "Inquiry" team worked beyond the parameters of the State Department and, at times, without the knowledge of others within the Wilson administration, let alone the public. Many members of the Inquiry team had personal connections with Wilson or House, including professors, prominent businessmen, lawyers, and public intellectuals who graduated from or worked for elite universities.[10] While many were well trained in historical methods and philosophy, few specialized in public policy or held expertise in the geographic regions under consideration. Meeting in secret first at the New York public library and, later, the offices of the American Association of Geographers, the Inquiry team advised the president on his most basic questions about the fate of the world.

By December 23, the Inquiry finished its first memorandum to the president.[11] In early January, after a brief Christmas break, House and Wilson discussed the memo and outlined its essential points—fourteen of them in all. Wilson could not have known it at the time, but the ideas that he and House crafted in January 1918 would shape the agenda for peace negotiations.[12] Before Wilson could unveil what they had developed, however, British prime minister David Lloyd George proclaimed the British War Aims on January 5, 1918. Lloyd George finished his speech with three objectives: upholding the "sanctity" of treaties, establishing territories "based on the right of self-determination or the consent of the governed," and forming an international body "to limit the burden of armaments and diminish the probability of war."[13] By introducing "self-determination" as a British war aim and by connecting it to "the consent of the governed," Lloyd George combined a revolutionary idea espoused by Vladimir Lenin and other Marxists with one embraced by Wilson and other Americans.[14] This turn of phrase set the stage for the long-term reception of Wilson's internationalist vision. Even though the concept of "self-determination" emerged within a Bolshevik context and Britain's prime minister articulated it anew, it would repeatedly be associated with Wilson.

On January 8, 1918, less than one year after the United States entered the war, Wilson delivered a speech to a joint session of Congress to outline the nation's war aims. Developed from the Inquiry team's memo, the speech came to be known as Wilson's "Fourteen Points." Wilson articulated a "program of the world's peace" that began with five general principles of international relations: open diplomacy that occurs "in the public view"; "absolute" freedom of the seas in both peace and war; free trade "among all the nations consenting to the peace and associating themselves for its maintenance"; reduction of armaments "to the lowest point consistent with domestic safety"; and "absolutely impartial adjustment" of colonialized lands that accounted for the interests of colonized peoples.[15] The next eight points pertained to more immediate territorial disputes and national development regarding Russia, Belgium, Alsace-Lorraine, Italy, Austria-Hungary, Romania, Serbia, and Montenegro, as well as the creation of the Turkish and Polish states. In these points, Wilson emphasized the importance of "autonomous development," gesturing toward Lloyd George's integrated notion of consent of the governed and self-determination yet without using either term. The final point, which Wilson purposefully moved to the end for emphasis, demanded the formation of "a general association of nations . . . under specific covenants for the purpose of affording mutual guarantees of political independence and territorial integrity to great and small states alike."

The scheme as a whole, especially Wilson's emphasis on the final point, served as the nation's objectives in the war. Once articulated, these principles also established the basic building blocks for what would eventually be known as "Wilsonian" internationalism. His "Fourteen Points" speech was not designed to be a timeless or a legally binding document. He crafted it with the hope of inspiring the world, solidifying American leadership in international affairs, and securing his vision for a new world order. As Russia and Germany began to negotiate their own separate peace, Wilson emphasized the creation of a league of nations with new urgency, remaining consistent with his earlier pronouncements. By administering the formation of this international body, Wilson believed the United States could serve as the ultimate spiritual and mediating force in the war. Wilson intended to make the most out of U.S. entry into the struggle by leveraging the Allies' common cause to exact America's moral conquest of the world.

White liberal Protestants embraced Wilson's announcement of U.S. war aims. In his speech, they saw themselves and their own ideological commitments, just as they had in his "Peace without Victory" speech one year earlier.[16] Wilson's insistence upon interdependence, or what others would call "collective security," resonated with social Christians. The Federal Council of Churches, for example, rallied behind the Fourteen Points as the proper application of the social gospel to global affairs. They had emphasized the interconnectedness of society through their own campaigns affirming how Christians should be their brothers' keepers in domestic social reforms. To these American Christians, Wilson's foreign policy was the natural extension of their reform efforts on the home front. Their assumptions about white Anglo-American servant leadership were implicit in Wilson's understanding of democracy. Neither Wilson nor the FCC needed to impress this view upon the other; it was understood as the obvious best course of action.

During the six years he had been in office, Wilson consistently drew upon social Christian ideals when describing his statesmanship and the role of America in the world.[17] His Fourteen Points offered a mounting crescendo in the global application of the social gospel. Only one year earlier, the FCC's Commission on Peace and Arbitration had released a report entitled *The Church and International Relations*, declaring, "The morality that ought to govern the conduct of nations is not different from the morality that ought to govern the conduct of individuals." Critics accused them of applying individual ethics to nation-states. In response, the commission asserted that separate moral codes for private and public life, or for individuals and nations, "is a sentiment so utterly false and contrary to Christianity, that it must always receive the indignant denial of the churches." The ethical principles for private and public life could not be at odds, nor could that of individuals and nations, because their interpretation of scripture led to the belief that one ethic applied to both. The kingdom of God necessitated a grand unity of these ethical systems. The purpose of Christianity, in this view, was "to extend the kingdom of God upon the earth, and to maintain the righteousness that exalteth a nation."[18] Christian thought and practice might begin with the conversion of individual souls, but for social Christians its ultimate goal rested upon the formation of ideal Christian nations in a unified global society.

Wilson made this ideology manifest by putting these social gospel principles into practice as an example for other nations to follow by law and, ideally, their own volition. The Fourteen Points speech bridged the gap between domestic and international applications of the social gospel by applying the same notions of service and democracy to both. The incongruity between how individuals and collectives, like nations or corporations, ought to act had long been a concern for social Christians, but they had not yet convinced others why it mattered. Wilson's war speeches provided fodder for this debate by drawing attention to both the problem of self-interested statecraft and a potential solution to it through disinterested collective security. Eugene Brooks, a social Christian professor at Trinity College, for example, explained when the sins of "selfishness and greed" animated international affairs it was an extension of individual sin to society. "False" religions perpetuated these sentiments through "tribal" doctrines, leading to the use of violence to protect one's own kin or nation.[19] Misguided statecraft and "false" religions shared the same problem: inward-facing, self-interested sectarianism. To social Christians, Wilson's internationalist vision removed the root cause by establishing one international system based on a nonsectarian collective good.

Writing around the same time, economist and social Christian reformer Richard Ely suggested that the greatest question of the twentieth century was, "How shall we avail ourselves of the superiorities of the few in the service of the many?" He looked to Christianity for the answer because, he claimed, as "the greatest of all religions," it provided an instructive standard to follow. Christianity was a tradition in which "the highest and best leader" dedicated his life to others.[20] Ely's Jesus-inspired ethos emphasized equality of *opportunity* alongside this ethic of service. He stressed the existence of an "inequality of capacities," the "fact" that all people do not possess the same characteristics, talents, or aptitudes. Those with the talents to serve must do so.[21] This "duty of leadership" reveals "wise and good" leaders because "*leadership of the wise and good* naturally follows from a recognition of the inequalities among men with respect to their powers."[22] Ely published this exposition of a Jesus-inspired democracy during the Great War, but he echoed the secular adaptations of similar biblical interpretations found in white, social gospel ministers' publications popularized a decade earlier.

Having studied under Ely at Johns Hopkins University, Wilson shared Ely's views of the relationship between democracy and equality. When Wilson insisted, "only a peace between equals can last, only a peace the very principle of which is equality and a common participation in a common benefit," he spoke from this social Christian framework. For Wilson and white Protestants of his ilk, all nations warranted respect, regardless of their territorial size or status in the global balance of power, but those same nations would, by design, play varying roles in world affairs. Wilson certainly believed that all nations depended on one another, but his conception of that dependence reified the superiority of "great" nations and the inferiority of "small" ones. This approach to international relations extended from his consideration of individuals within society, who could possess equal worth but not uniform positions within the nation. For nations to thrive, just as with individuals, all had to work toward the greatest public good regardless of how much—or little—it benefitted them individually.

The connection between Wilson's appeals for equality and Americans' experience of *in*equality under his administration was not lost among critics familiar with U.S. history. W. E. B. Du Bois, for example, reflected poignantly on the irony of the United States projecting itself as "a sort of natural peace maker, then as a moral protagonist in this terrible time." African Americans' experiences stood as a testament to Du Bois's assertion that "no nation is less fitted for this role" than the United States. "For two or more centuries," he explained, "America has marched proudly in the van of human hatred,—making bonfires of human flesh and laughing at them hideously, and making the insulting of millions more than a matter of dislike,—rather a great religion, a world war-cry."[23] It was obvious to Du Bois and generations of African Americans that U.S. society contained intrinsic inequalities sustained through active maintenance of racial difference.[24] American democracy, as Wilson conceptualized it and Du Bois experienced it, maintained social inequalities as a necessary component of a government based on "freedom," "equality," and "liberty."

In addition to Du Bois, other activists attempted to use Wilson's comments on equality to publicize their own case of unjust treatment under the law and, as much as possible, leverage the anticipated peace negotiations to improve social conditions around the world. The newly formed National Woman's Party (NWP), for instance, publicly displayed Wilson's appeals for the advancement of democracy in order to draw attention to the shortcomings of the United States. Led by Alice Paul, an international suffrage activist and Quaker, NWP members stood outside the White House holding banners addressed to "Kaiser Wilson" who supported the German people because they were not self-governed yet did not address U.S. women's lack of self-governance. Alluding to Matthew 7:3–5, the NWP implored Wilson to remove the "beam" out of his eye so that he may see clearly his hypocrisy before correcting anyone else. The unmistakable contradictions between Wilson's words and deeds, however, were hidden in plain sight to the president and other elite white Christians who failed to see the perpetuation of their own privileged status in the new world order.

Even Colonel House, who had helped Wilson draft the Fourteen Points, recognized that Wilson's proclamations of equality and collective action appeared at odds with his actions at home and abroad. This became a source of frustration for House when he, Wilson, and Secretary of State Robert Lansing did not see eye to eye. In September 1918, for example, Wilson and Lansing crafted a response to an Austrian proposal for peace without seeking House's input. When House learned of the plan, he wrote in his diary that "the President and Lansing both seem determined that it shall be known to the world that this country is acting independently of our allies. They blazon the fact to the entire world." This was a problem for House because he and Wilson had purposefully crafted a foreign policy in which the United States did *not* "stand aloof from world politics." If a league of nations designed around a "close political and economic unity throughout the world" was what the president wanted—which he did—then, House reasoned, the president and secretary of state were "wholly wrong."[25] To avoid this embarrassing inconsistency, he implied, the United States could not exert its own importance while also insisting upon equal union among nations.

Wilson and the white Protestants who shared his internationalist vision, however, saw no error in this approach. They saw instead a consistent application of social gospel truth from individuals and their nation to their nation and the rest of the world. Whereas House, Du Bois, and Paul saw contradictions in Wilson's goal of advancing democracy abroad and his record of limiting it at home, Wilson saw a uniform appeal to construct an overarching public good for the world. For Wilson, that goal required priorities and necessitated certain social concerns over others. Denying African American civil rights and delaying women's suffrage was a strategic decision that Wilson considered in the interest of the nation's wartime unity. Rather than an inconsistency, Wilson saw a gradual cultivation of the public good that adapted to circumstances. When Wilson urged the Senate to pass women's suffrage in September 1918, well after suffragists persistent appeals during both terms, he did so as a war measure that contributed to the development of his intended world order. In order to ensure its formation, Wilson devoted his efforts to the constitution of a grand structure that could be modified in due time rather than to ironing out the specific details that satisfied all parties at its inception.

These inconsistencies were consistently brought to Wilson's attention. He was rarely deterred or inspired to reconsider his positions. Wilson attempted to explain his focus on moral structure to William Howard Taft in March 1918. As the president of the League to Enforce Peace (LEP), the largest American organization devoted to establishing a league of nations, Taft wanted to aid Wilson in the development of the governing document for his proposed association of nations. Wilson, however, insisted that he would not craft precise language prior to any formal peace negotiations. To do so, he reasoned, could potentially "embarrass him." He preferred instead to discuss broad themes from which international law could develop. This process, he admitted, would be a gradual one, just as the development of common law had been within nation-states, requiring multiple international meetings. Wilson refused to talk specifics with Taft; instead, he emphasized the theme of guaranteeing the territorial autonomy of nations and the need for conferences to protect them. Wilson recognized that this kind of relationship between nations would require limitations because the Senate "would be unwilling to enter into an agreement by which a majority of other nations could tell the United States when they must go to war."[26] The final document, Wilson anticipated, would require meeting the probable demands of the Senate while establishing, as much as possible, the proper moral framework for global interaction.

Establishing God's Peace on Earth

In the early morning hours of November 11, 1918, the Wilsons remained awake and anxious in the White House residence. They waited to hear from Colonel House about the status of the armistice. From Paris, House sent the president a telegram announcing the Great War had come to an end: "Autocracy is dead. Advance [long live] democracy and its immortal leader."[27] Hostilities were officially to end later that morning, but the telegram signaled the White House could officially announce the armistice, leaving House and Wilson with the overwhelming feeling that democracy had prevailed. President Wilson told the nation, "A supreme moment of history has come. The eyes of the people have been opened and they see. The hand of God is laid upon the nations. He will show them favour, I devoutly believe, only if they rise to the clear heights of His own justice and mercy."[28] The war was over, but for Wilson peace had not yet come. He addressed a joint session of Congress later that day, informing the nation of the terms of the armistice. His speech was, above all, practical and straightforward regarding the end of hostilities. He ended by reminding the nation and the world that the goal of peace was not yet achieved and would not be achieved in one day; instead, he affirmed, the peace process would continue until the world established the terms for a lasting, permanent peace.[29]

Wilson had two agendas for the postwar peace: first, to settle the immediate territorial and power disputes related to the war, and, second, to reconstitute the entirety of global interaction into an international system whose order would be maintained through a partnership of democratic nations.[30] Wilson did not create these foreign policy platforms, nor was he the first to assert their import. Yet Wilson's articulation of them became synonymous with this model of internationalism. Wilson set the terms of the Paris Peace Conference by emphasizing nationhood over empire and by providing a shared language for international cooperation.

Much to the chagrin of the Senate, Wilson took it upon himself to negotiate the peace treaty with a U.S. delegation of his creation. Wilson even pledged to personally go to Paris to represent the United States in the world's negotiations. To that end, John Franklin Shafroth (D-Colorado) introduced legislation authorizing the president "to negotiate, and after ratification by two-thirds of the members of both Houses of Congress, to sign a treaty for the creation of an international peace-keeping tribunal."[31] Approval of the president's mission was not unanimous; Senate majority leader Henry Cabot Lodge objected to Wilson's leadership as a matter of principle and pragmatic statesmanship. He was skeptical of Wilson's diplomacy because the president focused on the global moral order over and above the specific territorial disputes that incited war. Convinced that Wilson would lose sight of the more pressing practicalities, Lodge warned against an attempt "to reach the millennium of universal and eternal peace" because territorial disputes promised to tax the delegates' time and energy."[32] If a lasting peace were to be established, Lodge reasoned, then Germany must be prevented from disrupting the global balance of power through future territorial conquest. Remaking the world was not on the Senate's agenda, even if it was on the president's.

Even though Lodge hoped to bring Wilson's vision down to earth, much of the world waited in anticipation of a global transformation. When Edith Benham arrived in Paris in December 1918, she witnessed this excitement firsthand, writing her beau and eventual husband with vivid detail. As part of the support staff for the Wilson family's trip to the Paris Peace Conference, Benham explained how President Woodrow Wilson, First Lady Edith, and others were honored with a parade through the streets of Paris. Under "a clear blue sky," Benham watched "the French soldiers in their blue, lining the way and keeping a broad path open for the President, and with the rest of the immense square packed and jammed with people," including wounded war veterans.[33] As the Wilson entourage traveled through the streets of Paris by motorcade, crowds of people shouted, "Vive Wilson!"[34] Trying to explain the scene, Benham divulged, "The pathetic desire of these

FIGURE 4.1. Looking up the Rue de Royal from the Place de la Concorde after the president had passed. The sign of welcome "Vive Wilson" across Rue Royal. The Madeline in the background. Paris, Seine, France. Dec. 14, 1919. Photo by Sgt. A. D. Chapman, S.C., 111-WT-2-3-62778. Courtesy of Army Signal Corps, Archives II, College Park, MD.

people to show honor to the President and the United States is just heartbreaking. . . . They look upon the President as almost divine and are always so deeply moved."[35] The experience overwhelmed Benham. No one in the delegation had expected a more enthusiastic reception in Paris than they received in the United States.[36]

Back home, many Americans protested the devotion their president received abroad. The National Woman's Party, for instance, burned copies of Wilson's speeches in "liberty bonfires" in Washington, DC. If Wilson would not acknowledge the contradictions of presenting himself as the "champion of mankind" while failing to cultivate democracy at home, then, these suffragists reasoned, perhaps the rest of the world would.[37] Meanwhile, as nation-states developed a new international apparatus for common council, nonstate organizations formed their own international networks for future activism. Du Bois, for example, traveled to Paris to report on the Peace Conference for the National Association for the Advancement of Colored People's magazine, *The Crisis*. While there, he organized the first Pan-African Conference. As Wilson tried to build a framework for international engagement in law, activists like Paul and Du Bois used the Wilsonian moment as international recourse for domestic social problems.

FIGURE 4.2. Crowd in the Plaza in front of the Philharmonic Club, Turin, Italy, awaiting President Wilson's appearance on balcony of the club where he is being entertained at dinner—crowd waited for more than two hours in pouring rain. 111-WT-5-1-63579. Courtesy of Army Signal Corps, Archives II, College Park, MD.

Across Europe, however, Wilson received a hero's welcome. Each country's citizens greeted Wilson with a fervor that aids like Benham compared to "a savior [who had] come to earth."[38] Irwin Hood Hoover, head usher for the White House, recalled that Italians "simply seem to worship him."[39] As Wilson journeyed from Rome to Genoa, Italians greeted him with signs that proclaimed his sacred role in history as the savior of Europe; they burned candles around Wilson's effigy and created shrines in his honor.[40] U.S. delegates and staff found similar reactions even in cities where the president did not travel. George Creel, head of the U.S. Committee on Public Information, reported to Benham that Polish and Czech support of the president could be found on posters that translated to "We Want a Wilson Peace." "Among the poor people," he explained, Wilson is treated "as a new popular Saint." Benham told her beau that "pictures [of Wilson] hung in many windows and the people told Mr. Creel that they wanted Wilson to reign over them."[41]

By the end of the Great War, the United States appeared to have rescued Allied nations from their common enemy, and President Wilson represented the dawn of a new era in global affairs. He was a national leader who expressed concern about the autonomy and advancement of all peoples, especially those living under an unwelcome authority. Wilson enjoyed this status because the war disrupted the geopolitical balance of power and an array of organizations worked to craft this message. The world's most powerful empires experienced major losses, including the loss of lives, capital, and prestige.[42] The United States benefited from these losses, gaining its own prestige as a source of stability in the world through both economic clout and political leadership.

Wilson had articulated a new vision for what could replace what was lost, a new world order based on international cooperation, from the very beginning of the war. It was not until his trip to Europe, however, that he finalized his plan. After the United States formally associated with the Allies, Wilson provided a clearer framework for his vision in the Fourteen Points. In doing so, he set the tone for the Paris Peace Conference. Once in Europe, Wilson finalized his draft of the Covenant of the League of Nations. As expected, Wilson emphasized national self-determination, open agreements, free trade, freedom of the seas, and collective security. When he reviewed the first draft, finalized by staff member David Hunter Miller, Wilson reiterated the importance of equality among nations and mutual dependence. He also removed any references to an international court.[43] The idea of a court as the primary arbiter of international disputes had gained credibility among American anticolonial and peace interest groups following the Spanish-American War. Most notably, Taft and his League to Enforce Peace proposed an international court as a necessary component to any formal partnership among nations.[44] By removing it, Wilson disappointed a longstanding source of American support for a league of nations and he opened himself up to the critique that this league of nations would lack an enforcement mechanism.

Wilson did not dwell on these criticisms but instead forged new partnerships in his development of the league, particularly with other Christian statesmen. Secretary of State Lansing noticed, for example, that South African–born British general Jan Christiaan Smuts gave Wilson a copy of his book *The League of Nations: A Practical Suggestion,* which "appealed mightily to the President."[45] Together, Wilson and Smuts considered the creation of a league of nations to be "'the heir of the Empires' since Imperialism was no more."[46] This idea that a partnership among nations would replace imperialism resonated with Wilson. He finalized his Covenant of the League of Nations according to it.[47] Prior to their meeting, Smuts had praised Wilson's approach to the war and the United States for being a model democratic nation. Smuts, like American social Christians, regarded Wilson's appeal to Congress in April 1917 as the best summation to date of the mission at hand. They agreed that the war was fought against an autocratic government on behalf of the German people who "wanted the spirit of Christian ethical civilisation to prevail."[48] Wilson's vision for the league, they believed, would establish this Christian ideal for all of global society.

America's allies in the British empire could see clearly a Christian influence just beneath the surface of Wilson's pronouncements. In addition to Smuts's efforts, the archbishop of Canterbury, Most Reverend Randall Thomas Davidson, invited the president to give an address as a part of "our joint effort to promote the League of Nations as an essentially Christian mode of policy and action." Speaking on behalf of all Protestants in England, Davidson appealed to Wilson to make their shared Christian mission explicit in his diplomatic mission.[49] The president politely declined three days later, citing his grueling Peace Conference schedule.[50] The issue, however, may have been weighing on the president's conscience, because he wrote Davidson a second letter, without having received a response from the archbishop. After once again declining to speak, Wilson clarified his stance on the issue, adding, "I believe that the solid foundation of the League of Nations is to be found in Christian principles and in the sustaining sentiment of Christian peoples everywhere, and it would be extremely stimulating to me to be privileged to address the representatives of the body of churches of whom you speak."[51] Just because the president believed Christianity to be the foundation of the league, however, did not necessarily mean that he wanted to make it explicit in the covenant establishing the League of Nations.

Wilson's drafts of the covenant included protections for religious liberty, especially among newly created states. Since he understood Christianity to be the foundation of a proper democracy, Wilson wanted to ensure that churches could flourish in the wake of the Austro-Hungarian and Russian empires; even so, Wilson's commitment to religion at the Peace Conference was limited.[52] He was not interested in grand proclamations about God or a universal guarantee of religious liberty as a primary objective of the United States. At several points during his stay in Paris, Wilson delicately brushed off clergy members who privately implored him to bring Christianity to the fore of peace negotiations. Désiré-Joseph Mercier, cardinal archbishop of Malines, wrote the president in March of 1919 to express his frustration with the Peace Conference. After three months of deliberations, there still had been no "public religious homage to God."[53] Mercier spent much of the war under house arrest, during which time he wrote an open letter, *Patriotism and Endurance*, that gave hope to many others who suffered during the war. Having survived the war, Mercier was shocked that the Peace Conference delegates, many of whom "represent a nation in which religion is honored," did not acknowledge God's role in any way. Mercier found President Wilson's statements and actions particularly disappointing. He pointed out the contradiction

FIGURE 4.3. Désiré-Joseph Mercier, cardinal archbishop of Malines, and President Wilson meeting during Wilson's European tour. 111-WT-2-1-61148. Courtesy of Archives II, Army Signal Corps, College Park, MD.

in a nation that simultaneously offered "national recognition to the Divine One" in the form of a Thanksgiving Day yet refused to make an effort to do so during historic peace negotiations.[54] Mercier, like Davidson, expected the president to not only lead this unprecedented meeting of nations, but, more importantly, to do so as a powerful representative of Christianity.

Mercier appealed to Wilson as a last resort, after his attempts to persuade French prime minister Georges Clemenceau had gone unanswered. Mercier urged Clemenceau to assemble Cardinals Gibbons, Bourne, Richelmy, and Amette, in addition to himself, in a preliminary peace treaty signing ceremony at the Church of Notre Dame. If God was not to be mentioned in the Covenant of the League of Nations, then at least the signing of the peace treaty could occur in a house of worship. Mercier hoped that Wilson, who he envisioned as standing between the people of God and pragmatic, secular statesmen, might allow Catholicism—which Mercier believed could represent "the religious conscience of humanity"—to play its part in the Paris Peace Conference.[55] President Wilson, however, disappointed Mercier, the archbishop of Canterbury, and thousands of lay Christians around the world. He did not demand the inclusion of the word "God" in the covenant; he did not insist that the Treaty of Versailles be signed in a house of God; and, when it came

to including universal protections for religious liberty within the League of
Nations, Wilson chose the creation of a nonsectarian league implicitly built
upon Christian principles over a league that explicitly named Christianity as
its sectarian moral and legal foundation.

The Crucible of God's Peace

For a moment, the world joined Wilson in his internationalist vision. As
historian Erez Manela persuasively argued, Wilson "captured imaginations
across the world," especially among colonized peoples.[56] Individuals and
ethnic groups subject to the authority of colonial power drew upon Wilson's
rhetoric and message and made it their own. Anticolonial nationalists in such
disparate places as Egypt, India, China, and Korea recognized a common
cause in Wilson's vision: the world must be made anew by ending colonial
empires and establishing new nation-states and novel forms of international
engagement. From anticolonialists in India to African American human
rights activists and women suffragists in the United States, Wilson's postwar
world order animated a variety of causes that fit within Wilson's discourse but
did not belong within what he imagined to be the new world order.

Both colonized people and emergent empires wanted to see an end to a
global order based on European imperialism. Japan, for instance, looked forward to a new world order in which it could strengthen its place in the world.[57]
Wilson named Germany as his primary target in ending imperialism, but
Japan's elite, which had modeled their state after Germany, felt threatened by
extension.[58] Not to be deterred, however, Japan's leaders used the Paris Peace
Conference as an opportunity to secure a position of authority among the
world's leading nations. By emphasizing national self-determination along
with collective security, Wilson offered a new strategy for "small" nations like
Japan to increase their power in international affairs without acquiring new
territory. In Wilson's model, interaction and engagement through trade and
goodwill became new markers of international power. Settler colonies, and
their human and resource exploitation, became signs of resistance to modernity and antiquated notions of governance. Rather than focus exclusively on
gaining territory—although this was still a concern—the Japanese delegation
also focused on participation in global trade and collective security as an
opportunity to gain a position of strength in Wilson's world order.[59]

Through a series of diplomatic negotiations, the Japanese delegation
revealed Wilson's preference for establishing a legal and moral structure
maintaining U.S.-inspired moral authority over the articulation of globally
binding creeds establishing international equality. The most telling of these

exchanges revealed the limits of what Wilson intended by his efforts to assert the equality of all nations. In his first draft for the Covenant of the League of Nations, a document only a handful of people read, Wilson wrote a provision that would obligate all *new* states to demonstrate legal and cultural equality between racial or national minorities and the racial or national majority.[60] Demonstration of racial equality would be a precondition for receiving international recognition of statehood. While many Americans and Europeans continued to assume nations comprised a distinct "people," Wilson acknowledged the need for racial minorities to be equal "both in law and in fact" to the racial majority for a new nation to thrive, a standard he resisted in the Reconstruction South.

By his second "Paris" draft of the covenant, Wilson added another provision intentionally crafting the culture of new nations. This new article accounted for religious liberty, a value that many Americans considered central to democracy. Article 21 in this draft of the Covenant of the League of Nations proposed:

> The High Contracting Parties agree to state that no obstacle shall be placed in the way of the free exercise of every belief, religion, or opinion, the practice of which is not incompatible with public order and morality, and that, within their respective jurisdictions, no one shall be disturbed in his life, liberty, or the pursuit of happiness by reason of his adhesion to such belief, religion, or opinion.[61]

Like the racial equality article that came before it, this provision upheld a principle of equality by requiring new states to agree to protect religious liberty as a condition of international recognition of independence and membership into the League of Nations.

This article reflected Americans' overwhelmingly nonsectarian Protestant culture. The article's language implicitly associated "religion" with "belief and opinion," an assumption American Protestants took for granted, often believing it to be the natural interpretation of religion. This association has a long history, dating to some of the earliest debates over religious liberty led by Thomas Jefferson and James Madison. Article 21 went one step further, however, in acknowledging American legal developments regarding religious liberty. Article 21 would not protect *all* religions, beliefs, or opinions, but rather only those compatible "with public order and morality." This distinctively American approach to religious liberty spoke the language of freedom while placing limits on who could receive protection. These limitations were well known to Americans—especially Latter Day Saints, Jehovah's Witness, Catholics, and Native Americans—but less well known to a global audience.

Wilson's draft of the covenant underwent a third revision, but neither the religious or racial equality articles received changes. This third draft was circulated more widely as Wilson hoped it could serve as the working draft at the conference. With this draft in mind, the Japanese delegates saw an opportunity to advance Japan's interests. This included securing possession of the Shandong province, improving the status of Japanese citizens in other nations, and ensuring Japan's position among the new concert of global power. To further these national interests, the Japanese delegation proposed an amendment to the article protecting religious liberty. Their proposal sought to prevent racial, national, and religious discrimination against citizens *and* foreign nationals within *existing* nations:

> The equality of nations being a basic principle of the League of Nations, the High Contracting Parties agree to accord, as soon as possible, to all alien nationals of State members of the League, equal and just treatment in every respect, making no distinction, either in law or fact, on account of their race or nationality.[62]

If all member states were equals, the delegation reasoned, then any citizen of a member nation should be treated equally within other member nations. As Baron Makino Nobuaki, a leading member of the Japanese delegation, argued, if the league were to protect citizens of member states from religious discrimination, then it ought to also protect them from discrimination based on other potential forms of prejudice. The Japanese delegation understood Japan, as a nation, to be composed of a distinct people. As a people, Japanese immigrants had overwhelming evidence of racial, religious, and national discrimination by American and European empires. Consequently, these three facets of an individual's identity seemed worthy of explicit international guarantees of correcting prejudices experienced in existing nations. If Wilson intended to make a good faith effort in establishing equality among nations, then the Japanese delegation intended to improve the condition of its citizens around the world.

This "racial amendment," as it came to be called, was one among numerous proposals on the negotiation table.[63] Each national delegation had its own priorities, reflecting their own states' interests; to the "Big Four"—the United States, England, France, and Italy—Japan's proposed amendment was inconsequential. According to U.S. delegate David Hunter Miller, the issue first entered into conversation between British and American delegates as an aside during territorial considerations. British ambassador Lord Cecil Arthur Spring Rice informed House that Great Britain would not agree to the Japanese amendment under any circumstances.[64] He then moved on to other

territorial considerations without further comment. To the British delegation, Japan's proposal required no discussion because territory was a more
important and feasible matter to consider.

Surprised by the British delegation's position, House attempted to revise
the amendment to make it more palatable to them.[65] Since the United States
delegation generally favored protecting religious liberty, House drafted a
revised statement based on the Declaration of Independence. (Apparently it
did not occur to him that the British delegation might not have been as fond
of this document as he and other Americans.) When House gave the revised
amendment to British delegate Arthur Balfour, Balfour dismissed it outright.
Balfour thought the proposal outdated, a product of the eighteenth century.
"It was true in a certain sense that all men of a particular nation were created
equal," he explained, "but not that a man in Central Africa was created equal
to a European."[66] Indeed, for Balfour, Rice, and even Wilson, all notions of
equality were not equal. Empires might have been ending, but colonial men-
talities continued.

To these two delegations, the kind of equality proposed by Japan was
absurd because equality could not be universally applied across humanity in
the way proposed. Colonel House did not disagree with Balfour, but he sym-
pathized with Japan as a nation that sought to expand its power: "The world
said that they could not go to Africa; they could not go to any white country;
they could not go to China, and they could not go to Siberia; and yet they
were a growing nation, having a country where all the land was tilled; but
they had to go somewhere." If they could not grow through territorial expansion, the next logical recourse was petitioning for the equality of its citizens
alongside those of the most powerful nations. Balfour understood House's
reasoning yet he refused to support the Japanese cause. His nationalism was,
at its core, a matter of excluding some but not others from full citizenship.[67]
This proposed system of *inter*nationalism was not intended to redefine or
fundamentally alter national identity. Indeed, it required the maintenance of
nationalism to stabilize global security and commerce.

The primary concern for Great Britain and the United States was the
precedent this would set. If Japan's amendment passed, then international
law could intervene in what the Americans and the British understood to
be national concerns. For instance, Wilson and Rice recognized that the
amendment might affect restrictions imposed on Japanese and Irish immigration, respectively.[68] If approved, the racial amendment would require the
reversal of immigration quotas and other discriminatory practices within the
national borders of the United States and Great Britain. This was, of course,
the intent of the amendment—to protect citizens of member nations against

the kinds of documented racial and religious discrimination Japanese immigrants experienced in the United States and Europe. Yet a racial amendment could, of course, also provide a legal basis for black South Africans and African Americans to challenge state-sanctioned discrimination as a violation of international law. The British and American delegates argued that such an approach would violate each nation's sovereignty by imposing an international standard over the will of its people. They found these kinds of impositions acceptable where the formation of a new nation was concerned, but not in places where they perceived the process of nationhood to be complete. In Wilson's conception, a league should protect national autonomy and strengthen the moral ties among brother nations; however, he did not want the latter to come at the expense of the former.

When the Japanese amendment came to a vote, Wilson served as the chair of the meeting. After several speeches, including ones from Makino and Rice,[69] only "yes" votes were counted. All but one party, Great Britain, voted in favor of the amendment. The United States abstained.[70] Wilson, as chair of the meeting, decided that unanimity was required in order for the amendment to pass. As a result, Japan's appeal failed. Without the United States formally voting against a provision that protected member nations against religious and racial discrimination, Wilson prevented this amendment from passing. By doing so, Wilson effectively ensured that the covenant did not protect the rights of religious freedom across *all* member states. Instead, religious liberty was only explicitly guaranteed within mandated territories developing their national autonomy. Protections against racial discrimination were removed from the covenant entirely. In the process, he reaffirmed the importance of sovereignty and self-determination over concerns of discrimination. The absence of these protections mattered little to Wilson because his notion of "equality" was already present throughout the covenant. As a whole, the document combined the "moral and physical strength of nations for the benefit of the smallest as well as the greatest. That is not only a recognition of the equality of nations, it is a vindication of the equality of nations. No one could question, therefore, the principle upon which this Covenant is based."[71] For Wilson, the equality established through the League of Nations was so obvious it could be—and should remain—assumed.

To Wilson, preventing the inclusion of universal legal protections for religion offered an alternative means to protect its free exercise. For Wilson and the white American Protestants who supported him, this amendment to prevent racial and national discrimination held the potential to sully the significance of the guarantees of religious liberty the document as a whole provided.

If all people who expressed any form of religious belief in the League of Nations were equal, and if international law prevented racial and national discrimination, then American social Christians and their understanding of democracy could lose their preferred social status in the United States and around the world. Despite their proclaimed aim of ending social barriers, American Protestant reformers like Wilson relied upon distinctions of race, gender, class, and religion. Wilson's particular understanding of democracy, like the British delegation's view of world order, assumed the superiority and authority of white Protestants to *properly* lead. White male leadership, especially by Protestants, was the fundamental assumption at the heart of the informal moral establishment that had made America exceptional and social Christianity a unique social justice enterprise. The racial amendment would undo their work.

The Japanese delegation recognized the new parameters for international engagement and adeptly tested Wilson's principles. They forced Wilson to choose between extending legal protections to other cultural identifiers, especially race and nationality, or losing Japan's support for the League of Nations. By declaring the need for unanimity for amendments to pass, Wilson chose unanimous support for the league rather than extending guarantees of religious, racial, *and* national nondiscrimination to all citizens of member nations. Despite the fervor of the parades, the devotion in the streets, and public rhetoric on signs and in speeches, religion at the Peace Conference was still a matter of diplomacy. It was a legal category actively in construction. For Japan and the United States, the form that legal category took served as a tool for diplomatic negotiations.

Most conventional histories of the Paris Peace Conference suggest that the defeat of the amendment represented straightforward Anglo-American discrimination, with consequences for Japanese nationalism in the 1920s and 1930s.[72] While Anglo-American discrimination against Japanese immigrants certainly played a part in defeating the racial amendment, it was not the only contributing factor. Another possible interpretation suggests that Japan misunderstood what Wilson meant with his religious article. After all, "religion" is not a native term.[73] It is a concept fraught with difficulties for translators. There is evidence to suggest, for example, that the Japanese delegation may have assumed religion, race, and nationality to be one and the same because the practice of Shinto, in the late nineteenth and early twentieth centuries, connected religion to the state.[74] Conversely, Wilson's Presbyterian background, coupled with American Protestant culture more generally, made it difficult for him to see the assumptions bound within his use of the terms "religion" and "race." Wilson would not see "religion," "race," or "nationality" as synonymous or interrelated identifications in need of legal protections because his location in the Protestant moral establishment reinforced the social and legal separation of each concept. And yet this explanation too falls short, as it neglects the history of Japanese elites studying Anglo-American conceptions of society and culture.[75] It also affords little agency to the members of the Japanese delegation, who began crafting their postwar peace agenda, like Wilson, well before the war ended.[76]

In 1919, Paris was the site of the purposeful, multilateral construction of a world order that held the potential to assert the sovereignty of nation-states over empires and to establish international cooperation through global commerce and security. For the Japanese delegates, the racial amendment was important, but so was securing a permanent claim to the Shandong province, a territory secretly acquired during the war.[77] As part of their negotiation tactics, Japanese delegates asserted that they would not join a league unless both interests were met. Japan's potential withdrawal over the racial amendment threatened the unity and long-term stability of the entire international system Wilson hoped to create. By suggesting this "right," Japan asserted its significance in world affairs—a call to end the discrimination of Japanese nationals wherever they may be. The Japanese delegation understood that Wilson could not support such equality—indeed would not—because white Americans would not participate in a league of nations that meddled in their national affairs. By suggesting it anyway, Japan put Wilson in a curious position. Supporting the racial amendment would place him in violation of his own long-standing southern evangelical principles (by agreeing to a clause that would give all religions equal status to Christianity) and radically alter American politics and culture (by allowing other nations to dictate domestic affairs). Not supporting it would undermine his international vision (by refusing to apply the religious nondiscrimination clause to all members rather than new states alone) and suggest that race and religion were not in need of legal protection from discrimination. Rejecting a universal application of racial and religious nondiscrimination would alienate Japan and lose the unanimous support he thought necessary for the league's stability.

At the Paris Peace Conference, then, religion, race, nationality, and the rights protecting each were the tools diplomats used to regulate international affairs. In the presence of Wilson's sincerely held belief and the *realpolitik* of peace negotiations, representations of and legal frameworks for religion and race were coconstituted with national interests. Religion and race were not only about the existence of theological beliefs or legal protection for religious exercise. The case of Japan demonstrates that asserting the international equality of religions and races was a matter of constructing, and then projecting, a national identity on the world's stage. The Japanese delegates asserted the integration of race and religion at the Paris Peace Conference in part because it more accurately reflected their national culture and in part because it better asserted their preferred role for Japan in the world. Likewise, Wilson resisted combining racial and religious protections against discrimination because American culture relied upon racial and religious segregation, as did Americans in the world, especially missionaries who depended upon the assumed superiority of Christianity and, often, whiteness. The struggle over race and religion at the Paris Peace Conference demonstrated how, to these dignitaries, race and religion had less to do with the existence of a basic, fundamental right and more to do with clarifying the parameters of national sovereignty and state power in an international system relying on collective security.

In this respect, legal protections for religion, race, and nationality were not only matters pertaining to the culture of the League of Nations but also bargaining chips at the table of international diplomacy—and ones the Japanese delegation played well. They succeeded in revealing the roots of Wilson's treatment of religion—it was a source of social order and cohesion and not an equal human right. In doing so, they also exposed Wilson's proclivity for upholding the structure of his league over specific details. This proved to be helpful as Japan demanded possession of Shandong province and supplied previously secret official documents legitimizing their claim. Even though the U.S. delegation intended to do everything in their power to return Shandong to China, Wilson upheld Japan's claim in order to maintain the integrity of official international agreements now in public view. Through both diplomatic issues, Japan demonstrated the extent of its influence relative to major powers. The most important victory for Japan, in this respect, was its legitimacy and respect acting alongside American and European empires.

The collective results of the Peace Conference disappointed many of Wilson's Christian supporters who assumed the establishment of a league of nations would be a crowning moment for Christian progress, global social salvation. C. H. Brent, senior chaplain of the American Expeditionary Forces, wrote the president on April 11—the same day that the racial amendment came to a vote—requesting that the president consider adding the word "God" or some other sort of reference to God in the Covenant of the League of Nations. "The more I have thought of the attempt which we are making to create world order," he explained gently, "the more I have concluded its hopelessness without looking to God to do that work above and beyond as well as through us which is necessary for anything permanent." Without overstepping the bounds of his rank, Brent suggested, he believed "it would tend to stabilize our idealism if the first mention of unity were referred to as the product and purpose of God's mind.[78] The president responded personally a few days later, thanking the reverend for his letter, and acknowledging what "it contains appeals to my heart." The president explained briefly that "it would be useless to propose such a sentence as you suggest for the Covenant of the League" because of the "peculiar" configuration of delegates.[79] Wilson was sympathetic, but after the debate over the racial amendment, and as territorial disputes were under negotiation, he knew additional sectarianisms would only further diminish the establishment of an international brotherhood. He would not risk losing unanimous support for the League of Nations even if it meant omitting "God."

For Wilson, the absence of "God" in the covenant mattered little because he believed Providence would determine the fate of the league *regardless* of whether or not the document acknowledged it. He was confident in this new organization because it reflected his understanding of democracy—all nations possess equal value but all do not share equal territorial size or distinction. Wilson insisted as much when he defended his decision about racial equality to journalists. He declared, "This League is obviously based on the principle of equality of nations. Nobody can read anything connected with its institutions or read any of the articles in the Covenant itself, without realizing that it is an attempt—that [the] first serious and systematic attempt made in the world to put nations on a footing of equality with each other in their international relations."[80] The manifestation of a principle of equality mattered more to Wilson than any finer detail outlined within the document. Moreover, he expected that the document both could and would be refined over time as humanity continued to breathe life into the organization. Future amendments would not be evidence of failure in the original but rather a continual demonstration of the strength of the league and the bonds that tied nations together. What he could not see, however, was how his particular understanding of equality belonged to a specific interpretation of Christianity that was, at the same time, peculiarly American.

"By the Hand of God Who Led Us"

On June 24, 1919, the president and his entourage celebrated. After sneaking into several official proceedings of the conference (because women were not allowed inside), Mrs. Wilson waited patiently at 11 Place des États-Unis to see if German diplomats would agree to sign her husband's chief foreign policy act. Around six o'clock that evening, she saw a French officer jump out of a car—she was sure while the car was still moving—only to run into the building. A few minutes later, the president himself arrived, announcing that Germany had indeed agreed to sign the peace treaty. What happened next was a blur to those at the heart of the celebrations; shots were fired in the air, sirens blared, and church bells rang, and in the midst of the excitement maids kissed whichever officer was nearest.[81] During dinner, American delegates and staff raised their glasses, and Edith Benham offered a toast to "the greatest man in the world and the greatest peace made by him." After "all drank heartily to it," the president offered his own toast, "To the Peace, and enduring Peace, a Peace under the League of Nations."[82] The celebrations continued through the night as, it seemed, the world had been made anew.

Though thrilling to his closest supporters, Wilson's performance at the Paris Peace Conference left many more Americans unsatisfied. In his diary, journalist Ray Stannard Baker confessed his criticisms of the president: "The only hope left of this Conference is that Wilson will come out with a last terrific blast for his principles, and their *specific application* & go down in the ruin. *I fear he won't.* And that is complete failure."[83] Baker, like many Wilsonians, was frustrated by the twists and turns of the peace negotiations. Each nation's delegates had fought for its *own* peace, a selfishness Wilson's peacemaking was expected to end. Baker assumed that Wilson's peace was the truest of them all, but he still had to confront the reality that the best ideas, and perhaps even the best men, do not always win. Their agenda to save the world was one partisan agenda among many. Based on what the president actually accomplished, Baker continued, "It now looks as though the League would be so weak, its foundations so insecure, that I could not myself support it. It will make very little difference *now* what peace is signed, for nothing essential will be settled."[84] For Baker, Christian internationalists, and League of Nations enthusiasts around the world, failure to win the peace in the way they had originally envisioned it sullied the triumph of ending the war.

In five months, Wilson had successfully convinced the leaders of belligerent nations to create, and then join, an international organization based upon principles he helped to outline. In the process, however, many of his ideas had been modified. Political egos, inter- and intranational rivalries, and arduous negotiations had blemished Wilson's vision for a new world order based on an international brotherhood. Conflict and controversy within the U.S. delegation certainly did not help. Colonel House embarked for Paris as Wilson's most trusted advisor, serving as Wilson's proxy in Peace Conference meetings when the president could not attend; he left Paris relegated to the sidelines of the Wilson administration and barely interacted with Wilson throughout the remainder of his tenure in office. As toasts were made in honor of the treaty and the Covenant of the League of Nations contained within it, many could not give their wholehearted approval. As John Maynard Keynes described it, "The proceedings of Paris all had this air of extraordinary importance and unimportance at the same time. The decisions seemed charged with consequences to the future of human society; yet the air whispered that the word was not flesh, that it was futile, insignificant, of no effect, disassociated from events."[85] Wilson did not breathe life into the peace he intended to create.

Knowing that the Treaty of Versailles did not contain all that he had hoped it would, Wilson had to convince the Senate that this peace was worth ratifying. The president had a daunting task in front of him. During his time in Paris, the U.S. Senate had grown more hostile toward the president and his plan. A handful of Republican leaders had written to Wilson, but he had not incorporated their suggestions in his negotiations. He had also ignored many suggestions from members of his own delegation, including House. As soon as the text of the treaty became fully known, many senators made clear that *if* they were to ratify the Treaty of Versailles, it would have to be done with reservations and amendments. The Senate would not let the president circumvent its constitutional power or its policy priorities. As knowledge of the cleft between the president and the Senate grew and the Peace Conference labored on, public opinion slipped out of the president's favor. Although broad support existed for *a* league of nations, by May the public and the Senate were skeptical of *this* one. This was not the peace upon which the American public had set their hopes.

The president began his presentation of the Treaty of Versailles to the Senate by reiterating his assessment of America's exceptional role in the conflict. Having joined the war effort "upon a different footing," the United States did not have a material interest in the war, nor was it legally bound to enter it. Instead, Wilson asserted, the United States entered the war on ideological grounds because "right everywhere" was "imperiled by the intolerable aggression of a power which respected neither right nor obligation" and ruled according to "autocratic authority." Again, he proclaimed, the members of the United States delegation were "the disinterested champions of right and we interested ourselves in the terms of peace in no other capacity."[86] This was, Wilson asserted, the height of American power in the world. The authority the United States had exerted since its rise to this new global status after the Spanish-American War, Wilson explained, consistently demonstrated the nation's disinterested approach to service and friendliness to other nations. This internationalist approach to foreign relations encouraged "weak peoples everywhere [to] stand ready to give us any authority among them that will assure them a likely friendly oversight and direction. They know that there is no ground for fear in receiving us as their mentors and guides."[87] Wilson did not shy away from the notion of the "weak" seeking the protection of the "strong." He embraced these differences as America's contribution to the world.

In what would be his final press conference, on July 10, 1919,[88] President Wilson fielded a variety of questions on the contingencies related to the treaty. White House correspondents asked President Wilson about various hypothetical scenarios that might occur if the treaty were ratified, including the use of the U.S. military in other nations' border disputes, potential changes to constitutional powers related to war and treaties, and relations with and between other nations. The meeting ended ominously, with one reporter asking, "Do you hold that if the Senate were to adopt reservations to the treaty of peace with Germany, the treaty could not be ratified?" Wilson replied, "I do not think hypothetical questions should concern us. The Senate is going to ratify the treaty."[89] His fight for peace, however, was far from over.

A Tale of Two Exceptionalisms

When Germany is beaten to her knees and the world is made safe by the arrangements
which I have suggested, then, and not before, we shall have the just and righteous peace
for which we fight. In this way and in no other shall we obtain it. We shall obtain it
because we are going to win. Let us be true to ourselves, and we shall not then be false
to any man.

— HENRY CABOT LODGE[1]

If world-peace is ever to come, it must be achieved by conscious Christian action directing the policies and activities of the state. Anything less involves failure to establish the
Kingdom of God in its fullness.

— SIDNEY L. GULICK[2]

By the eleventh hour of the eleventh day of the eleventh month in 1918,
President Woodrow Wilson appeared to be the most influential man in the
world. With hostilities over, it seemed clear that American intervention had
changed the course of the war. Even at this point, Wilson insisted that the
United States entered the war for a disinterested, ideological commitment
to humanitarian service rather than a self-interested militaristic quest for
power. Much of the world apparently agreed, expecting him to lead the peace
negotiations at Paris. While Wilson met with leaders of state at Versailles,
however, the U.S. political leader who held the power to determine America's
role in the postwar world was nearly four thousand miles away. According
to the U.S. Constitution, the president may negotiate treaties, but the Senate
is responsible for ratifying them. Since 1816, this responsibility specifically
belonged to the Senate Foreign Relations Committee. By law, Republican
senator Henry Cabot Lodge, the chair of the Foreign Relations Committee
and acting majority leader,[3] stood between President Wilson and his vision
for a new world order.

A born and bred "Boston Brahmin,"[4] Lodge appeared to be the inverse
of Wilson. Separated in birth by six years, both remembered fondly their
connection to the Civil War. Growing up on opposite sides of the Mason-
Dixon Line, each man held the opposing region and the political party that
dominated it in contempt. Secession caused Lodge to distrust southerners
on principle; Reconstruction led Wilson to vow he would never become a
Republican. For most of his life, Lodge would believe that the North was the

South's superior; Wilson would seek to restore the South's honor, despite supporting the outcome of the Civil War. Elite and educated, both men grew to revere American history. Each wrote their own histories of the United States, each of which emphasized its great leaders, especially the nation's first president.[5] Their respective heroes emerged in epic tales heralding the successes of great men. Thomas Jefferson looms large in Wilson's *A History of the American People*, while Lodge wrote biographies of Alexander Hamilton and Daniel Webster.[6] Despite their political and cultural differences, both considered American democracy to be a unique development in the course of human history and, accordingly, the answer to many of the world's problems. They believed the United States held a special purpose in the world that, over time, would be realized by all nations. The form and content of their American exceptionalisms, however, differed in practice.

The Great War provided a moment of crisis and opportunity for these, and other, men in power. Both Wilson and Lodge divided the history of the United States into the same epochs—the Revolutionary War, the Civil War, and the Great War—each with its own leader directing the course of history. As historians of great white men, Lodge and Wilson were keenly aware of their own place in history. Each wanted to be the great white man of the moment. Lodge, however, wanted to limit U.S. international engagement, while Wilson wanted to expand it in unprecedented ways. They were historians seeking to make their individual mark in the historical record; yet history remembers their political legacy as a pair, one in contrast to the other.

As is usually the case for histories of elite white men, the story is actually more complicated than this. The foreign policy debates between political leaders like Wilson and Lodge began with fundamental questions about Americans' orientation with the rest of the world and ended with a divided American culture. By the time the debate over the Covenant of the League of Nations ended, Wilson's predominant contribution to postwar international affairs came to represent a host of issues pertaining to American culture and its place in the world. U.S. participation in the League of Nations depended on the question of whether membership in such an international organization aligned with senators' conception of American identity. In this way, public debates about the postwar world were never limited to international concerns. The future of U.S. foreign policy relied upon the Senate reaching a consensus about the nature and purpose of America in the world. On Capitol Hill, in dining rooms around the country, and in closed-door hotel rooms scattered around Paris in 1919, elite white male Protestants like Wilson and Lodge debated—largely among themselves—the nature and direction of America's empire. Wherever it occurred, these discussions exposed theological, cultural, and political antagonisms that had developed among American Protestants.

Protestants' notions of proper religious thought and action shaped civic discourse about the Covenant of the League of Nations. The fulcrum on which the covenant's ratification rested—whether or not the United States should engage fully with the world or remain isolated from it—also held in the balance internal evangelical debates about whether or not Christians should be "of" the world or live "in" yet isolated from it. Wilson's internationalism called into question the nature of the intimate partnership white Protestants had cultivated between their nonsectarian Christianity and their nationalistic "Americanism." Rather than bring the nation together under the banner of democracy, internationalism, and Christianity, the debate over the Covenant of the League of Nations revealed the differences simmering beneath the surface of white Protestants' shared rhetoric of unselfish Christian service. As senators debated U.S. foreign policy, they relied upon contested notions of Christian ethics, cosmology, and millennial expectation. Each side rested its case for America's proper role in the world on competing interpretations of "true" Christianity.

Christianity on Capitol Hill

It is in an ironic twist that as Wilson gained favor abroad, he lost it at home. In less than a year, Wilson managed to breathe life into an international community and persuade it to create a league of nations that would serve as a moral establishment for collective global security. But even though most Americans supported the idea of a league of nations prior to the war, they rejected the League of Nations Wilson created in their image. As the chair of the Senate Foreign Relations Committee, Lodge became the public face of criticism facing Wilson and the League of Nations. He criticized the president for potentially entangling the United States in global affairs for perpetuity, yet he was generally supportive of *a* league of nations and had been since 1915.[7] Lodge disapproved of portions of the Covenant of the League of Nations through a list of reservations but was willing to negotiate to realize the overarching goal. Despite a series of newspaper articles and political cartoons that depicted Lodge as the person standing between Wilson and his global vision, Lodge was one problem among many for the president and league enthusiasts.

To the ire of both Lodge and Wilson, another partisan group formed to obstruct both men and their political parties. The most vitriolic opponents to the League of Nations were a band of senators who became known as the "Irreconcilables." The group Wilsonians called the "Battalion of Death" consisted of sixteen senators who refused to accept, on any terms, the Covenant of the League of Nations: William E. Borah, Idaho (Republican); Frank B. Brandegee, Connecticut (Republican); Albert B. Fall, New Mexico (Republican); Bert M. Fernald, Maine (Republican); Joseph France, Maryland (Republican); Asle J. Gronna, North Dakota (Republican); Hiram W. Johnson, California (Republican); Philander C. Knox, Pennsylvania (Republican); Robert M. La Follette, Wisconsin (Republican); Joseph Medill McCormick, Illinois (Republican); George H. Moses, New Hampshire (Republican); George W. Norris, Nebraska (Republican); Miles Poindexter, Washington (Republican); James A. Reed, Missouri (Democrat); Lawrence Y. Sherman, Illinois (Republican); and Charles S. Thomas, Colorado (Democrat).[8] These senators could not unanimously agree on anything but the need to thwart U.S. membership in the League of Nations.

The Irreconcilables considered their differences a strength rather than a weakness. They shared what they thought mattered most, a broad interest in upholding national sovereignty. Some did so out of a suspicion of world government, and others were frustrated with "idealism" guiding policy decisions. Despite focusing on different details in their arguments, Irreconcilables' objections to the covenant took a similar form, as each senator argued that Wilson's terms for the League of Nations violated "true" religion or the "natural" order to the world as God designed it. Their subject may have been foreign relations, but their policy decisions relied upon their identification and articulation of what they believed to be the ultimate nature of religion, nationalism, and American exceptionalism.[9] In Congress, an ostensibly secular public institution, senators debated the terms of American Christianity as a matter of foreign relations. The pages of the *Congressional Record* reveal the Senate debated the potential religious repercussions of the U.S. entering the League of Nations because, senators assumed, the United States was either an explicitly Christian nation or a crucial asset to global Christianity.

Wilson's detractors, no less than his supporters, belonged to a nonsectarian Protestant culture that enveloped their civic interests. The Irreconcilables hoped to "save" American society from an "idealistic" organization founded on "unnatural" order. Idealism, in their use of the term, carried negative connotations of being both secular, as opposed to truly or sincerely religious, and romantic and, therefore, unpractical or unrealistic. "Idealistic" possessed rhetorical benefits that served multiple partisan constituencies. Emergent "realists" understood idealism as fundamentally irrational and, therefore, an antiquated or flawed approach to public policy. For their part, premillennialist Protestants who opposed Wilson's vision understood his idealism to be a false interpretation of biblical concepts. The *Congressional Record* reports that one of the primary topics under debate in the Senate was the effect the league would have on America's "chosen" status among nations and, as a result, the advancement of Christianity. Differing conceptions of religion and politics collided as senators debated the proper relationship between God, nations, and citizens as a necessary precursor to proper U.S. foreign relations.

Irreconcilables particularly objected to the possibility that membership in the League of Nations would require the U.S. federal government to bind its citizens in an improper and unnatural allegiance to others. Membership in an international organization could violate individual conscience and disrupt one's loyalties to self, nation, and God. William Borah, the Republican "Lion of Idaho," made this point clear in November 1919 when he delivered the final Senate speech regarding the League of Nations. As the most vocal of all the Irreconcilables, Borah moved Lodge to tears with his opposition to Wilson's covenant. He argued that the covenant threatened U.S. sovereignty, its legitimacy constantly challenged by the existence of a league of nations. For Borah, America's independence from external pressures and its liberty to do as it pleased mattered not only in the post–Great War world but also as an eternal truth. On the Senate floor, Borah proclaimed, "Next to the tie which binds a man to his God is the tie which binds a man to his country." Borah's expression was not merely the dramatic flair of a senator looking to make a spectacle. He asserted that individuals were bound, under God's design, to exist in a world ordered by nationalism. He would not support any other world order, even those that are "ambitious and fascinating" if they threatened to "embarrass or entangle and impede or shackle [U.S.] sovereign will."[10] As an Irreconcilable, Borah would not let such a system come to fruition.

Borah framed this foreign policy issue as a matter that demanded citizens stand up for U.S. interests over their own partisanships or universalizing impulses. He acknowledged that history might judge him to be in error, but he would rather err by "exalting" his patriotism for the nation of Washington, Jefferson, and Lincoln than allow the United States to hold equal power and global position with other nations.[11] Borah's appeal to a trinity of national leaders reveals the intimate relationship between his theism and his nationalism. Individual identity as an American hinged upon a relationship to God and a nation-state. He exhorted his colleagues to the metaphysical nature of democracy, a balance between material and immaterial realities that depended upon a basic optimism in human progress through the nation-state. "Democracy is something more, vastly more, than a mere form of government," he explained. "It is a moral entity, a spiritual force" that depends upon the "moral instincts" of citizens. Government, as a civic authority, held a supernatural purpose to reflect the will of its citizens.[12] Borah's objection to the covenant relied upon white Protestant values of religion as both civic virtue and public good. Religion required nationalism to thrive, reinforcing the authority of the nation-state in the process.

Borah *and* Wilson believed American democracy was a spiritual force sanctioned by God to lead the world. Their ideas for leadership, however, took different forms. Wilson believed the United States served as the bearer of universal truths—the "truth" of democracy being the proper form of government, with white Protestant Christianity the "true," universally transcendent, form of religion. The United States must therefore involve itself in the affairs of the world to protect and defend the least among nations. Borah, in contrast, believed that the United States must remain separate and distinct from all other nations as a testament to the world's "natural" order. Borah feared that U.S. membership in the league might temporarily bring Americans to greater power but would ultimately result in a situation in which "we shall no longer be master of our own spirit." He objected to sharing global power among nations, a move that would strip the United States of sovereignty and "that fine sense of confidence in the people, the soul of democracy."[13] Paraphrasing Mark 8:36, "for what does it profit a man to gain the whole world, and forfeit his own soul," Borah applied his interpretation of biblical exhortations about individuals to his guidelines for statecraft. Borah, like Wilson, conceived of freedom and liberty as God-given rights to both nations and individuals; both understood international affairs to be a matter of building "a Christian world."[14] They disagreed, however, on the direction to which biblical history and theology pointed. Their differences reflected the underlying fault line among nonsectarian Protestants in the twentieth century: should Christians fully engage with the world (including its cultures, political entanglements, and modernization) or maintain distance from the world, especially from non-American cultures? Should the United States provide an example to the world by its actions in international affairs or by remaining removed from other nations? Should American Christians be merely "in" the world or also "of" it?

Irreconcilables confirmed and complicated these ideological tensions by expressing their convictions that foreign policy operated within a Christian world order. Consider, for example, the frustrations of Albert B. Fall, Republican from New Mexico. He saw the Covenant of the League of Nations as violating not only precedents in American history—precedents established by George Washington, expanded upon by James Monroe, and reaffirmed by Abraham Lincoln—but also God's order. If the United States supported this League of Nations, Fall asserted, "we have not only destroyed the Government of our fathers but, in my mind, we have committed a crime against the nations of the earth, against civilization itself, and retarded for more than a thousand years that reign of Christ which we all hope will eventually bring the people of the earth together."[15] For Fall, the United States was not only a part of the Christian progress of history; it was integral to it. This position required the United States to maintain an exceptional and separate status from all other nations.

Similarly, Asle Gronna, Republican from North Dakota, asserted that the Paris Peace Conference neglected to consider "the fundamental principles of Nature's God, which cannot be violated."[16] Gronna considered it unreasonable to ask citizens to forfeit their national patriotism in favor of a unified international identity. Referencing the biblical tale of the Tower of Babel in which God scattered the people of the earth and gave them different languages, Gronna affirmed that his reading of "history" confirmed the need to "keep these nationalities separate." Any attempt to unite the world "upon some altruistic and Utopian principle" would ensure its destruction rather than its progress.[17] In a clever turn of phrase, Gronna differentiated between two separate Christian interpretations of God's will. Identifying his own with "history," Gronna affirmed his position as natural and proper— legitimizing it through biblical narrative and the progress of time—while discrediting Wilson's position as man-made and, therefore, false "altruism." Gronna, and many other opponents of the league, signified Wilson's position as "Utopian"—that is, idealistic, secular, and unchristian—even as Christians around the world recognized Wilson as a Christian statesman and advocate for the social gospel.

Gronna's objection went beyond Wilson. He understood that Wilson did not create the notion of an essentially Christian international brotherhood from whole cloth, so Gronna extended his critique to Christian ministers who promoted the idea. Clergy who supported the league, Gronna claimed, preached a false doctrine by ignoring humanity's inherently sinful nature. He considered the possibility of a perpetual peace a cosmological and teleological impossibility. Even though optimism for the establishment of world peace cut across parochial lines—including, for instance, Wilson, Borah, Theodore Roosevelt, and Jane Addams—Gronna placed the blame of this "falsehood" on Wilson and the liberal Protestant clergy who perpetuated it. Their claim of a "war to end wars" was inconsistent with Gronna's interpretation of scripture: "We cannot claim that we advocate peace and at the same time do the things which we know will provoke war. We are either in favor of peace or we are in favor of war. We cannot serve two masters. We are either believers in the teachings of Christ or we are dissenters."[18] In Gronna's eyes, Wilson had undermined his stated commitment to a perpetual peace by writing a document that potentially committed America to future conflicts. To Gronna, this was not merely bad policy but false Christianity. True Christians, he believed, should oppose the league if they wished to be consistent in their calls for peace.

These types of complaints by Irreconcilables struck at the heart of Wilson's social Christian supporters, who formed the base of the pro-league fervor in both the United States and much of Europe. As historian Markku Ruotsila has explained, the "most typical religious argument" waged against the league was the accusation that liberal Protestants imbued the League of Nations with a millennial role that rightfully belonged to the church.[19] And indeed, liberal Protestant clergy infused their support of the league with postmillennial claims that required the actions of the state. They assumed that secular nation-states had a role to play in establishing the kingdom of God on earth. Democrats and Progressives influenced by this state-based social gospel supported the league because they were convinced it advanced the world toward the fulfillment of their Christian mission. Progress, for social Christians, required a national ethic of disinterested Christian service. They believed American democracy embodied this ideal, and its establishment through the League of Nations confirmed both American exceptionalism and Christian truth as they understood it.

Every partisan group considered the League of Nations as a clear "sign of the times," but each interpreted that sign for its own ends. In a debate with Senator Lodge, founding member of the League to Enforce Peace Abbott Lawrence Lowell, for example, affirmed the league as a reflection of the Bible—a sign that Christians were successfully establishing the kingdom of God on earth.[20] Christian internationalists like Lowell believed the league ushered the world closer to realizing a brotherhood of mankind under the fatherhood of God. In other words, the league as Wilson imagined it would be Christianity applied to international affairs. In his defense, Lowell used the same verse that league *opponents* often used, Matthew 16:3, "O ye hypocrites, ye can discern the face of the sky; but can ye not discern the signs of the times?" Reading the same text and witnessing the same current events, Irreconcilables like Borah saw the League of Nations as an aberration of God's will, while Lowell and other league proponents believed it fulfilled God's will.

American Christians did not hold a shared policy position as Christians; instead they shared biblical evidence and similar appeals to transcendent truth as justifications for their competing positions. Whether opponents or advocates for the league, U.S. politicians appealed to American exceptionalism and the spiritual force of democracy through Christian aphorisms. Philander C. Knox, an Irreconcilable Republican senator from Pennsylvania, for example, mirrored Wilson's rhetoric while opposing its content. The United

States was known around the world, Knox explained, as "a land of promise, flowing with milk and honey." Drawing on social Christian discourse, Knox acknowledged the unprecedented state of world affairs in which the United States stood at the brink of saving humanity, "pregnant with the political salvation of the world."[21] Because of its exceptional status, he reasoned, the United States must not forfeit its sovereignty to other nations. Altering the nation in such a way would violate God's design, because "to us, and for us, God has set up this one Government founded on the equality of man. Our feet must not depart from the paths He has marked for us. Ours is the duty to keep the faith untainted. We shall not wander after false gods."[22] For Knox, any departure from the historical narrative that began with the Israelites, progressed to the Puritans, and led the United States to enter the Great War for the benefit of humanity would violate God's clear will for what he imagined as the most exceptional nation on earth.

Both Republicans and Democrats subscribed to the extrabiblical drama that Knox articulated so clearly. Wilson and Christian internationalists, no less than Knox and other Republican Senators, believed that God chose the United States to fulfill a certain purpose in the world. Generally that purpose was to be an example, but the specific details were fodder for more than a century of debate that culminated in this standoff in the Senate over the fate of the League of Nations. Religion and politics were not separate spheres of consideration for Wilson or the Senate but rather two seamlessly integrated aspects of American identity. These political leaders held the state of Christianity in the world, and the application of biblical interpretation to American and international law, to be political and legal issues warranting civic debate. The question of how the United States could best embody Christianity in its foreign relations plagued the public. The solution would constitute the basis of American foreign relations for the remainder of the twentieth century.

Even individual senators who did not identify with a specific denomination or demonstrate a particularly strong level of religiosity were nonetheless steeped in this social Christian culture that drew upon an extrabiblical American narrative. Irreconcilable senator George Norris of Nebraska, for instance, objected to the proposed League of Nations because of the repercussions it would hold for Christianity. Convinced that an unamended version of the league covenant would endanger missionary work in Asia, Norris warned, "It is the Christian religion that is going to be blotted off the face of the earth over there."[23] Having heard stories of Chinese converts to Christianity being tortured by the Japanese government, Norris exhorted his fellow senators to consider the American Christian missionaries, the Chinese converts "who have given up their pagan religion," and the "heathen Government" that wants to persecute those who "have confessed to the religion of Jesus Christ."[24] Ratifying the treaty would, Norris worried, undo the progress he saw missionaries making in changing cultural, political, and social norms in China.

Senator Norris asked his colleagues to make a policy decision based on the interests of missionary endeavors, because, he assumed, the success of Christian missionary work was in the best interest of the nation. And vice versa. Senator Norris's concern for Christianity is all the more interesting because in the same speech he confessed, "I am not a member of any church; I am not a member of any religious organization." And yet, he avowed, "My hand shall wither and my lips shall be sealed in eternal silence before I will ever give my official approval to any act that will stamp out the religion of Jesus Christ and establish paganism in its stead."[25] Even though Norris was religiously unaffiliated, he was willing to defend the advancement of Christian missionary efforts as a *national* civic mission. The power of a nonsectarian American Protestant culture and the widespread influence of social Christian discourse wove the concerns of humanity, American nationalism, and Christianity into a secular vision for foreign relations. The custodians of those interests, however, disagreed about what precisely they were defending or advancing.

The Great War of the Protestant Establishment

Although Norris, Wilson, and countless others claimed to stand for Christianity, their claim—however universal they purported it to be—was contested by other Christians. Americans had a difficult time defining the relationship between Christianity and their nation, let alone reaching a consensus about what it meant for foreign policy. Their attempts to do so revealed the interchangeability of national and religious identities. American Protestantism had shifted dramatically within the lifetime of the policymakers deciding the fate of the Covenant of the League of Nations. Although denominational affiliations, like President Wilson's Presbyterianism, continued to hold meaning for adherents, the boundaries between church affiliations had blurred among Americans affiliated with religious groups. New forms of identifying and measuring one's Christianity had gained credence in American culture since the mid-nineteenth-century. Evangelicals, for instance, distinguished themselves from other American Christians by what they read, what political issues they supported, and which social activities they attended or protested. The more salient organizing principle for evangelicals in America was not which church one attended but the degree and form of piety one performed. This Great War in the twentieth century, much like the Civil War in the nineteenth, hardened these distinctions among American Protestants even as they shared a sacred text and a normative discourse.

The debate over the Covenant of the League of Nations exacerbated the growing tension over what constituted "true" Christianity in America. Even though conservative evangelicals supported the war and detested German autocracy, they largely attempted to abide by the nineteenth-century evangelical admonition to be "in" the world but not "of" it.[26] This meant refraining from political activity and interactions with any worldly influences that detracted from the development of individual Christian piety. The urge to separate from "the world" resulted from a myriad of theological positions, including the belief in total human depravity, biblical inerrancy, and premillennialism. Since human nature is inherently sinful, these conservative evangelicals reasoned, humanity cannot be expected to progress through individual volition. Likewise, they believed that collective will could not save or redeem humanity. Conservative evangelicals, therefore, considered any effort to transform the world or improve the human condition to be in vain. As a part of their general distance from any matters of culture, premillennialists asserted the need for Christians to maintain a purposeful aloofness from politics and social involvement outside of their religious community.

Wilson's successful advocacy for the League of Nations in Paris drove these conservative premillennialist evangelicals to participate in civic debates as a united sectarian movement. They noted their own change in the body politic by identifying themselves as "fundamentalists" and by insisting that their authority derived from their separation from political debate.[27] When President Wilson returned from Paris in July 1919, antileague organizations, like the League for the Preservation of American Independence, and fundamentalist figures, like *Christian Worker magazine* editor James M. Gray, encouraged Americans to prevent U.S. participation in the league. Although Gray feigned neutrality to maintain his evangelical piety, he advocated agitation against the league as "a political more than a religious question."[28] In Gray's eyes, opposing the league protected the United States and God's will in the world. Referring to this position as political rather than religious allowed him to take a policy position without disturbing his piety and, therefore, becoming too worldly. This insistence on creating a stark line between religion and politics allowed fundamentalists to enter public debate while maintaining a claim to being removed from American culture and its place in the world.

Well before the Scopes Monkey Trial in 1925, fundamentalists and their liberal counterparts began the ideological conflict that would influence much of American religious history in the twentieth century. The spark that ignited these battles was not public education but the place of America in the world. Throughout the war, postmillennial liberal Protestants criticized premillennialists for their distance from the American war effort. By failing to promote American democracy, they asserted, premillennialists revealed their empty patriotism and false theology. Premillennialists denied these attacks and shifted public discourse about Christianity in three important ways. First, fundamentalists counterattacked by accusing postmillennial Protestants of possessing a theology heavily influenced by German theologians, which rendered them both disloyal and unchristian. While their critique rings of wartime propaganda, the assertion is not without basis. German theologians who created the theoretical framework for biblical criticism significantly influenced postmillennial liberal Protestants in America. Second, premillennial Protestants charged postmillennialists with confusing human institutions with divine ones and, therefore, misunderstanding the Bible. Premillennialists considered state-based reforms to detract from the mission of the church, while postmillennialists understood state-based reform *to be* the mission of the church. Third, and most importantly, premillennialists engaged in public debates to reinforce their values while articulating a clear boundary between religion and politics. This rhetorical maneuver drew attention to the way postmillennialists conceived of politics as *an extension of*, rather than a distraction from, their piety.

Premillennial Protestants consciously engaged in public efforts to refashion American public life to adhere to what they understood to be the fundamental notions of biblical living.[29] In defending their claim to serve as the custodians of American culture, fundamentalists accused Wilson of not putting "America first." This allegation closely resembled statements from league opponents, like the Irreconcilables, who accused the president of prioritizing the needs of the world above his own country. This dictum, while seemingly patriotic, referred to only a portion of the nation. Fundamentalists' emphasis on "America" was a tacit demand to protect and defend *white* American Protestants like themselves before all others. Wilson's internationalism threatened the cultural authority of white upper- and middle-class Protestants in the United States and, by extension, their authority over other nations, races, and religions. Christian anti-internationalists, who often identified as fundamentalists and followed premillennialist eschatology, interpreted the world order Wilson and his liberal Protestant supporters proposed as the beginning of a unified world government, a "sign" they understood to indicate biblical end times. They espoused a policy agenda similar to Irreconcilables—that United States must not join the League of Nations under any circumstances—but they cast their position in cosmic terms.

Successful opposition to Wilson's internationalism required a consensus built upon an interpretation of American exceptionalism requiring distance from the rest of the world. Although he was respected broadly, Senator Lodge did not represent the majority of League of Nations skeptics or Wilsonian opponents. Irreconcilables represented even fewer Americans (indeed, no single Irreconcilable even represented the group of sixteen). Working together with fundamentalists, however, Irreconcilables and Republicans successfully challenged Wilson, liberal Protestant social gospel reformers, and internationalists more broadly. The general tide of isolationist-inspired policies and "in-the-world-but-not-of-it" Protestants crested in 1919 with the League Fight. The overwhelmingly internationalist perspective of the Wilson administration, along with the influx of immigrants in the opening decades of the twentieth century, contributed to a postwar backlash that sought to purify American identity by isolating the center of American culture. Movements like "100-percent Americanism" attacked "hyphenated" Americans or other perceived stains upon "native" white Protestant America.[30] In the racial and religious violence that erupted following the war, nativist white Protestants targeted African Americans, Jews, and Catholics as corrupting influences on the United States. Their call for a purified "Americanism" presumed American identities to be white, Anglo-American, conservative, anti-internationalist, and *premillennial* Protestant.

Wilson gave white Protestants plenty of reasons to fear the loss of their cultural capital. Jews, Catholics, and anticolonialists in the United States and around the world stepped forward to support the president's insistence upon the greater global good above national interests. He and his social-gospel-inspired league supporters thought of this goal—the full Christianization of the world by removing the power of partisan self-interest—as the ultimate expression of their Christianity. According to Grayson, Wilson had a different notion of how America could be first among all others. Believing that the United States entered the war "without selfishness, without purpose of gaining anything for herself," Grayson explained, Wilson considered it "almost inconceivable to him that his fellow-countrymen would not agree with the great purpose of the covenant of the League of Nations."[31] Indeed, Wilson believed he spoke for the nation, without even consulting Congress or the general public. He presumed to represent universal truths of patriotism, nationalism, and internationalism. He remained confident that the covenant would ensure American (that is white Anglo-American Protestant) leadership in the world rather than erode it. All nations belonged to this brotherhood of nations, but all were not called to be the custodian of civilization, the first among brother nations.

Wilson was conscious of the sea change underway in American Protestantism, but he proclaimed himself unconcerned. In an unusual moment of self-reflection during the Paris Peace Conference, the president spoke with Edith Benham about his own popularity and his predictions for the public's reception of the League of Nations plan. Specifically, she wondered, how could he claim to represent the will of the people during this unprecedented moment in world history and without any example to follow as his guide? The president replied, there is no need to follow precedent when the progress of the nation is at stake. Benham pressed further. How, if the president did not consult newspapers, did he know what the people wanted? Wilson replied that it was natural for him to know and understand the desires of the American people, as he and the American people were one and the same.[32] Seven years after taking office, the self-consciousness that had defined Wilson's private moments in the White House seemed to have disappeared. Wilson spoke with confidence of his ability to represent the United States, gaining assurance as a patriarch through his southern evangelicalism, confidence in his teleological purpose through his social Christianity, and legal confirmation in the Constitution.

Still unsatisfied, Benham pointed out that his approach was a matter of "deductions only," leaving her wondering, "don't you go deeper than that?"— perhaps implying *shouldn't* you? Granting Benham some leeway, Wilson replied, "possibly so," but Benham noted after some pause the president concluded he was filled with "American thought" enough to merely inform fellow Americans what came to his mind.[33] Benham informed the president of "the way the little people, the poor, look to him as a Messiah to give a new light in the world, possibly because they had not had a practical person to give practical expression to their aspirations." Wilson answered her skepticism about his ability to solve the world's problems with conviction. "He said the religious teaching hadn't found a practical solution for the troubles of the world and states and they must have someone to give them practical relief for their distress."[34] Wilson believed, with more confidence than he had when he entered office, that his foreign policy agenda (not he as a messiah) would provide that relief because such policies were based on what he was convinced were the universal truths expressed most clearly in his white Protestant social Christianity.

Threats to the Great American Mission

At the eleventh hour of the League Fight, Christian internationalists felt the heat from the myriad criticisms coming from all sides. Even social Christians were becoming less confident than the president in the eventual triumph of the League of Nations as the manifestation of America's light in the world. Liberal Protestants who supported the covenant began to recognize how intertwined domestic and foreign policy had become. For example, Sidney Gulick, a prolific member of the FCC's Wartime Commission, admitted in his own work that American democracy had to fulfill its own promises to Christianize American democracy fully before appeals to the rest of the world could be successful. The conversion of the world, Gulick reasoned, demanded high standards at home: "The success of foreign missions depends very closely on the success of Christianity in the towns and cities of Christendom. The wickedness of Christendom discredits Christianity everywhere. Foreign and home missions are inseparable."[35] Several constituencies shared this sentiment that the blemishes within American Christianity under Wilson's leadership affected the advancement of both Christianity and democracy abroad.

No one lobbied on this premise more than the National Colored Congress for World Democracy. Operating under the auspices of the National Equal Rights League (NERL), the National Colored Congress (NCC) crafted an "Address to the Country and the World" in December 1918. The NCC, which included notables like Ida B. Wells-Barnett, R. H. Singleton, and others acting on behalf of "colored America," emphatically congratulated "their fellow countrymen and their Government on being the instrument by which the God of Righteousness turned the tide of battle for the forces of liberty."[36] Notably, the Congress accepted the terms on which the war was fought and the religious framework surrounding this pivotal moment in history.[37] They did not, however, want this moment to pass by without reckoning with the oppressive and unrelenting discrimination experienced by a large contingent of American citizens.

The NCC looked to the creation of the League of Nations with great hope because its arrival signaled a new era of humanity. In a world with a League of Nations, "every denial or violation of justice, humanity, and democracy" could "become a matter for correction and abrogation on a world basis by a world court."[38] Speaking on behalf of all African Americans, the NCC impressed upon the U.S. Congress, the president of the United States, and foreign dignitaries the centrality of racial equality to extending liberty, democracy, and peace around the world.[39] Without correcting racial discrimination and oppression in the United States, the NCC asserted, "there will not be the dawning of a new day of democracy, nor of a new era of permanent peace."[40] The American mission of advancing of democracy would fail, the NCC warned, unless the United States fully established civil rights and social justice for its citizens of color.

Both NERL and Wilson considered the discussions of the Paris Peace Conference a potential triumph for the "brotherhood of man" and "fatherhood of God." NERL's vision of how that goal might be implemented, however, differed significantly from Wilson's and rested upon the organization's ability to persuade the Peace Conference to end racial discrimination in the United States as well as among the new concert of nations. To that end, William Trotter had traveled to Paris with Wells-Barnett and others to speak directly to the president and other foreign dignitaries. They held a common cause with the Japanese delegates' efforts to establish a racial equality amendment, but they traveled to Paris without the foreknowledge that such negotiations would occur. In fact, few delegations granted any meetings with the NERL. In response to being denied a seat at any diplomatic table, Trotter and his fellow activists instead issued a poignant open letter to the delegates of the Paris Peace Conference. They implored world leaders to recognize that a "color line," especially the one in the United States, impedes any cultivation of democracy around the world. As a way of making complex and systematic oppression recognizable on an individual level, the letter focused on the experience of a pregnant African American woman who was lynched in the United States.[41] While white internationalists and isolationists debated the terms of "true" Americanism and Christianity at home, Trotter attempted to make it clear to the international delegations at Paris that neither vision of American democracy was worth emulating in its current form.

After he returned to the United States, Trotter testified to the Senate Foreign Relations Committee in August 1919. In Washington, Trotter offered an amendment to the Treaty of Versailles, a potential fifteenth point to Wilson's Fourteen Points. Speaking as a representative of the NERL, Trotter explained that this war, according to the United States government, was fought for "world democracy, universal liberty, and universal humanity." Trotter reasoned that the terms of peace must not fall short of those aims. He therefore proposed that member nations "assure full and complete protection of life and liberty to all their inhabitants, without distinctions of birth, nationality, language, race, or religion, and agree that all their citizens, respectively, shall be equal before the law."[42] Following the Japanese delegation's efforts to prevent racial discrimination across member states, Trotter called for the United States to declare legal protections for minorities *within* member states. This amendment, he argued, was a necessary amendment for senators to pass before the United States ratified the Covenant of the League of Nations. If Lodge and other Republicans were making a list of reservations to be met before U.S. ratification, then racial equality ought to be considered among them.

Trotter's testimony to Congress implicated the majority race and religion in the United States. White American Protestants had a history of securing their own privileges and then masking that privilege as a matter of inherent individual rights while simultaneously denying those rights to others. The majority of African Americans were born in America, yet, as the peace negotiations made clear, they did not—and continually would not—experience "the enjoyment of full democracy, of full equality of rights, of full liberty, of full protection of life" or even the pursuit of happiness.[43] For Trotter and the African Americans he represented, the concepts and functions of race and religion intertwined to oppress, even as—and perhaps especially because— social Christians believed their interpretation of a Christianized democracy liberated humanity.

Additional testimony on behalf of the amendment came from Allen W. Whaley, an AME minister and graduate of Harvard Law School. Whaley insisted that the moral integrity of the nation required the correction of the social sin of slavery. A friend of Marcus Garvey and a supporter of the Universal Negro Improvement Association, Whaley encouraged a broader vision for social salvation. Lest there be any confusion as to why this amendment was needed now, Whaley explained, "the Declaration of Independence meant something to the white Americans, but it did not mean anything to the colored Americans."[44] While his own experiences of discrimination inspired his testimony, Whaley was careful not to appear to be speaking from self-interest alone but on behalf of justice for all: "We want our Constitution, beautiful as the language is, beautiful as the sentiments are, to be a real thing and not a mere sign of nothing."[45] His testimony revealed how the American exceptionalism Irreconcilables and Christian internationalists held so dear, preserved, rather than transformed, social injustices within American democracy by paternally reforming *others* rather than all of American society.

Whaley and Trotter were not the only voices being added to the *Congressional Record*. Together they constituted, however, a quarter of the speakers addressing "Negroes, Race Equality and Protection of, Etc."[46] Their testimony exists in the documented history of the Senate Foreign Relations Committee without further commentary. It is unclear to what degree senators contemplated racial discrimination or amendments proposed by these activists. Much of the written records reflect an interest in specific countries and their relations with the United States or, more broadly, the sovereignty of the United States. Correcting inequalities experienced by Americans or minority groups in the United States took a backseat to debates over the relative strength and reach of this nation in relation to that nation. Racial minorities or the victims of racial violence may have been "in" the nation, but senators, much like the president, disregarded their concerns as being "of" the nation. Underwritten by the white Protestant moral establishment, the league debates in the Senate and on Wilson's national tour concentrated on divisions *among* white Protestants, particularly the divisions between liberals and conservatives, as well as post- and premillennialists. He did not reconcile the disparities between the words and deeds of those representing American democracy.

The New Normal

Disappointed by Republicans' overwhelming resistance to the League of Nations, President Wilson undertook a cross-country speaking tour to drum up support. Pressed by a sense of urgency to recapture popular opinion before the Senate Foreign Relations Committee concluded its public hearings, Wilson maintained a vigorous schedule, even though his health had declined in Paris. The Wilsons traveled by train for three-and-a-half weeks, with Wilson speaking at over forty engagements, several of which included events in Irreconcilables' home states.[47] With Henry Ford funding much of the public relations efforts,[48] the tour attempted to bring significant exposure—and clarification—to the president's motivations behind the League of Nations.

Wilson continually returned to three themes: the importance of Article X, the preservation of the Monroe Doctrine, and the centrality of the League of Nations to establishing peace. Article X guaranteed that member nations would "respect and preserve" the territorial integrity of other member nations. Irreconcilables interpreted it as a nullification of the Monroe Doctrine by allowing European nations to potentially interfere in the "American hemisphere." This interpretation exacerbated the fear that the United States would be "entangled" in future wars that did not directly threaten its territories or interests. In Wilson's interpretation, Article X bound all nations together in a new world order in which the threat of territorial conquest for one nation was a threat to all. The idea was to maintain the sovereignty of all nations by honoring national borders through collective security. If all nations entered this covenant, then Article X would be the cornerstone that prevented future wars because it was in no country's best interest to gain power by military conquest. Instead of threatening American sovereignty and prerogatives in the western hemisphere, Article X, to Wilson's mind, protected both by making it mutually beneficial to prevent war altogether. Even as Irreconcilables developed their arguments on the Senate floor, the tenor of Wilson's appeals remained unchanged. He insisted that the League of Nations was the natural conclusion to America's entry into the war, the embodiment of American ideals, and the fulfillment of America's purpose—in his eyes, its promise—to the world. By creating and leading this new world organization, Wilson believed the United States would "save" the world.

Despite Wilson's publicity tour, critics continued to oppose the League of Nations from all sides. Irreconcilables, like Borah, would not ratify the treaty (in whole or in parts) under any circumstances. Reservationists, like Lodge, believed that the Treaty of Versailles could be ratified without the League of Nations and with certain amendments, leaving the Senate to consider the two issues separately. Premillennial, antistatist evangelicals likewise opposed the Covenant of the League of Nations but not necessarily the peace treaty. They considered the covenant a product of human folly, a foolish errand to Christianize the social order when, as they understood it, that mission belonged to the church rather than any state. African Americans and women's suffragists spoke powerfully against both the league and the treaty because its design did not fulfill its stated aims. First- and second-generation immigrants from Europe and Asia opposed Wilson's league because they saw little benefit to the United States being a part of it. To these distinct yet often overlapping constituencies, Wilson's position was untenable and idealistic.

Wilson soldiered on. Refusing to accept idealism as a source of weakness, Wilson asserted the importance of making one's ideals manifest in public policy. As he explained in Sioux Falls, South Dakota, in September, "That is the way I know I am an American. . . . America is the only idealistic nation in the world." As he had in his private conversation with Benham, Wilson proclaimed his authority as the primary representative of American ideals. He had "saturated" himself "in the records of that spirit," learning "everywhere in them there is this authentic tone of the love of justice and the service of humanity."[49] Wilson exhorted his audience to realize and embrace the assurance U.S. involvement in the war brought to other nations. If the United States did not lead the world "in this new enterprise of concerted power," "mankind would have no other place to turn. It is the hope of nations all over the world that America will do this great thing."[50]

When serving other nations failed to resonate with his audiences as a public good, Wilson insisted more narrowly upon serving fellow Americans by supporting the Treaty of Versailles and the Covenant of the League of Nations. In Pueblo, Colorado, later that month, Wilson pleaded with his audience not to allow the death of their doughboys to be in vain. The covenant, he asserted, was not an "absolute guarantee" against any future war but was an instrument through which Americans could "make good their redemption of the world. For nothing less depends upon us, nothing less than the liberation and salvation of the world."[51] By explaining his motivations and his interpretation of the league, Wilson was confident that "men will see the truth." He assumed this truth in particular would appeal to Americans because "it is going to lead us, and through us, the world, out into pastures of quietness and peace such as the world never dreamed of before."[52]

Although it was not scheduled as such, Pueblo, Colorado, proved to be the final stop of Wilson's western tour. It would also prove to be the last public address of his political career. En route to Wichita, Kansas, Dr. Grayson worried over the president's head pain, fatigue, and general discomfort. He had the train stop several times so that Wilson could walk and get some fresh air, yet the president's symptoms only worsened as the night went on. Edith stayed at her husband's side, witnessing what historians now recognize as the warning signs for a probable stroke. Much to the chagrin of the president, and with questionable constitutionality, his secretary, physician, and wife decided on his behalf to cancel the tour and return to Washington.

Five days later, on October 1, 1919, Wilson suffered a stroke that impaired the functionality of his left arm and leg, limited his vision, and diminished his mental acuity. Wilson's recovery made little progress during October and November, the very months in which the Senate wrapped up its debate on the league. Edith and Grayson limited visitors, trying to hide the severity of the president's condition. Their efforts largely failed as both contemporaries and later historians recognized that something was very wrong with the president. An already heated situation was made worse as senators' messages to the president—from both Republicans and Democrats—went unanswered. As Senator Borah gave the final speech of the league debate, President Wilson laid in bed at the opposite end of Pennsylvania Avenue. The White House was silent.

On November 19, the Senate rejected the Treaty of Versailles even though it included Lodge's fourteen "reservations." After some deliberation on procedure, senators voted again on the treaty, but this time without Lodge's reservations. Both with reservations and without reservations, the Senate fell short of the two-thirds majority needed to ratify the Treaty of Versailles. With enough senators still unsatisfied, the Senate reconsidered the treaty in March 1920. The third version of the treaty, which included reservations, also failed. Wilson struggled to cope with the fate of the league, his nation, and his own political career. Daily, the president would have either Edith or Grayson, sometimes both, read scripture to him. When he learned that his own nation did not join the league, Wilson specifically requested 2 Corinthians 4:8–9, "We are troubled on every side, yet not distressed; we are perplexed, but not in despair; Persecuted, but not forsaken; cast down, but not destroyed."[53] Grayson later recalled that verses similar to this one became frequent recitations during Wilson's final year in the White House. Grayson, who defended

Wilson's character to the very end, admired the president for his emphasis on forgiveness. He knew well the president's consuming disappointment, yet he did not dwell on it. Grayson would never admit it, but forgiveness may not have come as naturally to Wilson as he first thought. In this moment of his life, Wilson asked repeatedly to be *reminded* to forgive.

A Separate Peace

What Wilson expected to be a triumph for humanity, Christianity, and the United States proved popular on the world's stage but failed on a national level. Despite the "crusading spirit" of the war and nationalist fervor, Wilson failed to unite all Americans behind his new world order. Elite white Protestants like Wilson claimed to speak on behalf of all Americans, but they failed to prove that they were, indeed, the custodians of American identity and statecraft. The Covenant of the League of Nations exposed the underlying sectarianisms supporting white Protestants' politics of American exceptionalism. National debates over the Covenant of the League of Nations divided Americans along more complicated divisions than isolationists and internationalists or Republicans and Democrats. As the world struggled to decide the terms of postwar international relations, Americans questioned their own established moral order; they questioned their own ideological commitments vis-à-vis the rest of the world; they questioned the veracity and superiority of their truth claims; they reflected on the ways in which other nations perceived their choices; and they reconsidered their self-made and self-defined purpose in the world.

White Protestants, in particular, could not agree on whether or not the league represented or destroyed global Christianity, if the United States was integral to the progress of the world, or if progress was even a teleological possibility. The question of whether the United States should join the League of Nations drew attention to the plurality of American Protestant identities and their divergent interpretations of scripture. Rather than embolden the American social Christian ideal of an international brotherhood, the results of Wilson's peace negotiations hardened the boundaries between competing white Protestant claims to American identity. White liberal postmillennial Protestants felt acutely under attack, as Irreconcilables, Republicans, and fundamentalists critiqued their interpretation of Christian progress and American exceptionalism. Speaking a rhetoric of universality, liberal postmillennial Protestants, like Wilson and other Christian internationalists, expected to advance a world order that integrated religion and the state. Instead, a variety of partisans united to construct a world order that separated religious ends from the powers of states.

6

The Crucifixion and Resurrection of Woodrow Wilson

In 1920, we witnessed the crucifixion of Wilson's ideal of peace, but soon in the providence of God we will behold its resurrection.
— J O S E P H   T U M U L T Y [1]

During the ten-year respite which we had after 1918, many people easily concluded that Wilson had failed. Then in September of 1931, the series of aggression began which spread until a billion people were engulfed and the entire world was at war. With each aggression the voice of Woodrow Wilson became more tragically prophetic.
— B E R N A R D   B A R U C H [2]

In March 1921 the world witnessed the formal transfer of power between Democratic president Woodrow Wilson and Republican president Warren Harding. In anticipation of Harding's inauguration and the official end of Wilson's presidency, Edward Martin, an editor of *LIFE* magazine, wrote President Wilson to explain why he continued to be a Wilsonian Democrat. During the presidential election, the Republican Party had challenged the basis of Wilson's credibility, and, thus, his legacy. Martin disputed this account, writing, "It has always seemed to me that your politics were Christianized and I think that Christianization of politics is not only the world's best bet, but its only chance."[3] Martin was "fairly satisfied" with Wilson's performance as a statesman, yet he confessed to not being entirely certain of what specific Christian principles guided Wilson's statecraft. When opponents listed the president's failures, Martin admitted, the claims were reasonable, but he could find nothing to substantiate the idea that Wilson's administration was a mistake. Even when Wilson appeared to lose a political battle, he seemed to be winning a larger war.[4]

Martin was—and is—not alone in his struggle to evaluate Wilson's presidency. Wilson's reform agenda reflected significant changes in the way Americans conceived of the purpose of the federal government and the relationship between individual citizens and their nation. Historians and public figures have debated Wilson's legacy since before his term even ended. Whether these debates primarily concern Wilson's policies or his character more generally, they often rely on the same evidence to reach separate conclusions. Irreconcilables criticized the validity of Wilson's idealism because they considered it a misguided, or even false, conception of the natural order

to the world. Martin and many other devoted followers remained committed to Wilson's internationalist vision because they understood his idealism
to be the application of Christianity to foreign affairs. The idea that Wilson's
League of Nations represented a Christian utopia served as both a blessing
and a curse to Wilson's legacy.

Americans made sense of the new place of the United States in the world by
debating Wilson's religion. The significations ascribed to Wilson—Christian,
idealist, utopian, and the like—are not neutral, ahistorical ideas but interpretive choices. Identifying Wilson's internationalism as utopian or idealist,
Christian or unchristian, American or un-American legitimized a particular
narrative of American culture while discrediting alternatives. Wilson's supporters were not casual observers in these cultural and political debates about
Wilson and the public role of his Christianity. Wilsonians actively shaped the
public perception of Wilson and the internationalism he, and they, sought to
establish. Rather than retreat from public activism following the 1920 election, Wilsonians, including especially administration insiders, reformulated
Wilson's internationalism for the postwar era and the context in which they
lived. The war abroad did not disenchant Christian internationalists from the
pursuit of a brotherhood of mankind. The overwhelming presence of racial
discrimination, sectarianism, and isolationism at home, however, led to their
disillusionment with evangelicalism. In the process, Wilsonians continued
to focus their reform mission on the state and public life rather than on the
church or individual souls.

The "Crucifixion" of the Anointed One

Wilson was not running for a third term in 1920—indeed he could not physically endure a campaign—but Americans nonetheless grappled with his
appearance in another presidential election. The general election was a refer-
endum on his ideas for world order. Making sense of Wilson's legacy required
Americans to consider a matrix of policy issues regarding "Americanism," a
national self-understanding defined formally through domestic and foreign
policy and informally through public discourse. In 1920, this American "way
of life" centered upon reactions to the Great War and Wilson's internationalist response to it. The existence of the League of Nations, and Wilson's role
in constructing it, recast fundamental questions about American democracy
in a world struggling to construe an *international* geopolitical order. Americans were ready for the end of European empires, but policymakers struggled
with lingering questions about what the new world order should look like:
What constitutes a legitimate nation? How should nations interact? Is the

League of Nations necessary to that system of interaction? If so, how should the organization be constituted? Different parties' answers to these questions revealed the competing philosophies about American democracy in the years immediately following World War I. Throughout the campaign season, Wilson served as a powerful symbol for these contested visions for America in the world.

When it came to foreign policy agendas, both Republicans and Democrats agreed that international cooperation was necessary "to preserve the peace of the world."[5] Beyond that basic premise, however, the two parties could not find common ground. "The outstanding features of the Democratic administration," the Republican Party platform explained, "have been complete unpreparedness for war and complete unpreparedness for peace."[6] In particular, the GOP condemned Wilson's foreign policy from his engagement with Mexico in his first term to the Paris Peace Conference in his second. Republicans argued that Wilson disregarded the precedents established by previous presidents and, therefore, failed to put Americans and their interests first. Republicans considered his actions not only deplorable but also unconstitutional by denying senators a role in negotiating the terms of the Treaty of Versailles. They found the Covenant of the League of Nations deeply flawed and in need of numerous amendments if the United States were to eventually join. Republicans framed their platform as a "return" to the "normal" Americanism that existed prior to the war. This message appealed to voters across partisan lines who were anxious to turn away from the direction President Wilson had steered the nation.[7]

The Democratic platform, in contrast, fully endorsed President Wilson and pledged to continue his policies. Democrats viewed Wilson's actions in Paris as laudable and a necessary step in reconstituting world order. Rather than obfuscate Wilson's break with "traditional isolation," the party praised his bravery in doing so. The problem, Democrats argued, was essentially a clash of personalities between the president and senators, especially Henry Cabot Lodge, who were envious of Wilson's leadership and the Democratic Party's success. If elected, Democrats promised to ratify the Covenant of the League of Nations without the Senate's amendments. Under Democratic leadership, the United States would join the league immediately "to aid effectively in the restoration of order throughout the world." The nation's honor, they alleged, would then be restored "in the front rank of spiritual, commercial and industrial advancement."[8] Even without Wilson at the helm, the Democratic Party proclaimed, Americans should stay the course.

Wilson's vision of service to mankind had united a broad array of interest groups during the war, but this consensus fell apart when the president attempted to bring his words to life. Wilson's attempt to project a unified Americanism on the world's stage exposed numerous divisions on the home front. Democrats and Republicans, isolationists and internationalists, doves and hawks, postmillennialists and premillennialists, modernists and fundamentalists, as well as "native" (white) and "hyphenated" (immigrant) Americans could agree that they should serve the common good of the world, but they could not agree on precisely what constituted the common good or the necessary means of achieving it. While Wilson presented it as a universal and international vision, his proposed world order was undeniably partisan. Its roots were national and its fruits were sectarian. Even though it could be translated abroad, other Americans recognized the cultural fault lines separating Wilson supporters and detractors. Many Americans, including other self-identified Christians, could not bear full realization of a Wilsonian world order because it did not represent America as they knew it.

In the election of 1920, several of these disparate groups coalesced to reject Wilson's world order in an overwhelming popular and electoral vote for Republican Warren Harding. The Democratic Party nominee, Ohio governor James Cox, only captured the southern states. The Republican margin of victory was so large—seven million votes—that Harding reversed his campaign promise to join the League of Nations with reservations. Once elected, he proclaimed his intent to *further* isolate the United States from foreign entanglements. Premillennial Protestants rejoiced in Harding's victory, which they read as the result of their efforts to repudiate postmillennial Protestants who hailed the League of Nations as the culmination of Christian progress. With this victory over Wilson (and, by extension, the Democratic Party and liberal postmillennial Protestants), Republicans, and Christian "fundamentalists" reinscribed isolationism—U.S. detachment from the rest of the world—as a core principle of Christian and American values.[9]

Self-described fundamentalists' claims to represent the essence of Americanism and Christianity, and subsequent debates over who had the authority to make such a claim, haunted the postwar period.[10] Their insistence on their centrality to American Christianity came in response to the tide of postmillennial endeavors that had followed Reconstruction. Between Reconstruction and the Great War, white middle-class social Christians sought to align the state with their interpretation of the social gospel. After the fight over the league, however, premillennialists insisted that Christian identity belonged outside the secular endeavors of the state and inside the religious mission of the church. Their assertion drew upon scripture, but their interpretation was relatively new in American culture. Signifying oneself as evangelical in this way reformulated the boundaries of church and state beyond what had informed American evangelicals since the antebellum era. It excluded state-based reform as a fulfillment of the mission of the church and narrowed the bounds of Christian missions to privatized, individual conversion experiences. Wilson and the culture that shaped his religion and politics were caught in the balance, reconstituted as Americans attended to the realities of the United States in a post–World War world. Along the way, the measure of Wilson's Christianity shifted from the mission of his statecraft to his individual piety and moral character.

The defining feature of American evangelicalism—the impulse to be in but not of the world—contributed to the intensity of the League Fight. It shaped one's perspective on world and "worldly" affairs. The big tent of evangelicalism housed both ends of the internationalist and isolationist spectrum, but it had not fully reconciled how evangelicals could root opposing approaches to the world according to the same dictum. By bringing attention to this intra-evangelical disagreement on proper Christian living, the League Fight dissolved the nonsectarian consensus white middle-to-upper-class Protestants had cultivated since the nineteenth century. White Protestants shared a love of the gospel and the privileges of whiteness, but by 1919, they could not resolve their different approaches to the common good in national and global affairs. The parochial and political partisanships among white Protestants on whether or not the United States should join the league drew public attention to the functional ideological differences among them. Historians of American religion, too, have noted how these fractures in the Protestant landscape became more visible at this time, using terms as varied as "liberal," "conservative," "premillennial," "postmillennial," "social Christian," "Christian socialist," "fundamentalist," "modernist," "progressive," "mainline," and "radical" to describe white Protestants. The struggle to make sense of white Protestantism in the early twentieth century exists because the significations used by both historical actors and historians are *relational* and depend upon these ideological shifts brought to light by the creation of the League of Nations.

With the Great War not yet faded from view, Harry Emerson Fosdick drew attention to these distinctions and the increasing pressure many white middle-class Protestants felt to justify their support of internationalism and the war more generally. In his 1922 sermon "Shall the Fundamentalists Win?" Fosdick contended that nonsectarianism had been a prevailing feature of American Protestantism until recently when fundamentalists incited sectarian discord.[11] The points of contention fundamentalists raised were not new—indeed "everybody knows that they are there," he explained—but the time had come for liberal "modernists" like himself to confront them directly. Fosdick acknowledged that Christians held divergent approaches to the so-called fundamentals of their faith, noting, for instance, that "side by side with those to whom the second coming is a literal expectation, another group exists in the evangelical churches," a group who believes Christ's second coming "will be worked out by God's grace in human life and institutions." The differences may be theological or may be in temperament, Fosdick clarified, but, nevertheless, they mattered. Where fundamentalists wanted to narrow and limit who belonged in Christian churches, Fosdick asserted, liberal modernist Protestants wanted to remain open and tolerant of others. In either case, he urged likeminded Protestants "in Christ's name and for Christ's sake" to recognize the "immeasurable folly" in the fundamentalist movement. It challenged a century of evangelical reform in secular institutions and thwarted the necessary human effort to establish a brotherhood of humanity.

Fundamentalists were undaunted by Fosdick's appeals. They questioned postmillennial evangelical assumptions about the need to Christianize the United States or the world. Theologically, fundamentalists believed that the millennium could not occur through human effort; the expected march of human progress was, for them, an inherently mistaken view of humanity. As evidence against optimism in human progress, they cited, among other things, the havoc wrought through trench warfare. The violence of the Great War illustrated the inability of any nation—or human institutions more generally—to be "saved" or Christianized.[12] This, for premillennial fundamentalists, was not a failure that needed to be corrected but rather a descriptive truth of the human condition. As a result, they obstructed the mission of Christian internationalists as a false interpretation of scripture. Fundamentalists purposefully engaged in public debate on this topic, dedicating time and money to publications, speaking engagements, and new faith-based organizations to redirect Christian identity away from state-based reform on both national and international levels. With such a thorough and persuasive assertion of their views as the true representation of Christian doctrine, fundamentalists could no longer be marginalized in American Christianity.

As Wilson's presidency came to an end, the white Protestant moral establishment experienced its own great war. The restructuring that followed relied upon a relational and prescriptive understanding of what it meant to be Christian, and even religious, in the United States. Rather than designating an adherence to a set of fixed, ahistorical doctrines or a coherent organized body of believers, describing oneself or others as "evangelical" was a way to identify a relationship *among other* American Protestants. In the political climate of 1920, *premillennialism* and *antiliberalism* became new markers for belonging to American evangelicalism. From the 1920s forward, identification as an evangelical more narrowly referred to premillennial, antistate, and antiliberal manifestations of Protestant Christianity, excluding postmillennial, state-based liberal Protestants from the fold. American evangelicals increasingly disassociated their religious identity from a set of churches or denominations with a shared transatlantic ideological or institutional heritage tracing to the Protestant Reformation; instead, they increasingly made sense of their Christian identity according to their place in American culture and politics. Theology mattered as an organizing ideology for American evangelicalism, but evangelicals' defining features reflected these national concerns.

The shifting currents of religion in American culture unmoored white Protestants who supported Wilson for applying their interpretation of Christianity to the state. During this postwar period, Wilson and other liberal postmillennial Protestants were both pushed *and* pulled from the Protestant moral establishment. The fundamentalist movement, especially its premillennial and antistate elements, narrowed the parameters of evangelicalism to purposefully push postmillennial social gospel-inspired Protestants out from under the banner of American evangelicalism. Fundamentalists mobilized with the intent of solidifying and reinscribing what constituted an evangelical worldview according to their interpretation of proper Christian doctrine. Social Christians and other liberal Protestants, for their part, challenged fundamentalist interpretations of a singular Christian doctrine, insisting upon historical-critical interpretations of scripture as the common-sense approach to Christian living. Their methods of interpreting scripture and their place in contemporary U.S. politics pulled them away from the current markers of evangelicalism. In this political and theological climate, they drifted toward a new "mainline" identity.[13] The cultural tyranny of "100-percent Americanism" and the corresponding increase in Ku Klux Klan activity pushed these white liberal Protestants to forge new interfaith alliances with Jews and Catholics.

In this respect, Wilson and the social Christians who supported him through two elections reformulated the public expression of their Christian mission beyond its white Protestant roots. With the formerly unmarked whiteness of the Protestant establishment now exposed, Wilsonians began to emphasize their internationalism as a step toward establishing a brotherhood of mankind rather than an attempt to Christianize the world. The theological underpinnings of their mission did not change, but its public presentation did. In this postwar context, Wilsonians wrung out the decidedly evangelical elements of Wilson's new world order to separate themselves from Protestant fundamentalists, Christian nativists, and white supremacists. The postwar culture pulled Wilsonians away from the evangelical milieu that inspired Wilson's vision. This shift occurred subtly as Wilsonians separated the man from the mission. In his supporters' tributes to his accomplishments, Wilson remained a devout Presbyterian, but his faith became a more private affair while his foreign policy vision became a universal political enterprise. In these reformulations of the recent past, Wilson, the civil servant, served the world by sacrificing himself for the sake of humanity. In the process, he, and the Christian identity he would have known, died so that *Wilsonian* internationalism could be born again.

Wilsonians Bear Witness

On November 10, 1923, families gathered around their home radios and in school auditoriums to hear the former president address the nation.[14] On the eve of Armistice Day, Wilson asked his fellow Americans to remember the soldiers who sacrificed their lives to spread democracy around the world. He also reminded the nation that they stopped short of the ideals he articulated for the Great War, a failure he knew could become his legacy for generations to come. After two years of living in Republican-led "normalcy," Wilson admonished those who wanted to celebrate the anniversary of armistice. "We turned our backs upon our associates and refused to bear any responsible part in the administration of peace," he asserted. The nation chose "a sullen and selfish isolation which is deeply ignoble because [it was] manifestly cowardly and dishonorable." Until the nation decided to "return to the true traditions of America," he added, any reminder of the war should be a national embarrassment.[15]

With another presidential election only one year away, Wilsonian Democrats welcomed the reprimand and the tacit encouragement. The following day, twenty thousand people marched to Wilson's home. These Armistice Day "pilgrims" paraded through Washington, DC, to celebrate the anniversary of the end of the Great War with the man they believed was responsible for ending it and, hopefully, all future wars. Outside the Wilsons' S Street home, the leader of the event, Senator Carter Glass, thanked Wilson for his service. When Wilson unexpectedly emerged from his home, Glass announced that the crowd gathered "to renew our faith and to signify the unabated loyalty of millions of Americans to that immutable cause which you, more than any other man on earth, so impressively personify."[16] Once the applause died down, Glass continued praising the former president, letting him know that with each new Armistice Day anniversary he and other Americans "are coming more and more to realize what a shocking mistake it was to have permitted a conspiracy of racial animosities and selfish politics to cheat the nation of honorably participating in that permanent guarantee of peace for which our boys died and the country sacrificed."[17] Glass and the Armistice Day pilgrims

FIGURE 6.1. "Pilgrims" gather outside the Wilsons' S Street home in Washington, DC, on Armistice Day 1923. Courtesy of the Library of Congress, Prints and Photographs Division, National Photo Company Collection, LC-F8-27241.

would not let the day pass without making it known that Wilson's vision was alive and well, or at least on the mend.

The marching band began playing music when Wilson motioned to address the crowd—something he had not done in person for quite some time. Spontaneously, he announced that he was not concerned whether or not his vision would stand the test of time. "I have seen fools resist Providence before," he explained, "and I have seen the destruction, as will come upon these again—utter destruction and contempt. That we shall prevail is as sure as that God reigns."[18] Wilson spoke more frankly than he ever had about the role he saw for himself and his political opponents. He continued to believe his foreign policy aligned international relations with God's order to the world, but this time he stated so plainly. This event marked one of the relatively few times that Wilson explicitly mentioned God in a public speech. With this direct invocation, Wilson expressed the relationship between his Christianity and his civil service. He associated his public record with eternal truths he found in scripture. The assurance with which he spoke about the role of Providence resembled comments he had made in publications during college, in his private correspondence throughout his life, and in his public speeches as president. But even as Wilson's rhetoric displayed continuity with previous pronouncements, it also reflected the ways the American religious landscape had changed.

Wilson, like his social Christian supporters, asserted anew the way religion informed his politics. He had to find new ways of articulating what for so long had been obvious to him and his supporters because alternative interpretations of his religious identity had gained strength. Outnumbered and outwilled at the polls in 1920, Wilsonian Christians found comfort in biblical metaphors and used them to cultivate sympathy across partisan divides. Wilsonians developed a sense of mission through a prolific outpouring of letters, pamphlets, books, radio addresses, and magazine interviews. Their postwar appeals to the *spiritual* and *religious* basis of the League of Nations (rather than a parochial evangelical Protestant interest) became embedded in historical memory through their shared efforts to vindicate their own position in American culture. With a wider appeal to religious Americans who read their sacred texts with a theologically liberal lens, Wilsonians forged new alliances against Republicans, fundamentalists, and anti-internationalists.

Those closest to Wilson delighted in sharing stories and newspaper clippings hailing the former president or skewering the Republican Party. Experiencing a moment that met both criteria, James Cox, the Democratic Party's unsuccessful 1920 presidential candidate, enthusiastically reported to Wilson in 1923 that he met an "Episcopalian clergyman, a Republican, but an independent thinking one," who attempted to understand current events according to scripture. Cox explained that as the conversation turned to international affairs, the minister concluded, "If Jesus wept over Jerusalem, so He must now be weeping over Washington."[19] Cox hoped that he, Wilson, and like-minded Christian internationalists would continue "to preach the gospel." He did not remark on whether the gospel was Christianity or Wilsonian internationalism. "Centuries after the name of Henry Cabot Lodge has passed into mere historic nothingness," he prophesied, "the children of republics all over the world will gratefully acclaim the name of Woodrow Wilson."[20] While the rest of the world moved closer toward realism in international affairs, and while fundamentalists realigned evangelicalism around premillennialism and an antistatism, Wilson and his ilk felt compelled to vocalize the truth they saw in their internationalism.

The narrative they developed in their own private and public print culture insisted that Wilson attempted to conduct international affairs as Jesus would have. They concluded that a powerful few rejected him at the cost of the many. Journalist Ray Stannard Baker, who traveled with Wilson to the Paris

Peace Conference, produced journal articles, pamphlets, and books attesting to the Christian foundations of Wilson's foreign policy. Writing for the *New York Times* in 1924, Baker explained that, when the president confronted critics in Paris, "underneath it all was a strange, deep, all-pervading certainty of mind" that the Covenant of the League of Nations "is right; it is true; it cannot fail." Wilson, Baker claimed, saw himself as its "Covenantor."[21] Baker's references to Wilson's nightly Bible reading, his righteous determination, and his calling as a prophet reinforced the idea that the league, as Wilson conceived of it, rested upon a Christian foundation, without saying so directly. Baker's inferences were not lost on his audience. Contemporary readers would have opened their newspaper to see Baker's words accompanied by "The Crusader," a drawing of Wilson dressed as a medieval knight, standing at attention while holding a sword, bearing an image of a cross on his chest, and flanked by George Washington to his right and Abraham Lincoln on his left.[22] Wilson as the "Covenantor," with the establishment of the League of Nations as his "crusade," became a dramatic symbol for social Christians who considered Wilson to stand for the postmillennial progress of American democracy and Christianity in the world. Its success depended upon the piety of individual defenders of faith, not least of all Wilson.

Wilsonians close to the administration or active in faith-based institutions, like the Federal Council of Churches, mediated Americans' remembrances of the Great War and Wilson's leadership during it. Deeply troubled by the strength of Republican and fundamentalist opposition to Wilson's internationalism, the FCC offered to publish and circulate Baker's articles on the president. This opportunity, Baker told Wilson, "seems to me excellent. We can thus get a tremendous circulation among church people, who are the sincerest supporters of your principles."[23] Indeed, the FCC remained on the front line of Wilson's defense against his critics. In 1921, the FCC executive committee adopted a declaration against war and in favor of churches and lawmakers doing their part to "establish a peace system."[24] In straightforward language, the committee proclaimed, "We condemn all proposals to change or annul existing treaties by mere Congressional legislation."[25] They were convinced that the will of the people remained with Wilson, regardless of what Congress decided. Accordingly, the declaration encouraged "equipping [laymen] for public work in the new [international] realm of endeavor for establishing the Kingdom of God on Earth as it is in Heaven."[26]

That same year, the FCC's War Time Commission bestowed President Wilson with the first of its medals to honor chaplains of exemplary service. As commander in chief, the commission declared, Wilson served as the highest chaplain of all, consecrated "to the sacred tasks of democracy in the United States and the world."[27] Together, Wilson's closest friends, administration insiders, and the FCC marshaled their resources to reassert a Wilsonian world order that was Christian in spirit if not in the letter of the law. Their examinations into the recent past appealed to American Protestants who participated in the Great War on two fronts: one waged in Europe "to make the world safe for democracy" and the other in the United States to determine the place of "social salvation" in American culture. Chronicling Wilson's service and asserting the religious framework behind the war effort helped many American Protestants—particularly liberal postmillennialists—make sense of World War I and reaffirm their decision to support it.[28]

From far and wide, in handwritten letters and telegrams, Wilsonian Christians sent notes of adoration to the Wilson family, even though the league and the Democratic Party had fallen out of popular favor. Mrs. Gertrude Farrell Kelly, who hailed from "violently bitter Anti-Wilson" Wisconsin, for example, wrote to Joseph Tumulty to share that Wilson "was an instrument of God to bring about that harmony of souls for which Christ died." Despite the current place Wilson held in American culture, she believed "he will be worshipped throughout the world."[29] Likewise, Dr. John Frazer, pastor of Central Methodist Church in Spartanburg, North Carolina, wrote the former First Family to share how he exhorted his congregation to take seriously the retirement of the president. Wilson was "as truly a creature of the church as of the state," he explained, and, as such, "Wilson will represent to future generations a splendid ideal of Americanism and Christian statesmanship, and a gallant soldier who fell fighting in the war against war, for the peace of the world."[30] These and similar letters give insight into how Wilsonians conceived of themselves and their place in the body politic and religious landscape. Between clergy like Frazer, lay Christians like Kelly, and administration insiders like Baker, Wilsonians collectively remembered the war as the epitome of social Christian impulses and American values.

These Protestants, however, were not alone in fortifying Wilson's vision as an *American* ideal. Despite the origins of Wilson's foreign policy in a specific white middle-class Protestant movement, his internationalist message appealed to many Americans outside of his demographic. Editorials to the *Jewish World,* for instance, indicate the verve with which American Jews rallied behind the former president. An unnamed contributor declared "the great principles with which [Wilson's] name is identified—the principles upon which he urged that Peace should be established when the war closed— are those to which every thinking, or rather right thinking, man is bound to subscribe."[31] The writer condoned this "right thinking" because Wilson's

postwar vision rested "upon foundations of love and justice and brotherhood," as "he thought to banish international greed and to enthrone international goodwill."[32]

Writing for the *Peace Advocate*, Rabbi Samuel Schulman of Temple Beth-
El in New York City similarly explained that he believed—like Wilson and
social Christians—that "America has a great trust for humanity." According to
Shulman, the United States was the only nation that based its identity on "the
recognition of the rights of men and the dignity of our common humanity.
It, therefore, has a destiny as a teacher to the world which is greater and more
prophetic than that of any other people on earth."[33] Wilson and social Christians identified with Schulman's notion of America in the world because, as
white middle-to-upper-class Protestants, they considered themselves responsible for the fulfillment of America's mission to the world, designated by God
to save the world. Schulman, as a Russian Jewish immigrant, welcomed this
notion of America's destiny in part because of his experiences of antisemitism.
Being a citizen of a nation with a government based on the will of the people
appealed to Schulman as a member of a group that experienced systematic
discrimination and oppression.[34] Schulman and Wilsonians, then, shared a
language of expectation for America's service to the world, even though it
appealed to them for radically different reasons.

Between his nomination of Louis Brandeis to the Supreme Court, his
relationships with Rabbi Stephen Wise and Felix Frankfurter, and his public
support of the Balfour Declaration, Wilson received letters of support from
numerous Jewish Americans.[35] Albert Kaufman, for instance, thanked him
for his service, "through which your name will be linked in the history of
the Jewish people."[36] This sentiment led many prominent American Jews to
express disappointment with the Senate's decision not to join the League of
Nations. The ideological framework expressed in Wilson's Fourteen Points,
particularly his insistence on the consent of the governed and the autonomy
of all nations, gave voice to ethnic and religious groups who often suffered
as minorities within nations or in powerless ethnic enclaves within colonial
empires. Alongside white liberal Protestants, American Jews, especially Zion-
ists, contributed to the developing narrative that Wilson, as an embodiment
of the United States, served humanity. Echoing the adoration Wilson received
from American Protestants, Rabbi Wise, for instance, declared that Wilson
left the White House "physically a broken man, but morally and spiritually
unconquered and unconquerable" as the "great moral captain of the world."[37]
Although he did not intend to make Wilson a messiah, Wise's sentiments
paralleled social Christian descriptions of Wilson, which *were* intended to
draw comparisons to Jesus.

These shared sentiments about Wilson mediated many of the cultural differences that often kept religious groups at odds in matters of public policy.
Conscious of their need to defend themselves against an anti-internationalist
majority, Wilsonians from different corners of American culture described
their cause and its architect with transcendent language. For white middle-
class Protestants, this meant proclaiming not just a biblical foundation to Wilson's foreign policy but also reasserting their earlier claims to the ostensibly
universal truths that they believed internationalism entailed. Their universal
moralisms resonated with American Catholics who agreed with the message of
international brotherhood but had often been excluded from white Protestants'
conceptualizations of it. Catholic intellectuals like Columbia professor Carlton
J. Hayes, for example, aided this Wilsonian effort. In his own history of the war,
he explained the war "dealt a body-blow at those doctrines of materialism and
determinism." Rather than creating a "revival" for any one sectarian idea or
institution, he concluded, it promoted "spiritualism" and the notion "that all
men are brothers and that in unselfish cooperation lies the hope of humanity and civilization."[38] This postwar sentiment, from religious figures and from
public intellectuals, challenged nativist and isolationist interpretations of the
proper lessons stemming from the war. It also bridged some divides that white
middle-class Protestant reformers erected during the late nineteenth century.

In their attempt to refashion their internationalism above sectarian
divides, Wilsonian Protestants welcomed these Jewish and Catholic interpretations of the war and of America. Rather than consider Wilson's foreign
policy to be the highest expression of a white paternal global order, Wilsonian Jews and Catholics helped to refashion Wilsonian internationalism as
an expansion of American pluralism. Effectively using the language of service, equality, and democracy, Jews and Catholics challenged the assumed
white Protestant center of American culture and Wilsonian internationalism. Believing this to be evidence that Wilson transcended social distinctions, white liberal Protestants embraced Jewish and Catholic faith leaders
as partners and fellow "champions of the rights of mankind." American
Jews and Catholics had supported Wilson's war effort through service to the
nation, but they did so for complex reasons that were often at odds with white
middle-class Protestants' assumptions about the inherent value of Wilson's
world order. First- and second-generation Jewish and Catholic immigrants,
for instance, endorsed Wilson's insistence upon self-determination and
equality among nations based upon direct experiences and shared narratives
of persecution. Others felt compelled to do so, by law or by social mores, in
order to demonstrate their patriotism and assimilation within mainstream
white American culture. Others still embraced the same myth of religious

freedom that white middle-class Protestants created and sustained. After the war, with white Protestant culture uprooted, liberal Protestants, Catholics, and Jews attempted to advance their status in American culture through a shared endorsement of Wilson's liberal internationalism.

The Exalted Saint

As Wilsonians began crafting an internationalism palatable to a religiously plural audience, Wilson continued his assertions of providential design, attempting to revive public knowledge of the Christianity that had inspired him. Writing for *The Atlantic Monthly*, Wilson attempted to make sense of the Russian Revolution and set straight the path he charted. In "The Road Away from Revolution," Wilson explained that "the world has been made safe for democracy," but "democracy has not yet made the world safe against irrational revolution."[39] "That supreme task, which is nothing less than the salvation of civilization," he explained, falls upon the United States, "as the greatest of democracies" and as "a Christian civilization." He insisted the United States must use "a Christian conception of justice," which requires "becoming permeated with the spirit of Christ and being made free and happy by the practices which spring out of that spirit" to fulfill this vision. For Wilson, the completion of this transformation required the sincere cooperation of churches, political institutions, and capitalists.[40] To his mind, the new world order based in social Christianity was still unfolding through civic progress.

After interviewing the former president in his home in October 1923 (just weeks before the pilgrims' march), journalist James Kerney became convinced that Wilson possessed an unwavering sense of mission. "Whatever historians may do," he wrote, "there can never be a doubt of [Wilson's] own intense conviction that his place was to fight what he was fond of terming the spiritual battles of humanity and democracy. It was a passion with him."[41] Kerney explained that "to the zero hour Woodrow Wilson regarded himself as the spiritual leader of a cause only temporarily lost."[42] Certainly, Wilson maintained his internationalist vision, a world held together by a moral compulsion, but in this, his final interview with the press, Wilson attempted to refashion his constituency. Having seen his political foes tarnish his policies and his reputation, Wilson divulged, "I realize that I am everywhere regarded as the foremost leader of the liberal thought of the world," and the small nations of the world "are looking to me to lead them."[43] Five years after developing the Covenant of the League of Nations, Wilson considered himself the servant not just of American citizens but also the leader of liberal internationalism. His body, however, would not go where his spirit led.

Wilson engaged in this public discursive offensive because he planned to run for a third presidential term. His health, however, continued to fail him. In January 1924, he took a turn for the worse. Citizens from all over the country expressed their sympathy to the former First Family. Clergy members like Reverend Francis Young promised to pray for the former president's health during church services.[44] As a priest, Father Young did not hesitate to dedicate a Mass to the president because Wilson had proved to be a friend to causes many Catholics held dear, even as he personally continued to hold deeply anti-Catholic views. Hundreds of people kept vigil outside the Wilson home, praying for his recovery. By the end of the month, a wave of condolence letters poured in as newspapers prematurely reported the president's death. Numerous letters expressed sentiments similar to those of Samuel Gompers, who attempted to lift Mrs. Wilson's spirit in a time of distress: "The spiritual leader of America and the world is at rest. But his voice and ideals will live on so long as man shall aspire to a nobler concept of human brotherhood."[45] The family filed this telegram and hundreds more away in scrapbooks, leaving a trail of sympathy from politicians, activists, farmers, missionaries, and everyone in between.[46]

On February 4, 1924, President Wilson died with his wife, his physician, and one of his daughters at his side. His death solidified popular perceptions of Wilson as a prophet who championed a righteous, yet unpopular, message for the world. Memorials and eulogies at the official services in Washington, DC, secured Wilson's place in social Christian memory as a Christlike figure who sacrificed his life for the betterment of humanity. Services at home and abroad shared this theme even though his death was five years removed from the league debates. In his formal eulogy for the president, David Hunter Miller, for instance, bore witness to the "inner light" that inspired Wilson. Since Miller served on the American delegation to the Paris Peace Conference, he explained how he knew well the inspiration behind the Covenant of the League of Nations, which they drafted together. In Miller's retelling, Wilson performed miracles—"the miracle of the draft [of the Covenant of the League of Nations], the miracle of the four million men, the miracle of the two millions in Europe, the miracle of thirty billions of money; and . . . the supreme miracle of winning the war."[47] Alluding to numerous biblical allegories, Miller affirmed Wilson's perseverance through the trials and tribulations of his office, refusing to be led astray by those who tempted him to "abandon his ideals, break his solemn word, betray the honor of his country and leave the ruins of the war to smolder in hate."[48] Above all else, Miller avowed that Wilson gave the ultimate sacrifice by being "perfectly willing to die for the League of Nations."[49] Miller unapologetically presented Wilson as a man who lived and died for the sake of the world, not just America.

This sort of reimagining of Wilson and U.S. debates about the League of Nations was not limited to former Wilson administration employees. Wilson's preeminence reached across the Atlantic, where parishioners who gathered together for a regular weekly church service in Westminster Abbey found themselves in a memorial for the fallen U.S. president. After reading Revelation 21:1–7, which begins with the proclamation, "and I saw a new heaven and a new earth," mourners joined together in singing the "Battle Hymn of the Republic." The world's foremost proponent for the League of Nations may have passed, but these Anglicans recited, "His truth is marching on." The congregants affirmed, "As he died to make men holy, let us die to make men free. While God is marching on. Amen." The rituals performed in Wilson's honor around the world confirm a remarkable trend in the public's perception of Wilson's presidency—that his commitment to serve humanity caused him to give his life.

Churches around the United States memorialized Wilson not only as a Christlike figure but also as a great example of Christian statesmanship. For instance, in Wilmington, North Carolina, one of Wilson's childhood homes, the local chapter of The Daughters of the American Revolution erected a plaque dedicated to the late president inside the First Presbyterian Church. The plaque commemorated not only the "sacred" memory of the commander in chief but also recognized Wilson as "The Father of the League of Nations. A Scholar Statesman and Christian Lover of Righteousness."[50] In Wilson's own church in Washington, DC, Reverend James Taylor heartened mourners by honoring the "prophet of peace" they knew so well.[51] Beginning his address with 2 Samuel 3:38, "know ye not that there is a prince and a great man fallen this day in Israel," Taylor asserted the incomparable stature of his president and congregant: "Perhaps no man in history who has occupied a position of such authority and power has been willing, while he was exercising that power, to give himself so unreservedly to the great cause of peace."[52]

Eulogies, of course, are intended to offer praise. The handful of men who delivered such speeches were friends of the president, men who had watched his health and political reputation deteriorate. Their desire to offer the highest praise they could think of is only to be expected. More telling, perhaps, were similar comments offered by Wilson's opponents. Burying President Wilson led to a moment of reflection even in states that overwhelmingly voted Republican. *The Inquirer and Mirror* (Nantucket, MA), for instance, evinced the same sensibility of Wilson's passing:

His was the voice that into the astonished ears of the great nations poured a promise of eternal peace on earth and lasting good will towards all men. Five years ago he stood like a Colossus above the blood-drenched world and

rebuked that world for its sins. And the world wept and repented and promised to sin no more. For his one little hour he uplifted the hearts of millions
and purified them in the crucible of unquenchable faith.[53]

History has shown that Americans consistently mythologize presidents following their deaths. What is unique about Wilson's story is that Americans
exalted him for his failures instead of his successes. Unlike George Washington, Wilson did not triumphantly lead a nation into a new era. Wilson
completed his term in office after the Senate refused to ratify the defining
document of his career. In contrast to fellow Virginian Thomas Jefferson,
Wilson did not express seemingly timeless principles that defined the republic for centuries. His pronouncements were contested both during and after
his lifetime. Unlike Abraham Lincoln, Wilson did not die immediately after
uniting the nation; instead, he died four years after leaving office, with the
nation divided over, among other things, the meaning of democracy and the
role of the United States in international affairs. Wilson did not fulfill his
promise to America nor, for many, the promise *of* America; yet many people,
both in the United States and beyond its borders, honored Wilson in death
for symbolizing the ideals just beyond their grasp.

Counterintuitively, Wilsonians considered Wilson's failures as a proof
text for the truths behind his aims. They hailed him as a sacred figure in
world history.[54] As Dr. Grayson explained over thirty years later, death "set
its sacred seal upon his mission, and we know beyond question that his principles were right. In the present confusion of the world there is scarcely a
straight-thinking man who does not realize that by the spirit which Woodrow
Wilson sought to introduce to the world, the world must be saved."[55] Grayson
postulated that when the world would look back on Wilson's "war speech," all
would be reminded "of the faith that was in Woodrow Wilson, the faith that
God had selected this epoch for the liberation of mankind."[56] The transcendent language Wilsonians used to describe Wilson was, despite their efforts
to indicate otherwise, a direct result of their time and place in American history. The memorials and eulogies of Wilson were messages to the living and
not the dead.

In death, as in life, Americans associated Christianity with Wilson's
presidency even as the meaning of his religious identity—and religion more
generally—had changed dramatically. In 1870, "Tommy" was thoroughly
steeped in southern Presbyterian culture; in 1912, "Woodrow" was a part of
the so-called Calvinist ticket; in 1917, he was the voice of social Christianity and its great hope in the Covenant of the League of Nations; by 1924, he
was still considered "religious," but his most ardent supporters stripped his

legacy of the parochial influences he found formative. Divisions among white American Protestants colored the eulogies in honor of the twenty-eighth president. The abundant language casting Wilson as a savior come to earth reflected the tenuous place liberal, postmillennial Protestants held in American Christianity. By lauding Wilson as a Christian ideal, Wilsonians pushed back against critics who opposed their efforts to connect the United States to a postmillennial world vision. They refuted fundamentalists by asserting Wilson as the epitome of evangelical efforts to convert the world. But Wilson's death did not vindicate liberal Protestants as "true" Christians. Instead, Wilsonians laid to rest their public claims to an evangelical mission when they buried Wilson at Washington National Cathedral. Wilson's attempts to save humanity may have been Christlike, but those who followed in his steps now knew Christianity in America had fundamentally changed. They sought instead to do what they thought Wilson would.

The Resurrection of Wilsonian Idealism

Wilson's specter loomed as Democrats struggled to define themselves in the aftermath of war. The unity the Democratic Party displayed in 1920 was lost by 1924. At the Democratic National Convention in New York City, delegates split over whether or not to endorse the League of Nations as a necessary means of achieving world peace. No longer Wilson's vision alone, the League of Nations now possessed its own record of achievements and failures. Americans witnessed the league struggle to oversee mandated peoples and territories and to complete significant global policy initiatives, such as disarmament and prohibitions on child labor. Wilsonian Democrats regretted not having a full part in those decisions, but—if electoral results are any indication—most Americans preferred a comfortable distance from international engagement. Endorsing the league continued to be a political liability in the postwar world. By 1924, the issue even divided Democrats.

Democrats could not agree on America's role in the world because they could not agree on what it meant to be an American citizen. The expansion of the Ku Klux Klan and its terrorism in the name of white Christianity plagued the United States. The Democratic Party was patient zero.[57] As a voting bloc, the KKK held prominent positions within the party and openly campaigned against one contender for the Democratic nomination, New York governor Al Smith. The KKK objected to Smith because he was Catholic, fearing that Smith's supposed allegiance to the Pope would undermine his loyalty to the United States. The KKK instead endorsed William McAdoo, Wilson's son-in-law as well as his former secretary of the treasury and chairman of the Federal

Reserve Board. McAdoo did not condemn the endorsement; he briefly benefited from it without comment. After the convention became deadlocked between these two nominees on the first day of voting, the Klan held a public "picnic" in nearby New Jersey where members dressed in their hoods and defaced effigies of Smith. The initial success that McAdoo experienced as a Protestant, prohibition-supporting Democrat fell apart in an extended primary race against this Catholic, prohibition-opposing Democrat. After ninety-nine ballots, both "frontrunners" removed themselves from the race, stepping aside so that the party could (theoretically) unite behind another candidate, John Davis, former solicitor general and ambassador to the United Kingdom under President Wilson. By November, however, this goodwill gesture on behalf of party unity no longer mattered. The United States elected another Republican president, Herbert Hoover.

The factions within the Democratic Party mirrored the tensions present in Wilson's administration and the white nonsectarian Protestant culture that had informed it. Both remained at a crossroads as nativist white supremacists battled with paternal, ecumenical Protestants. African American Christians remained largely on the outside of this infighting among Democrats and church-affiliated organizations, offering poignant critiques of both sides' efforts to uphold American values built upon racial inequality. They, and other minorities, were infuriated with the intolerance and violence of the Klan and disappointed with ostensibly liberal and progressive Protestants' failure to fully include ending racial discrimination in their vision of social salvation. With Democrats moving away from the ideal state they had envisioned in the previous decade, social Christians, as vocal proponents of many of the progressive efforts of the Democratic Party, shouldered the weight of these criticisms. This was with good reason. After the war, Americans generally rejected the efforts to Christianize the nation and the world through state-based reform. "Uplift" efforts—from the League of Nations to Prohibition—were not proving to make the United States the more perfect union reformers promised.

Elite Protestant ministers took many of these criticisms of their social gospel message to heart. Shailer Mathews, for instance, reconsidered his support of the war and reflected upon the social salvation he had sought to realize in postwar reflections like *The Validity of American Ideals*.[58] Likewise, in *The Religion of Democracy*, Henry Ward tempered his wartime zeal but maintained his basic belief in democracy as the way in which the world would achieve the progress necessary to see the kingdom of God on earth.[59] Others, like Reinhold Niebuhr, admitted their deep disappointment with the role religion played during the war and sought to outline a new orthodoxy.[60] With this reinvigorated publishing enterprise, liberal Protestant ministers maintained the impulses animating their social reform movement. They continued to adapt their message of salvation by focusing on the transformative processes of social life informed by the gospel message and experienced through modern culture.[61] This iteration of liberal Protestant reform responded to the postwar challenges to their cultural capital but did so using familiar tactics.

In light of the nation's turn toward isolationism, amusement, nativism, and fundamentalism, liberal Protestants refocused their efforts to apply their interpretation of Christianity to the present age. The FCC, for example, established a new committee to investigate why Americans might join the Klan.[62] The committee concluded that the bigotry characterizing the KKK and its sympathizers stemmed from ignorance and misinformation. As a result, the FCC established a Committee on Good Will and invited Catholics and Jews to the cause of correcting religious intolerance and discrimination in the United States. If progress were to be made abroad, then the effort must begin at home. With Protestants comfortably at its helm, the FCC's Committee on Good Will made tenuous advances toward a new Americanism, a national culture committed to building a brotherhood of mankind.

Following the Scopes Monkey Trial in 1925, the Protestant leaders of the Committee on Good Will began to disagree about the role of proselytization in their partnerships with other religious affiliations.[63] The FCC's conservative members firmly believed that the primary purpose of interfaith work was converting Catholics and Jews to their interpretation of Christianity. Moderate and liberal Protestants of the FCC disagreed about the role and purpose of ecumenical social action. In response, more liberal members of the FCC formed a separate organization in 1927, one that did not hold Protestantism above other traditions. The resulting faith-based institution, the National Conference of Christians and Jews (NCCJ), reflected what historian Kevin Schultz described as a "trifaith" identity. The structure of the organization illustrated as much, with equal Jewish, Catholic, and Protestant cochairs: Roger Straus representing Judaism, Carlton J. H. Hayes representing Catholicism, and Newton D. Baker, President Wilson's former secretary of war, representing Protestantism. With Presbyterian minister Everett Clinchy serving as the founding president, the NCCJ had the tools necessary to craft a new "Americanism" that appealed to a broader array of Americans.

Its mission statement, formally adopted in 1935, made clear how it could be distinguished from other religious organizations of the time:

> The National Conference exists to promote justice, amity, understanding, and cooperation among Jews, Catholics, and Protestants in the United States and to analyze, moderate and finally eliminate intergroup prejudices which

disfigure and distort religious, business, social and political relations, with
a view to the establishment of a social order in which the religious ideals of
brotherhood and justice shall become the standards of human relationships.[64]

In order to prevent theological conflict, the NCCJ focused on what Protestants, Catholics, and Jews had in common, a phrase that echoed of an earlier time: "the brotherhood of man under the fatherhood of God."[65] All three
faiths could claim their traditions promoted both the brotherhood of man
and the fatherhood of God. Indeed, William Howard Taft had drawn upon
the phrase two decades earlier when trying to demonstrate how his Unitarianism belonged within a larger Protestant consensus. Taft drew upon this sentiment then for much the same reason that the NCCJ now did—the principles
of brotherhood resonated with Americans as a nonsectarian value that all citizens could support regardless of their faith affiliation. Much like twists and
turns of the 1912 election and the League Fight of 1919, this phrase appealed
to many Americans but held a special meaning to social Christian activists.

Throughout the interwar period, Wilsonians attempted to bridge the
divide between liberal Protestant ideals and Democratic Party initiatives.
The relationship Wilson had cultivated with the FCC lived on and thrived in
the 1930s through the work of the NCCJ. Wilsonians, whether they worked
primarily through the Democratic Party or the NCCJ, recast the relationship between reform, religion, and the state by emphasizing Wilson's internationalist vision as a wholly unique expression of his individual faith. Newton
Baker, who held positions of leadership in the NCCJ and Democratic Party,
proved pivotal to this process. During a Jefferson Day event sponsored by
the Democratic National Committee at Washington Cathedral, in April 1932,
Baker offered his perspective on the recent past while standing near Wilson's tomb. Twelve years removed from the horrors of war but in the midst
of a devastating economic depression, Baker reminded his audience that the
world war was ultimately self-inflicted by an imperial system of global power
built upon a "frail materialist philosophy." In this turmoil, he explained, Wilson developed an international doctrine that applied "the Christian ethic
long accepted as the ideal of individual action, that he who would be greatest among men must achieve that eminence by his service to his fellows."[66]
Baker confirmed what Wilsonians had long known—Wilson's internationalism was the social gospel applied to foreign policy—but he attributed the
Christian basis of the mission to Wilson alone. In this narrative, Wilson drew
his inspiration from personal piety rather than from a collective movement of
middle-class white Protestants who sought to remake global order based on
their interpretation of a Christianized democracy.

With Baker's help, the Democratic Party distanced itself from exclusively Christian doctrines and institutions while maintaining the piety of individual figures. Baker reaffirmed the idealism Wilson was known for, insisting that the Depression "chastened" the country's "disposition to discount the thing called idealism" and would "vindicate afresh the inadequacy of a purely materialistic foundation for a modern society."[67] Rearticulating the story of the war and Wilson's faith allowed Baker and others to separate the policies and positions of the Democratic Party from those of the most vocal Christian groups of the day: the KKK and premillennial fundamentalists. If the Klan and fundamentalists represented true Christianity as they claimed, then Baker and Wilsonian Democrats wanted to keep their distance. What the world will remember from the war, Baker posited, is "the struggle of a nation moved by no selfish purpose and led by a statesman who dared to foresee as the result of the conflict a new world in which the principle of liberty would be safe, the principle of justice established, and conference arbitration, conciliation and adjudication substituted in international disputes for the arbitrament of war."[68] Clinging to a Wilson-inspired ethic of service to the world, Baker called for a new generation of Democrats to renew their faith in Wilsonianism, the source of *their* idealism. He abandoned any insistence upon Wilson's vision being an embodiment of a Christian ethic of service or evangelical mission.

Baker's 1932 address was a part of his larger effort to free the definition of "Americanism" from the grasp of nativist white Protestants, whom he considered insular influences on the United States and Christianity. In 1936, supported by the NCCJ and the Williamstown Institute of Human Relations, Baker and his colleagues Everett R. Clinchy and Roger Straus published *The American Way*, a striking attempt to define American identity along Wilsonian principles. In the introduction, the authors wrote that they "enter[ed] the border land of human relations among nations, races and classes" by focusing on "a single area of the whole problem," the "cultural divisions known as Protestants, Catholics, and Jews in America."[69] Their "prayer for America" was to move the nation closer to an "American way" in which other nations turned toward the United States as an example to emulate, "where reason and harmony prevail, welding us together into the most powerful people in the world—not powerful by the sword, but spiritually powerful, by our having attained knowledge, sympathy and tolerance for the people who live in the same street with us, and for all our fellow citizens in this continental country."[70] Closely resembling the social gospel message espoused by Gladden, Rauschenbusch, and Wilson, *The American Way* differed from these earlier pronouncements in one notable way. The ultimate expression of America's strength would not be the paternal care and "uplift" of others by "great" white Protestant servants alone but rather the social harmony of upper- and middle-class Protestants, Catholics, and Jews.

Drawing from the deep well of social Christian thought, Baker's "American Way" was based upon Wilsonianism but not a message espoused by Wilson himself. As historian Kevin Shultz has shown, white Protestants began to realize in the interwar period that the principles of American democracy— "inalienable individual rights, principles of brotherhood, negative liberty, freedom of expression"—did not belong exclusively to American Protestants.[71] Even though they held up "American" values as primarily Christian (and tacitly Protestant) during the Great War, by the mid-1920s white liberal Protestants like Baker began to emphasize that those same values could be found in Catholicism and Judaism. This shift in perception was due in part to the efforts of Catholics and Jews to actively combat popular stereotypes of their traditions, ethnicities, and, in some cases, countries of origin. Interfaith organizations like the NCCJ, the organization most responsible for promoting the idea that American culture was based on a "Judeo-Christian" tradition, also deserve credit.[72]

Through this effort, Wilsonians—comprising Protestants, Catholics, and Jews seeking to establish an internationalist American culture based on a brotherhood of mankind under a fatherhood of God—created a Wilsonianism that transcended many of the partisan divides that led to Wilson's failures. This reformulation, constructed out of an evolving historical memory of Wilson, belonged to a new era. Indeed, it was this broader vision of Americanism, as well as Wilsonianism, that helped bring the Democratic Party's 1932 presidential candidate to the White House. It was fitting, and quite telling, that Franklin Roosevelt's campaign song was "Happy Days Are Here Again." Roosevelt embodied a national ideal modeled after Wilson, but not espoused by Wilson, a new vision that could serve as the basis of foreign policy ideals in the remainder of the American century.

By Roosevelt's presidency, American public intellectuals and policymakers began to discuss the League of Nations as a flawed organization, but one whose principles reflected, rather than rejected, American values. For his part, President Roosevelt took a conciliatory approach to Wilson's legacy even though his career and Democratic reform could be traced to Wilson's administration. In his State of the Union speech in January 1941, for instance, Roosevelt advised the public, "We need not overemphasize imperfections in the Peace of Versailles. We need not harp on failure of the democracies to deal with problems of world reconstruction." Rather than focus on past mistakes, by either listing them outright or debating the severity of any errors,

Roosevelt encouraged citizens to remember what united them. A "new order of tyranny" threatened the world and "the American people have unalterably set their faces against that tyranny."[73] Roosevelt reformulated Wilsonian internationalism as a "high-minded" international system based on *American* values. He did so with ease because of interfaith organizations like the NCCJ and the concerted effort of Wilsonian Jews, Catholics, and liberal Protestants to construct an American culture they valued. This subtle shift in the public discourse relocated internationalism, Wilson, and Wilsonians upon a new Judeo-Christian foundation rather than the social Christianity of Wilson's White House.

Spreading the Wilsonian Gospel

The twentieth annual board meeting of the Woodrow Wilson Foundation (WWF) in 1942 had a feeling of triumph. The committee decided "two deep currents" had taken hold among Americans: widespread acceptance of Wilson's notion of international cooperation and complete rejection of isolationism. "The unprecedented scope and danger of the present situation," confirmed for the board "the triumph of Mr. Wilson's international philosophy."[74] As Americans struggled to understand the Second World War, Wilson's vision for the United States in the world became a blueprint for American action. Public commentators, like *United States News* founder David Lawrence, returned to Wilson's legacy as Americans faced another world war.[75] Looking back on the recent past, Lawrence argued that Americans were mistaken to reject Wilsonian internationalism in 1920. The current war brought Wilson's vision into focus, "as the lives of America's finest are being offered again on all continents and over the seven seas in a second great crusade to establish once and for all that man is indubitably his brother's keeper."[76] Whereas the nation turned its back on Wilson in 1919, Lawrence asserted that now "the peace of the world, must rest upon the spirit, if not the letter, of Woodrow Wilson's memorable pledges to mankind."[77]

This Wilsonian gospel animated Democrats who felt Wilson's haunting presence in contemporary domestic and international affairs. Wilsonians again stood ready to mediate the message. On the twenty-fifth anniversary of Armistice Day, in 1943, Samuel Huston Thompson, U.S. attorney general during the Wilson administration, proclaimed that the United States and the world were merely "wandering in the wilderness" since Wilson's presidency.[78] Standing inside Washington Cathedral, he placed the current world war in a context that centered on Wilson. When "Democracy and Liberalism disappeared over the horizon," he narrated, "Woodrow Wilson arose to battle for the cause of Democracy." In Thompson's rendering, Wilson was a prophet who dared to speak to those brave enough to listen. World events, he fore-warned, pointed toward a unified system. Convinced that the Second World War proved Wilson's interpretation of the First, Thompson exhorted other torchbearers to complete Wilson's vision.

While most Americans did not share Thompson's optimism that Wilson would receive the accolades due to him, this war presented another oppor-tunity to compare the Americanism of the First World War with the current role of America in the world. Much had changed in American culture since 1917, including an economic depression, Prohibition's ratification and repeal, gang wars, race riots, and women's suffrage. As Americans contemplated the origins of World War II, they reconsidered Wilson's internationalism, doubt-ing the wisdom of isolationism. As the face of internationalism, Wilson too received a second look from policymakers and American popular culture.

The Woodrow Wilson Foundation was especially invested in promoting a revised version of Wilsonian internationalism to the American public. In 1944, Americans who flocked to their local cinema could, courtesy of Twenti-eth Century Fox, watch a feature-length film about Woodrow Wilson. Begin-ning with his tenure as the president of Princeton University and ending with the Senate failing to ratify the Treaty of Versailles, Darryl F. Zanuck's *Wilson* brought the twenty-eighth president into the contemporary conversation. Zanuck had earned his stripes as a movie mogul during the height of the studio wars, working on films like *The Jazz Singer* (1935) starring Al Jolson and *The Grapes of Wrath* (1940) starring Henry Fonda. For *Wilson*, Zanuck worked directly with the WWF, which requested a "fair balance between the favorable and the unfavorable" elements of Wilson's career. The partnership proved successful, as *Wilson* was well received by film critics and the WWF. Arthur Sweetser, then president of the WWF, considered the film "a great public service at a crossroads of our history."[79]

Wilson notably does not depict the twenty-eighth president as an ardent believer. Wilson's principled actions are divorced from his faith and his intel-lectual heritage as a Presbyterian. The film does not begin with Wilson's boy-hood or the relationship he had with his father, Reverend Joseph Wilson. Instead, it opens with the "scholar president" holding the highest office at Princeton University. Wilson the film character is introduced as more of an impartial intellectual swayed only by reasoned debate and exposition than as a Christian statesman seeking to serve—or save—humanity. In this way, Zanuck's *Wilson* was certainly more appealing to a World War II audience than an accurate portrayal of Wilson's actual views would have been. During the First World War, Theodore Roosevelt and others criticized Wilson for failing to fully prepare the country for war through militarization; the 1944 film version of Wilson, however, takes an assertive stance against Germany. Far from an idealist who insisted upon a "peace without victory," the fictional Wilson, speaking to a World War II–era audience, challenged German ambassadors in the White House and indicted German *kultur* as a whole. The American leader who promoted an international organization lacking any ability to formally enforce its own covenant was curiously missing from *Wilson*.

The film similarly reformulated Wilson's relation to historical precedent. In 1919, Wilson's opponents accused him of straying from a traditional American foreign policy valuing national sovereignty. On film, however, Wilson was commemorated for carrying on the principles of the nation's most cherished presidents. As Zanuck's Wilson contemplated potential entry into the Great War, viewers watch him pace the halls of the White House, visiting the portraits of both George Washington and Abraham Lincoln. Resolved to act, and with history on his side, Zanuck's Wilson continued his uncompromising campaign against German indecency after the war. Zanuck brought to life the popular belief, which poignantly emerged after Wilson died and again during World War II, that Wilson would be enshrined in American memory alongside Washington and Lincoln.

In Zanuck's treatment, Wilson's fight with the Irreconcilables becomes a way to show the dangers of religious zealotry dictating foreign policy. Zanuck's Wilson reminded senators, particularly Henry Cabot Lodge, that they supported the notion of a league prior to America's entry in the war. Zanuck's Lodge counters by saying that, while he did support a league previously, he has been "converted" to the other side. He also reminds the president that many converts, namely St. Paul, had gone on to do great things. The potent revision of history contrasts the fictional Lodge with the fictional Wilson by portraying the Republican leader as the only figure who turned to religion when making his foreign policy decisions. Not coincidentally, Zanuck presented Lodge as a misguided political leader who stood on the wrong side of history. Twenty-five years after the actual league debate, Zanuck portrayed Lodge—and Christianity—as sectarian, narrow-minded, and resistant to change. In doing so, he effectively erased the culture that informed Wilson's foreign policy. With these few onscreen minutes, Zanuck rendered the dominant cultural assumption—in full Technicolor brilliance—that religion, properly understood and lived, remained private and separate from politics.

Wilson was a cultural victory for Wilsonians. The film presented audiences with the Wilson they hoped Americans would see—a statesman who held American idealism over and above any other sectarian ideology. Likewise,

Wilson gave Wilsonians the Republicans they wanted Americans to see—a party that followed its own misguided truth to the detriment of the collective good. *Wilson* received acclaim from general audiences and critics alike. Summing up the attraction of the movie, one reviewer explained, "The film is pleasing throughout: the kind of pictures of themselves which Americans like to see."[80] Americans entangled in World War II found the film's explanation of world affairs particularly compelling. Recognizing that some viewers considered the film to be propaganda, especially since the WWF helped fund the film, Sweetser rebutted, "To the average man, the film gives the plain and simple story of what we fought for and lost in the last war and what we are fighting for and can still win in this war." Noting that even an isolationist paper in New York recommended that "every American who can should see it," Sweetser especially encouraged "old 'Wilsonians'" "who kept alive the spirit of international cooperation" to attend. Sweetser found Zanuck's rendition of Wilson and World War I–era United States "almost providential" at "this moment when America is facing her second chance."[81]

The movie was not intended for an audience well versed in recent history. Instead, it was designed for an audience vaguely familiar with Wilson but without a dominant impression of him. Those who were too young to remember Wilson's presidency on their own were now old enough to be fighting in the current war. Or, as the *New York Post* put it, "The history of Wilson's failure has been the history of [current soldiers'] lives. They are giving their lives to find the answers to the questions that haunted Wilson. They are fighting to rewrite the end of Wilson's story into lasting peace."[82] For these younger viewers, watching *Wilson* was not merely a lesson in history but a reflection on the present crisis, as many viewers noted, "the same problem faces us today."[83] Once they understood Wilson's contributions in this preferred context, the WWF hoped, this new generation of Americans could return a prodigal nation to its rightful mission.

What the *Post* appreciated about Zanuck's portrayal was that "Wilson was not a lonely, slightly cracked idealist. He rose to power as the mouthpiece of the hopes of the great mass of the American people."[84] In this way, *Wilson* challenged the dominant isolationist memory of the Great War, offering in its place a revised image of President Wilson to its World War II–era audience. Wilson, the character based on a reimagined version of the historical figure, made the current war more personal by outlining an American narrative that resonated with those fighting in a new world war. In this imagining, the Second World War could correct the errors Americans made through the First. "If the lesson of Wilson's losing fight with the Senate is to be fully grasped," as one review explained it, "we must understand how that mistake came to be made. . . . We must understand that Wilson's failure was the people's failure, that the villain was not Henry Cabot Lodge, but you and I and our fathers before us."[85] With this view, embraced and funded by Wilsonians, the past and Wilson's place in it was not a distant memory but a present concern for Americans of every age.

Making the lesson of the film explicit, Josephus Daniels wrote in the *News and Observer* (Raleigh, North Carolina): "No lover of peace could see this picture—and it ought soon to be shown all over the country—without highly resolving to unite with all lovers of peace this time declaring: 'We will win the peace which partisanship and isolationism gone to seed denied us after World War No. I.'"[86] With Wilson's religion written out, Wilsonians claimed they represented universal values held by all. By speaking for "we" Americans, however, Daniels spoke on behalf of his own personal experience and his vested interest in rewriting the public perception of the Wilson administration and its internationalism.

Despite Zanuck's creative liberties in narrating the past, critics hailed *Wilson* as an innovation in filmmaking. They praised the use of Technicolor, the inclusion of what seemed to be "thousands" of extras (for scenes like a Princeton football game and the 1912 Democratic convention), and the reproduction of the White House interior. *Wilson* surpassed Hollywood hit *Gone with the Wind* in production costs but could not rival the latter's profits. Despite its low earnings, Zanuck's vision earned five Oscars, including Best Art Direction, Best Cinematography, Best Film Editing, Best Sound, and Best Writing for its original screenplay. *Wilson,* however, lost the 1945 Oscars for Best Picture and Best Director to *Going My Way*, a film starring Bing Crosby as a young Roman Catholic man who leaves his life of "sports, song, and romance" to become a priest whose unconventional approach to the priesthood departed from an earlier generation. As the Academy Awards indicate, critics and popular audiences did not dislike religion in film per se but rather preferred certain forms of religious identity on screen.

Wilson lost to *Going My Way* on a number of fronts. As part of a wave of films that centered on Catholic characters, *Going My Way* and other Crosby films were what film studies scholar Anthony Burke Smith described as a "veritable Catholicization of the American imagination" that occurred between the Great Depression and post–World War II period.[87] Through films like these, the American public consumed a new vision of American identity that embraced Catholicism as a legitimate expression of American civic and religious identity. Not only did *Wilson* lose at the box office and Academy Awards but also Wilson's religion, which had been crucial in two successful elections, no longer typified how Americans imagined him. Indeed, *Going My*

Way and *Wilson* were part of a larger effort to refashion American identity in such a way that included Catholics and Jews in the American mainstream.

Both *Going My Way* and *Wilson* affirmed the dominant cultural norms regarding religion in the United States. Crosby's character appealed to American audiences because the film presented religion as an individual experience that minimized partisan difference in order to serve the public good. In microcosm, *Going My Way* illustrated the generational and cultural transitions experienced within Catholic parishes and in their surrounding neighborhoods at midcentury.[88] It was a favorable depiction of Catholicism in particular and religion in general, both approved for mainstream audiences and endorsed by box office profits. In contrast, *Wilson* presented religion exclusively through the character of Lodge, one of the film's villains rather than its hero. On screen, Lodge brandished his Christianity and biblical knowledge as a display of his sectarianism, a weapon used to defeat the Covenant of the League of Nations. Religious identity was not problematic itself, but this fictional performance of it cut against an American standard of faith. *Wilson*'s Lodge was an antagonist because his religious identity was the ultimate expression of self-interest coming at the expense of the public good. Both of these cinematic notions of religious experience had been applied to President Wilson during his lifetime. The former, depicted through *Going My Way*, was how he understood his own religious identity. The latter, depicted in *Wilson*, was how his Irreconcilable and fundamentalist opponents described him in 1919. By the 1940s, however, neither of these onscreen conceptions of religion were applied to public depictions of the former president. The silver screen erased the religious identifications of Wilson's past in an effort to shape the relationship between religion and politics among his followers in the present.

By the mid-twentieth century, Catholics, Jews, and Protestants were well versed at using a variety of new technologies to reformulate their ethnic, religious, and national identities. Immediately after World War I, Catholics and Jews, especially first and second generation immigrants, endured frequent attacks regarding their loyalty to the nation as well as their ability to assimilate into American culture. In the process, Jews and Catholics actively asserted their place in American culture through a variety of public venues. Catholics, for instance, actively repackaged their relationship to American culture through film. Many parishes reorganized or offered new services that expanded the presence of Catholicism in surrounding neighborhoods. Similarly, Jews utilized the burgeoning radio industry and new sociological theories to explain Judaism and what it means to be Jewish to non-Jewish audiences. Using these methods, American Jews successfully redefined public knowledge of "Jewishness," altering public perception of religion, race, and

ethnicity by dominating the airwaves.[89] These efforts to display and rearticu-
late the proper form of religion in public life became the key to gaining legitimacy in America's trifaith culture. Together, they recharacterized nativism,
white supremacy, and religious fundamentalism as *un*-American.

Wilson is but one part of this movement to encourage an American Judeo-
Christian identity during the twentieth century. *Wilson,* as a Hollywood
narrative of recent U.S. history, was a method of reformulating Wilson's idealism as inclusively *American*, rather than exclusively Protestant, ideals. This
endeavor, sponsored by the institution responsible for maintaining Wilson's
legacy, purposefully shifted the nature of public debate about liberal internationalism away from Christian sectarian strife. The film, along with an
extensive liberal Protestant publication network and two decades' worth of
Wilsonian memorializations, helped to make internationalism appealing to
more Americans. By the time the United Nations held its first general assembly in January 1946, President Roosevelt's widow, Eleanor Roosevelt—who
was an American delegate to the UN in her own right—completed this popular interpretation of the recent past by invoking both her late husband and his
mentor in the Democratic Party. President Wilson, she told fellow delegates,
"is being vindicated today since we are meeting again to carry on his idea."[90]
This meeting, she explained, completed her husband's vision for the war. Near
the end of the speech, Eleanor encouraged the delegates to seek "the spark of
divine intelligence," drawing upon an idea found across the New Testament
Gospels, "whosoever will save his life shall lose it but whosoever will lose his
life for my sake the same shall save it."[91] Without naming Christianity or the
Bible as her source of inspiration and without declaring for whose sake lives
would be saved, Eleanor ensured Wilson's and Wilsonians' internationalism
permeated the United Nations, exhorting, "We must build faith in the hearts
of those who doubt, we must rekindle faith in ourselves when it grows dim,
and find some kind of divine courage within us that will make us keep on till
on Earth we have Peace and Good Will among Men."

The State of the Church

The continued debates about international order and the tensions of the
interwar period revealed to white Protestants the dividing lines embedded
beneath and alongside their coreligionists. Postmillennial internationalists,
quickened by a white middle-class paternalism, viewed the state as an acceptable means of achieving eschatological ends. They applied their international
service ethic to national institutions, including the U.S. State Department and
armed forces. They purposefully entangled their religious impulses with the

affairs of the state and were deeply disappointed when their religious hopes
hung on a cross of party politics. Premillennialist anti-internationalists, some
of whom also exhibited a strong inner current of white nativism, refused to
acknowledge any effort at wedding a universal church to a global state as
fundamentally Christian. At the cost of their own feelings of purity from
the stains of civic activism, premillennialist Protestants engaged in public
discourse to insist that Christianity should remain separate from the state
because, if the United States were to be a Christian nation, it must be isolated
from the world as an example of its chosen status.

Throughout the interwar period, conservative Protestants and fundamentalists attacked President Roosevelt as a continuation of Wilsonian internationalism.[92] Their efforts to do so were a continuation of white Protestants'
great war following World War I. Pushed out of evangelicalism by their conservative counterparts and pulled away by their commitment to international
humanitarianism, Wilsonians no longer identified their ideologies as explicitly Christian. By World War II, the center of American life had shifted from
white Protestant "100-percent Americanism" to a trifaith Judeo-Christian
consensus that valued religion generally (a "faith in faith") rather than white
evangelical Protestantism specifically. For Wilsonians in the 1940s, Wilson's
vision was valid only so far as it expressed the core values of America, not
social Christianity in particular or humanity in general. It proved convenient
that, a generation earlier, Irreconcilables and fundamentalists had separated
Wilson's internationalism from "true" Christianity. Rather than insist upon
a Christian foundation to the twenty-eighth president's policies, World War
II–era internationalists accepted and applauded the more generic term "idealism" to describe the president's vision. To midcentury ears, Wilson's idealism could still be inspired by his *personal* commitment to Christianity, but it
did not necessarily mean that his vision was *exclusively* Christian in practice.
Instead, it could be supported by the new Judeo-Christian consensus, because
idealism belonged to people of all faiths. As Wilsonianism became less firmly
rooted in Christianity and white superiority, Wilson's internationalism could
be an example of Americanism in the world. It would transform the world
by advancing American democracy, appealing to all through a commitment
to equality and service. The universal appeal of American democracy is, of
course, what Wilson assumed his vision for America in the world possessed
all along.

Conclusion

Formulations of Church and State

> To conquer with arms is to make only a temporary conquest; to conquer the world by
> earning its esteem is to make permanent conquest. I am confident that the nations that
> have learned the discipline of freedom and that have settled with self possession to its
> ordered practice are now about to make conquest of the world by the sheer power of
> example and of friendly helpfulness.
>
> — WOODROW WILSON, "Armistice Speech," November 11, 1918[1]

Between Reconstruction and World War I, white middle- and upper-class Americans frequently discussed the nation's "ills." Like parents caring for a sick child, white Protestants took the temperature of American culture and grew increasingly concerned. They prescribed themselves—their bodies, their ideas, and their well-intentioned efforts—as the solution to the self-diagnosed "problems." More often than not, these ills concerned groups of people—women, blacks, immigrants, and laborers—who frightened and fascinated white Protestant reformers. These white Protestants' habit of articulating their concerns as "immigrant," "Negro," or "woman" problems reveals their presumed cultural authority, their position on a pedestal of their own creation. This discourse was not benign, because it relied upon a conception of civic service actively constructing a form of American life in which certain groups care for those they deem weaker and in need.

These Americans sought to remake the world by curing what they considered to plague them, whitewashing perceived blemishes. Elite white Protestant evangelists of the social gospel conceived of their role in American society as similar to Jesus's relationship to the church. They considered themselves to be servants whose piety and status colored their paternalism as necessary, morally justified, and, therefore, welcome. From novels dedicated to proper Christian living to volunteer organizations devoted to political activism on a range of concerns, public outreach through civic service defined American Protestantism from the mid-nineteenth century forward.

Despite their claims otherwise, white middle-class Protestants did not hold a monopoly on American culture during this time period. Between 1860 and 1920, the United States experienced the Civil War, the Spanish-American War, the Great War, and military interventions in Mexico, Haiti, and Russia.

At the same time, the face of American citizenship changed and remained deeply contested. Freedmen gained the right to vote but were met with discriminatory and violent acts that prevented them from exercising this right. Jews and Catholics emigrating from Europe wrestled with the legal and social process of naturalization in relationship to whiteness and blackness as well as ethnic and religious identities. Transatlantic travel, and growing knowledge of the wider world, shifted white Americans' gaze beyond U.S. borders, making other places and people both more familiar and strange. White social Christians perceived these changes as treacherous. They attempted to navigate this new cultural terrain by asserting their authority in maintaining both Christianity's established place in American culture and America's role in Christian history.

By 1920, this informal white Protestant establishment realigned itself according to the sectarian battles between liberal ecumenist internationalists and conservative fundamentalist anti-internationalists. This division was not a binary between two clear sides but several cultural conflicts fought in transcendent ideological terms. Protestants who believed in universal truths found in an inerrant Bible and who anticipated an impending apocalyptic end had little in common with Protestants who embraced science, ecumenism, and historical-critical biblical interpretations. President Woodrow Wilson lived through and alongside these deepening fault lines. Accordingly, the historical record is a rhetorical minefield in which patient and diligent care must be given to what appears to be straightforward statements based on such terms as "fundamental," "evangelical," "liberal," "conservative," or "mainline." These contestations over religious identity were not separate from the debates regarding American culture or U.S. foreign policy but constitutive to the development of American nationalism in the early twentieth century. The essence and functions of religion, politics, race, and the state were coconstituted as Americans determined the role of the United States in the world.

As Woodrow Wilson and the ideological heritage of Wilsonian world order demonstrate, American religion, domestic politics, and foreign relations in the early twentieth century were closely related to one another. Indeed, thinking about these concepts as separate components obscures the way in which U.S. foreign relations and religion drew from the same set of assumptions about how Americans should live in the world. Wilson's articulation of American identity and the nation's ostensible purpose for global social salvation projected his particular Christian worldview as naturally, and obviously, American as well as universal and transcendent. His pronouncements on this topic elicited not just *a* firm opposition but several *kinds* of opposition, most forcefully from fundamentalists, the Republican Party, Socialists,

civil rights activists, and others who did not drink from the same postmillennial evangelical wellspring. Like Wilson himself, his detractors were shaped
by religion in American culture, the product of a century of postmillennial
evangelicalism that dominated the spirit and form of reform-minded politics.
Opponents to the League of Nations, at church pulpits and on the Senate
floor, passionately sought the demise of Wilson's Covenant of the League of
Nations to maintain both the sovereignty of the United States *and* their own
particular understanding of Christianity.

These perspectives on American sovereignty in an international system
reverberated back upon those least able to have a voice in the construction of
a new global order. A decade after Israel Zangwill depicted the United States
as a "melting pot," race, religion, gender, class, and the tensions inherent in
each social category boiled to the surface as international affairs added fuel
to the flames of these domestic concerns. The League Fight in 1919 revealed
not only America's inability to serve in an international body but also its bro-
kenness as a national body politic. Contrary to the longstanding myths of
U.S. religious freedom and pluralism, the nature of religion and politics had
divided Americans by the second decade of the twentieth century. Wilson's
internationalism and its legacies are products of the tensions within the history of America's informal moral establishment.

With Wilsonian internationalism as an instructive example, it is clear
that the idea of religion and conflicting formations of religion play several
competing roles in the history of U.S. foreign relations. Wilson's vision for
America in the world belongs within a historical context in which liberal
Protestants sought to Christianize America and the world. His emphasis
on "equality" and "the advancement of democracy" is best understood as
an expression of white middle- and upper-class social Christian notions of
proper world order. Likewise, postwar changes within American evangelicalism shaped the legacy of Wilsonians' reinterpretation of Wilson's internationalism. Premillennialists' and Republicans' efforts to delegitimize the
Covenant of the League of Nations led Wilsonians to reframe their vision for
America in the world based on new postwar realities. By reducing religion
to morality, applied ethics, affect, or religious affiliation alone, scholars may
miss how cultural, legal, and diplomatic formations of religion influenced
both domestic and foreign affairs.

If a central component of American foreign relations is articulating the
role and mission of the United States in the world, then studies of religion
are constitutive to those practices, as religious identities often define what
it means to be American. When Wilson attempted to spread U.S. empire,
conservative premillennial evangelicals challenged Wilson's foreign relations

on biblical and nationalistic grounds. Social Christians were pushed from the American evangelical norm as premillennialists decried the League of Nations as unchristian and as nativism reemerged as an integral component of white evangelicalism. New interpretations of American identity also pulled liberals away from the established Protestant mainstream. White liberal Protestants defended their Americanism and reformulated their religious identity according to a new Judeo-Christian—rather than white evangelical—norm. Moving from evangelical Christianization efforts to mainstream humanitarian reform, white liberal Protestants retained their emphasis on individual authority, biblical criticism, and adaptation to the modern age even as their place within American culture shifted.

As some white Protestants espoused nativism and racial superiority following the war, most forcefully through membership in the Ku Klux Klan, nonsectarian organizations like the Federal Council of Churches of Christ in America increasingly reached out to Jews and Catholics. With time, it became clear that religious identity could provide the necessary tools for political consensus. Together, these Protestants, Catholics, and Jews reformulated public discourse about American nationalism and internationalism. In the process, the assumed authority of whiteness did not receive major reconsideration; instead, "white" grew to encompass former immigrant groups, including those once discriminated against as racial outsiders. The enemy to achieving a more perfect union on earth proved *within* American Protestantism, not *outside* of it. Sharing the values of brotherhood, this new Judeo-Christian coalition upheld Wilsonian internationalism based upon American ideals rather than the Christianity Wilson espoused. Liberal Protestants ceased to describe themselves as evangelical, but they maintained their relationship to the state as the proper means of achieving social salvation. Liberals embraced the nation, and its public sphere, as their own to advance their mission of establishing a "brotherhood of man." At the same time, premillennialists narrowed the meaning of "evangelicalism" to refer to their particular brand of antistate, premillennial Protestantism. Both were so successful at this verbal shift that, by the second half of the twentieth century, most common usages of "evangelical" assume a conservative bent.

When scholars, pundits, and schoolteachers describe Wilsonianism, they often describe it as moralistic or idealistic. This simple association often ignores Wilsonianism's roots in these heated cultural debates among white Protestants in the first half of the twentieth century. Employing "Wilsonianism" in this way can perpetuate the aims of both conservative and liberal Protestants of Wilson's era without revealing its contested history and purposeful construction. Understanding Wilsonianism as idealistic, rather than

Christian, endorses premillennial Protestants' aggressive naming and claiming of American evangelicalism and, at times, Christianity as a whole in 1919. It simultaneously upholds Wilsonians' reformulations of liberal internationalism and Americanism in the 1920s and 1930s. Presuming Wilson's foreign policy to be secular or, at least, intentionally distanced from his personal piety is a measure of Wilsonians' successful renarration of Wilson's religious life. Much like Wilson, Wilsonian internationalists and their opponents did not feel the need to explicitly state their reliance upon or connection to Christianity because it seemed obvious to them. They believed their cause to be a matter of universally transcendent truth.

Wilsonians sacrificed their relationship to American evangelicalism so that their ultimate goal could be met through U.S. foreign relations. The social salvation they sought was not an otherworldly life for individual souls but rather a global society modeled after American democracy. As the United States established its empire through peaceful, brotherly relations, these Americans believed social salvation would follow. Wilson and the Covenant of the League of Nations, then, paved the way for social Christians to make a peaceful conquest of the state to fulfill the ends of the church. Abandoning an evangelical and, in some cases, Christian affiliation to pursue international security and stability may appear outside the scope of considerations of *religion* in foreign relations. Yet this is the case with the history of religion in Wilsonian world order. The mission proved too broad and too historic to belong entirely to what became a limiting conception of religious identity. Domestic politics and a contested national culture contributed to a new context in which religion itself seemed in need of reform. When the spotlight shines too brightly on the sincere belief of an individual, on the defining characteristics of a group, or on an imagined reality, much more remains in the shadows. When the study of religion in foreign relations includes how religion is socially and legally constructed, marshaled through the resources of state and nonstate actors, or sanctified through public discourse, new perspectives come to light.

Notes

Introduction

1. "Annual Baltimore Conference of the Methodist Episcopal Church, South, March 25, 1915," *The Papers of Woodrow Wilson*, ed. Arthur S. Link, vol. 32, *January 1–April 16, 1915* (Princeton, NJ: Princeton University Press, 1980), 32:430.

2. "Luncheon Address to the Chamber of Commerce of Columbus, Ohio, December 10, 1915," *The Papers of Woodrow Wilson*, ed. Arthur S. Link, vol. 35, *October 1, 1915–January 27, 1916* (Princeton, NJ: Princeton University Press, 1980), 35:327. (Hereafter shortened as PWW.)

3. Ibid., 328.

4. Ibid.

5. New York: Macmillan, 1913.

6. Ibid., 125.

7. Ibid.

8. See Walter Rauschenbusch, *Dare We Be Christians* (New York: Pilgrim Press, 1914).

9. "Address to the Federal Council of Churches, Columbus, Ohio, December 10, 1915," *PWW*, 35:335–36.

10. Historian David Sehat emphasizes the "public relevance of evangelical moral ideals" in a national context in *Myth of American Religious Freedom* (New York: Oxford University Press, 2011), 52.

11. Andrew Preston introduced this concept of Wilson being "steeped" in the social gospel in *Sword of the Spirit, Shield of Faith: Religion in American War and Diplomacy* (New York: Anchor, 2012).

12. "Wilsonian moment" is Erez Manela's term in his award-winning book, *The Wilsonian Moment: Self-Determination and the International Origins of Anticolonial Nationalism* (New York: Oxford University Press, 2007).

13. See Kevin Schultz, *Tri-faith America: How Catholics and Jews Held Postwar America to Its Protestant Promise* (New York: Oxford University Press, 2011).

14. While many books draw upon this theme, I was persuaded by Frederick Dickinson, *War and National Reinvention: Japan in the Great War, 1914–1919* (Cambridge, MA: Harvard University Asia Center, 1999), 4.

Chapter One

1. Edwin Alderman, "Woodrow Wilson: Memorial Address Delivered Before a Joint Session of the Two Houses of Congress, December 15, 1924, in Honor of Woodrow Wilson Late President of the United States" (Washington, DC: Government Printing Office, 1924), 16, Cary T. Grayson Papers, Woodrow Wilson Presidential Library (hereafter referred to as WWPL), Staunton, Virginia.

2. *The Souls of Black Folks*, 5th ed. (Chicago: A. C. McClurg, 1904), 1–2.

3. Visitors to the Boyhood Home of President Woodrow Wilson in Augusta, Georgia, will hear this story while standing on the steps of the manse. See also, A. Scott Berg, *Wilson* (New York: Putnam, 2013), 31–32; John Milton Cooper Jr., *Woodrow Wilson: A Biography* (New York: Vintage Books, 2009), 16–17.

4. "Thomas Woodrow Wilson" reflects several family names. To minimize confusion, "Reverend Wilson" or "Reverend" will refer to Joseph Wilson. "Tommy," "Woodrow," and "Wilson" will refer to Thomas Woodrow Wilson, reflecting his own choice in nomenclature at different stages of his life.

5. There is some debate about the status of the Wilsons' domestic worker. Dr. Cary T. Grayson concluded that the Wilsons probably paid $6–8 per month for a domestic worker ("The Religion of Woodrow Wilson" [n.p.: unpublished manuscript, 1924] Cary T. Grayson Papers, WWPL). Since Reverend Wilson supported slavery, it seems unlikely that he would have given this person a wage in addition to room and board prior to Reconstruction. Most likely the Wilson family participated in the customary arrangement of southern ministers "borrowing" or "leasing" slaves from parishioners rather than owning slaves themselves.

6. Grayson, "The Religion of Woodrow Wilson."

7. Ibid.

8. For more on this white southern culture, see: Edward Blum, *Reforging the White Republic: Race, Religion, and American Nationalism, 1865–1898* (Baton Rouge: Louisiana State University Press, 2007); Paul Harvey, *Freedom's Coming: Religious Culture and the Shaping of the South from the Civil War through the Civil Rights Era* (Chapel Hill: University of North Carolina Press, 2007); Christine Leigh Heyrman, *Southern Cross: The Beginnings of the Bible Belt* (Chapel Hill: University of North Carolina Press, 1998); Ted Ownby, *Subduing Satan: Religion, Recreation, and Manhood in the Rural South, 1865–1920* (Chapel Hill: The University of North Carolina Press, 1993); Art Remillard, *Southern Civil Religions: Imagining the Good Society in the Post-Reconstruction Era* (Athens: University of Georgia Press, 2011); Chad Seales, *The Secular Spectacle: Performing Religion in a Southern Town* (New York: Oxford University Press, 2013); and Bertram Wyatt-Brown, *The Shaping of Southern Culture: Honor, Grace, and War, 1760s–1880s* (Chapel Hill: University of North Carolina Press, 2000).

9. See Grayson, "The Religion of Woodrow Wilson." For more on the relationship between Scott and southern white men, see Peter Schmidt, "Walter Scott, Postcolonial Theory, and New South Literature," *The Mississippi Quarterly* 56, no. 4 (2003): 545–54. For the influence of racial theologies on Dixon and the South, see Edward Blum, "Race as Cosmic Sight in Souls of Black Folk," in *W. E. B. Du Bois: American Prophet* (Philadelphia: University of Pennsylvania Press, 2009), 61–97.

10. See also Chad Seales's *Secular Spectacle* for the importance of play in southern culture.

11. Woodrow Wilson, "Address to the Presbytery," April 20, 1915, in *Woodrow Wilson in Church: His Membership in the Congregation of the Central Presbyterian Church, Washington, D.C., 1913–1924*, ed. James H. Taylor (Charleston, SC: Walker, Evans, and Cogswell Company, 1952), 18–19, courtesy of the Presbyterian Historical Society, Philadelphia, PA.

12. Ibid.

13. Ibid, 19.

14. Eleanor Wilson McAdoo and Margaret Y. Gaffey, *The Woodrow Wilsons* (New York: The Macmillan Company, 1937), 40, HathiTrust Digital Library, http://hdl.handle.net/2027/uc1 .b62115.

15. Joseph R. Wilson, *Mutual Relation of Masters and Slaves as Taught in the Bible: A Discourse Preached in the First Presbyterian Church, Augusta, Georgia, January 6, 1861* (Augusta, GA: Steam Press of Chronicle & Sentinel, 1861), 7.

16. Ibid., 21.

17. Woodrow Wilson, "The Politics and the Industries of the New South" (revision of an unpublished article, ca. April 30, 1881), *The Papers of Woodrow Wilson* (hereafter PWW), vol. 2, *1881–1884* (Princeton, NJ: Princeton University Press, 1967), 2:51. The *New York Evening Post* rejected an earlier form of this essay. After significant revisions, Wilson successfully published in the *New York Evening Post* a year later (PWW, 2:31n).

18. For more on this notion of reforging, see Blum, *Reforging the White Republic.*

19. The Wilsons illustrate the thesis of Christine Heyrman's *Southern Cross* as a multigenerational example of how evangelicals "translated" their faith into southern culture. Woodrow and Ellen, as southerners born in the mid-nineteenth century, belonged to southern evangelicalism so strongly that when they moved to the North and had their own children they feared losing their southern identity rather than their evangelical one.

20. McAdoo and Gaffey, *The Woodrow Wilsons,* 90.

21. Michelle Brittain, *The Politics of Whiteness: Race, Workers, and Culture in the Modern South* (Athens: University of Georgia Press, 2004); Mathew Frye Jacobson, *Whiteness of a Different Color: European Immigrants and the Alchemy of Race* (Cambridge, MA: Harvard University Press, 1999); Angie Maxwell, *The Indicted South: Public Criticism, Southern Inferiority, and the Politics of Whiteness* (Chapel Hill: University of North Carolina Press, 2014); Nell Irvin Painter, *The History of White People* (New York: W. W. Norton, 2011); David Roediger, *Working toward Whiteness: How America's Immigrants Became White: The Strange Journey from Ellis Island to the Suburbs* (New York: Basic Books, 2006); and Matt Wray, *Not Quite White: White Trash and the Boundaries of Whiteness* (Durham, NC: Duke University Press, 2006).

22. Arthur Link, "Woodrow Wilson: The American as Southerner," *Journal of Southern History* 36, no. 1 (1970): 11.

23. For an extension of Link's reasoning, see Berg, 309–10. More in-depth analysis of Wilson's segregationist policies can be found in Eric Yellin's *Racism in the Nation's Service: Government Workers and the Color Line in Woodrow Wilson's America* (Chapel Hill: University of North Carolina Press, 2013).

24. Cooper, *Wilson,* 4–5, 23–25, 410–11.

25. Woodrow Wilson, "The Union" (draft of a speech) November 15, 1876, PWW, vol. 1, *1856–1880,* 1:228.

26. See Blum, *Reforging the White Republic,* and Remillard, *Southern Civil Religions.* Whereas Blum examines the construction of a new and renewed white Protestant ethnic nationalism following the Civil War, Remillard draws attention to nonwhite and non-Protestant national identities and their discourses as they developed after the Civil War. Wilson espoused the white Protestant ethnic nationalism Blum described, but he must be placed in the larger historical context that Remillard provided.

27. Ellen Axson Wilson to Woodrow Wilson, May 23, 1886, PWW, vol. 5, *1885–1888,* ed. Arthur S. Link (Princeton, NJ: Princeton University Press, 1968), 5:251.

28. Letter from Reverend Dr. Joseph R. Wilson to Reverend Dr. James Woodrow, June 19, 1884, Ray Stannard Baker Papers, Joseph R. Wilson folder, Manuscript Division, Library of Congress, Washington, DC (hereafter LOC).

29. See Matthew Hedstrom, *The Rise of Liberal Religion: Book Culture and American Spirituality in the Twentieth Century* (New York: Oxford University Press, 2012); Candy Gunther Brown, *Word in the World: Evangelical Writing, Publishing, and Reading in America, 1789–1880* (Chapel Hill, The University of North Carolina Press, 2004); John Modern, *Secularism in Antebellum America*; Christopher G. White, *Unsettled Minds: Psychology and the American Search for Spiritual Assurance, 1830–1940* (Berkeley: University of California Press, 2009); Catherine L. Albanese, *A Republic of Mind and Spirit: A Cultural History of American Metaphysical Religion* (New Haven: Yale University Press, 2008); Seales, *The Secular Spectacle.*

30. See Kathryn Lofton, "The Methodology of Modernism: Process in American Protestantism," *Church History: Studies in Christianity and Culture* 75, no. 2 (2006): 374–402.

31. These form the basic features of liberal Protestantism in the Gilded Age and Progressive Era. See Cara Burnidge, "Protestant Liberalism," *Encyclopedia of Religion in America*, eds. Charles Lippy and Peter Williams (Washington, DC: CQ Press, 2010), 3:1782–90.

32. Catherine A. Brekus and W. Clark Gilpin, eds., *American Christianities: A History of Dominance and Diversity* (Chapel Hill: University of North Carolina Press, 2011).

33. Martin Marty, *Righteous Empire: The Protestant Experience in America* (New York: Dial Press, 1970), 177–87.

34. Wilson settled on this pen name after much thought ("Shorthand Diary, July 19, 1876," PWW, 1:156, 1:156n2); "A Religious Essay: Work-Day Religion," August 11, 1876, PWW, 1:176–78; this essay was also printed in *North Carolina Presbyterian* (Wilmington), August 16, 1876, two months after his father became editor of the journal (PWW, 1:147n1, 1:253n1).

35. See "Shorthand Diary, August 9, 1876," PWW, 1:174; Wilson, "A Religious Essay: Work-Day Religion," PWW, 1:177.

36. Ibid.

37. (New York: Houghton, Mifflin, and Company, 1886). Many historians consider Washington Gladden one of the fathers of the social gospel for this and other works, such as Jacob Henry Dorn (*Washington Gladden: Prophet of the Social Gospel* [Columbus: Ohio State University, 1968]), Gary Dorrien (*Social Ethics in the Making: Interpreting an American Tradition* [Malden, MA: Wiley-Blackwell, 2009]), and Gary Scott Smith (*The Search for Social Salvation: Social Christianity in America, 1880–1925* [Lanham, MD: Lexington, 2000]). Heath Carter expands these narratives of social Christianity by drawing attention to working-class Christians who developed the thought and practice of social Christianity *prior to* Gladden (*Union Made: Working People and the Rise of Social Christianity in Chicago* [New York: Oxford University Press, 2015], 1–8, 48).

38. Wilson, "A Religious Essay: Work-Day Religion," PWW, 1:176–78.

39. Woodrow Wilson, "A Religious Essay: The Bible," PWW, 1:185.

40. Brown, *Word in the World*; Modern *Secularism in Antebellum America.*

41. William Hutchinson, *The Modernist Impulse in American Protestantism* (Durham, NC: Duke University Press, 1992).

42. Woodrow Wilson, "A Religious Essay: The Positive in Religion," PWW, 1:211.

43. Ibid., 212.

44. Ibid.

45. For an interpretation of Wilson that emphasizes the role of eschatology, see Milan Babik, *Salvation and Statecraft: Wilsonian Liberal Internationalism as Secularized Eschatology* (Waco, TX: Baylor University Press, 2013).

46. For more on this divide and its place in American evangelicalism, see Matthew Bowman, *The Urban Pulpit: New York City and the Fate of Liberal Evangelicalism* (New York: Oxford University Press, 2014); George Marsden, *Fundamentalism and American Culture* (New York: Oxford University Press, 2006); Matthew Avery Sutton, *American Apocalypse: A History of Modern Evangelicalism* (Cambridge, MA: Belknap Press, 2014).

47. Woodrow Wilson, "A Religious Essay: Christ's Army," PWW, 1:180; also printed in *North Carolina Presbyterian* (Wilmington), August 23, 1876.

48. "A Religious Essay: A Christian Statesman," PWW, 1:188; also printed in *North Carolina Presbyterian* (Wilmington), September 6, 1876.

49. Ibid.

50. Ibid., 189.

51. For examples of this popular literature see Edward Bellamy, *Looking Backward* (London: William Reeves, 1887); Charles M. Sheldon, *In His Steps: What Would Jesus Do* (Chicago: Advance, 1896); and, later, Bruce Barton, *The Man Nobody Knows* (Indianapolis: Bruce-Merrill, 1925). For more on this genre, see Paul Gutjahr, *Popular American Literature of the 19th Century* (New York: Oxford University Press, 2001); Gregory S. Jackson, *The Word and Its Witness: The Spiritualization of American Realism* (Chicago: University of Chicago Press, 2009); David S. Reynolds, *Faith in Fiction: The Emergence of Religious Literature in America* (Cambridge, MA: Harvard University Press, 1981); Erin A. Smith, *What Would Jesus Read? Popular Books and Everyday Life in Twentieth-Century America* (Chapel Hill: University of North Carolina Press, 2015).

52. *Congressional Government* (Boston: Houghton Mifflin, 1885); *The Study of Administration* (New York: Academy of Political Science, 1887); *The State: Elements of Historical and Practical Politics* (Boston: D. C. Heath, 1889); *An Old Master and Other Political Essays* (New York: Scribner's and Sons, 1893); *George Washington* (New York: Harper Brothers, 1896); and *A History of the American People*, 5 vols. (New York: Harper Brothers, 1901–1903).

53. "Letter to the Editor: 'Anti-Sham' No. 1," January 25, 1882, PWW, 2:98.

54. Irwin Hood Hoover, *Forty-Two Years in the White House* (Boston: Houghton Mifflin Company, 1934), 112.

55. In *What the World Should Be: Woodrow Wilson and the Crafting of a Faith-Based Foreign Policy*, Malcolm Magee brought these streams of thought together, rightly noting that Wilson objected to Catholicism as an institution and not, except in rare instances, to individual Catholics ([Waco, TX: Baylor University Press, 2008], 30–32).

56. For an example of this kind of argument about the nature of anti-Catholicism, see Bruce Lincoln, "Revolutionary Exhumations in Spain," in *Discourse and the Construction of Society: Comparative Studies of Myth, Ritual, and Classification* (New York: Oxford University Press, 1992), 103–30.

57. See David Sehat, *The Myth of American Religious Freedom* (New York: Oxford University Press, 2011).

58. For more on covenant theology and its role in Wilson's ideology, see Mark Benbow, *Leading Them to the Promised Land: Woodrow Wilson, Covenant Theology, and the Mexican Revolution, 1913–1915* (Kent, OH: Kent State University Press, 2010); Malcolm Magee, *What the World Should Be*; Magee, "Wilson's Religious, Historical, and Political Thought," in *A Companion to Woodrow Wilson*, ed. Ross A. Kennedy (Malden, MA: Wiley-Blackwell, 2013), 38–54.

59. Elizabeth Fenton, *Religious Liberties: Anti-Catholicism and Liberal Democracy in Nineteenth-Century U.S. Literature and Culture* (New York: Oxford University Press, 2011), 59.

60. "Letter to the Editor: 'Anti-Sham' No. 1," PWW, 2:97–98.

61. "Letter to the Editor: Anti-Sham No. 3," March 22, 1882, PWW, 2:115.

62. See Jay Dolan, *In Search of American Catholicism: A History of Religion and Culture in Tension* (New York: Oxford University Press, 2002); Andrew Henry, *Southern Crucifix, Southern Cross: Catholic-Protestant Relations in the Old South* (Tuscaloosa: University of Alabama Press, 2012).

63. Jenny Franchot, *Roads to Rome: The Antebellum Protestant Encounter with Catholicism* (Berkeley: University of California Press, 1994); Tracy Fessenden, *Culture and Redemption: Religion, the Secular, and American Literature* (Princeton, NJ: Princeton University Press, 2006); and Fenton, *Religious Liberties*.

64. "Wilson's Notes and Topical Headings on Professor [Lyman] Atwater's Lectures on Civil Government," Lecture Seven, November 1, 1878, PWW, 1:427.

65. See Sehat, *Myth of American Religious Freedom*.

66. *Princeton in the Nation's Service* (Princeton, NJ: The Alumni Princetonian, 1896), 37–38.

67. Ibid.

68. Ibid., 35.

69. Wilson, *Princeton in the Nation's Service*, 36.

Chapter Two

1. Samuel Zane Batten, *The Christian State: The State, Democracy and Christianity* (Philadelphia: Griffith & Rowland Press, 1909), 10.

2. "Memorandum," (n.d. [1912]), Ray Stannard Baker Papers, Yates, Mr. and Mrs. Fred and Mary folder, Manuscript Division, Library of Congress, Washington, D.C. (hereafter LOC).

3. Ibid.

4. Eleanor Wilson McAdoo and Margaret Y. Gaffey, *The Woodrow Wilsons* (New York: Macmillan, 1937), 180, HathiTrust Digital Library, http://hdl.handle.net/2027/uc1.b62115.

5. Ibid., 180–81.

6. Ibid.

7. See William Hutchinson, *Between the Times* (New York: Cambridge University Press, 1990); David Sehat, *Myth of American Religious Freedom* (New York: Oxford University Press, 2011).

8. Tracy Fessenden, *Culture and Redemption: Religion, the Secular, and American Literature* (Princeton, NJ: Princeton University Press, 2006).

9. See Fessenden, *Culture and Redemption*; John Lardas Modern, *Secularism in Antebellum America* (Chicago: University of Chicago Press, 2011).

10. "Orthodox in Religion, Straight in Politics: The Ticket Named in Baltimore and Incidents of Its Making—Young Men in Politics," *New York Times*, July 7, 1912, 10, ProQuest Historical Newspapers: The New York Times (97264478).

11. Theodore Roosevelt and Progressive Party National Convention, *Theodore Roosevelt's Confession of Faith before the Progressive National Convention, August 6, 1912* (New York, Allied Printing, 1912), 32.

12. "'Hail New Party in Fervent Song: 'Battle Hymn of the Republic' Sways 1,000 Delegates," *New York Times*, August 6, 1912, 1, ProQuest Historical Newspapers: The New York Times (97301651).

13. "Roosevelt Named Shows Emotion: 'Of Course I Accept,'" *New York Times*, August 8, 1912, 1, ProQuest Historical Newspapers: The New York Times (97350333); "Roosevelt Seeks Aid of Democrats: Progressives of Both Parties to Be on His Committee," *New York Times*, June 24, 1912, 1, ProQuest Historical Newspapers: The New York Times (97236268).

14. "Armageddon Not Mythical but Real Battlefield," *New York Times,* August 11, 1912, SM1, ProQuest Historical Newspapers: The New York Times (97271670). For more on the role of apocalypticism in American culture, see Matthew Avery Sutton, *American Apocalypse* (Cambridge, MA: Belknap Press, 2014).

15. "President Defends His Religious Faith: Refused to Deny Belief in Unitarianism," *New York Times,* April 24, 1911, 5, ProQuest Historical Newspapers: The New York Times (97158803).

16. Ibid.

17. "Calls Taft True Christian: Dr. Hill Also Says Prayer Is the Secret of His Control," *New York Times,* September 23, 1912, 2, ProQuest Historical Newspapers: The New York Times (97344968).

18. The "Channing School" refers to William Ellery Channing who outlined American Unitarianism with his Harvard graduation sermon, "Unitarian Christianity," in 1819, sparking the first "Unitarian Controversy" throughout Boston and the New England area.

19. "Calls Taft True Christian," 2.

20. For more on this transatlantic history, see Leslie Butler, *Critical Americans: Victorian Intellectuals and Transatlantic Liberal Reform* (Durham, NC: University of North Carolina Press, 2007); Mina Carson, *Settlement Folk: Social Thought and the American Settlement Movement, 1885–1930* (Chicago: University of Chicago Press, 1990); Allen Freeman Davis, *Spearheads for Reform; the Social Settlements and the Progressive Movement 1890–1914* (New York: Oxford University Press, 1967); Gary Dorrien, *The Making of American Liberal Theology*; and Paul T. Phillips, *A Kingdom on Earth: Anglo-American Social Christianity, 1880–1940* (University Park: Pennsylvania State University Press, 1996).

21. For more on social Christianity, see Matthew Bowman, "Sin, Spirituality, and Primitivism: The Theologies of the American Social Gospel, 1885–1917," *Religion and American Culture* 17, no. 1 (2007): 95–126; Bowman, *The Urban Pulpit: New York City and the Fate of Liberal Evangelicalism* (New York: Oxford University Press, 2014); Heath Carter, *Union Made: Working People and the Rise of Social Christianity in Chicago* (New York: Oxford University Press, 2015); Gary J. Dorrien, *Soul in Society: The Making and Renewal of Social Christianity* (Minneapolis: Fortress Press, 1995); Brantley Gassaway, *Progressive Evangelicals and the Pursuit of Social Justice* (Chapel Hill: University of Northern Carolina Press, 2014); George Marsden, "The Gospel of Wealth, the Social Gospel, and the Salvation of Souls in Nineteenth-century America," *Fides Et Historia: Official Publication of the Conference on Faith and History* 5, no. 1 (1973): 10–21; Gary Scott Smith, *The Search for Social Salvation: Social Christianity and America, 1880–1925* (Lanham, MD: Lexington Books, 2000).

22. Ralph Luker, "The Social Gospel and the Failure of Racial Reform, 1877–Present," *Church History* 46, no. 1 (1977): 80–99; Luker, *The Social Gospel in Black and White American Racial Reform, 1885–1912* (Chapel Hill: University of North Carolina Press, 1991); Ronald C. White, *Liberty and Justice for All: Racial Reform and the Social Gospel (1877–1925)*, The Rauschenbusch Lectures (San Francisco: Harper & Row, 1990).

23. For more on the role of urban space and evangelical reform, see Bowman, *The Urban Pulpit.*

24. Samuel Z. Batten et. al., *A Social Service Catechism* (New York: Federal Council of Churches of Christ in America, 1912), 1.

25. Ibid.

26. Ibid., 3.

27. "Wilson an Example of the World's Need: 'Give Us Men!' Is the Cry of Speakers at British Universities' Congress," *New York Times,* July 7, 1912, C4, ProQuest Historical Newspapers: The New York Times (97268123).

28. Udo J. Keppler, "The Good Samaritan," *Harper's Weekly* 72, no. 1858 (October 9, 1912), centerfold, courtesy of Library of Congress Prints and Photographs Division, Washington, DC, LC-DIG-ppmsca-27883.

29. See Heather Curtis, *Faith in the Great Physician: Suffering and Divine Healing in American Culture, 1860–1900* (Baltimore: Johns Hopkins University, 2007); R. Marie Griffith, *Born Again Bodies* (Berkeley: University of California Press, 2004); Pamela Klassen, *Spirits of Protestantism: Medicine, Healing, and Liberal Christianity* (Berkeley: University of California Press, 2011); Joseph Williams, *Spirit Cure: A History of Pentecostal Healing* (New York: Oxford University Press, 2013); Clifford Putney, *Muscular Christianity: Manhood and Sports in Protestant America, 1880–1920* (Cambridge, MA: Harvard University Press, 2001).

30. Men and Religion Forward Movement, *Messages of the Men and Religion Forward Movement*, Volume 2: Social Service (New York: Association Press, 1912), 2, 3.

31. Ibid., 3.

32. Ibid.

33. Ibid., 4.

34. Quoted in Paul T. Phillips, *A Kingdom on Earth: Anglo-American Social Christianity, 1880–1940* (University Park: Pennsylvania State University Press, 1996), 223.

35. As quoted in Neil Salzman, *Reform and Revolution: The Life and Times of Raymond Robins* (Kent, OH: Kent State University Press, 1991), 140.

36. "William I. Haven, Rivington D. Lord, and Charles S. Macfarland to Woodrow Wilson, March 5, 1913," PWW, vol. 27, January–June, 1913, ed. Arthur S. Link (Princeton, NJ: Princeton University Press, 1979), 27:153–54; also printed in *Presbyterian Advance* (Utica, NY) vol. VII (March 13, 1913), 31.

37. See "Woodrow Wilson to Charles S. Macfarland, March 26, 1913," PWW, 27:231.

38. "From Felixina Shepherd Baker to Woodrow Wilson, March 3, 1913," PWW, 27:147.

39. "Woodrow Wilson to Mary Allen Hulbert, March 9, 1913," PWW, 27:167.

40. "From James Henry Taylor to Woodrow Wilson, April 24, 1913," PWW, 27:357.

41. "Woodrow Wilson to Mary Allen Hulbert, August 10, 1913," PWW, vol. 28, *1913*, ed. Arthur Link (Princeton, NJ: Princeton University Press, 1979), 28:135.

42. Presidents James Madison, John Quincy Adams, Andrew Jackson, James K. Polk, Franklin Pierce, James Buchanan, Ulysses S. Grant, and Grover Cleveland attended services at First Presbyterian Church. First cultivated a strong relationship with Capitol Hill as indicated by its 1948 rededication as National Presbyterian Church.

43. Central was originally located near the intersection of Third and I Streets. While in office, Wilson laid the cornerstone for a new location at 15th and Irving Streets.

44. "Woodrow Wilson to Mary Allen Hulbert, August 10, 1913," PWW, 28:135.

45. Ibid.

46. Ibid., 28:135–36.

47. Ibid., 135.

48. Ibid.

49. "Address on Preparedness to the Manhattan Club," November 4, 1915, PWW, vol. 35, *October 1915–December 1915*, ed. Arthur Link (Princeton, NJ: Princeton University Press, 1981), 35:171.

50. "Woodrow Wilson to Mary Allen Hulbert, June 29, 1913," PWW, 28:13–14.

51. Ibid., 13.

52. Ibid., 13–14.

53. "Woodrow Wilson to S. Townsend Weaver, September 7, 1916," PWW, vol. 38, *August 7–November 19, 1916*, ed. Arthur Link (Princeton, NJ: Princeton University Press, 1982), 38:157.

54. Ibid.

55. Grayson, "The Religion of Woodrow Wilson" (n.p.: unpublished manuscript, 1924) Cary T. Grayson Papers, WWPL.

56. William R. Hutchinson, *The Modernist Impulse in American Protestantism* (Durham, N.C.: Duke University Press, 1992).

57. See also Fessenden, *Culture and Redemption*; Modern, *Secularism in Antebellum America*; Lofton, "The Methodology of the Modernists: Process in American Protestantism," *Church History: Studies in Christianity and Culture* 75, no. 2 (2006): 374–402; Talal Asad, *Formations of the Secular: Christianity, Islam, Modernity* (Stanford: Stanford University Press, 2003).

58. Woodrow Wilson, "Remarks Upon Signing the Tariff Bill," October 3, 1913, PWW, 28:351.

59. Ibid., 28:352.

60. Ibid.

61. "Charles Ernest Scott to Woodrow Wilson, May 31, 1913," PWW, 27:489–90.

62. Woodrow Wilson, "Address to Berea College," February 24, 1915, PWW, vol. 32, *January 1–April 16, 1915*, ed. Arthur Link (Princeton, NJ: Princeton University Press, 1980), 32:284.

63. Woodrow Wilson, "Address to the Federal Council of Churches in Columbus, Ohio, December 10, 1915," PWW, 35:334.

64. Ibid.

65. Ibid.

66. Walter Rauschenbusch, *Christianity and the Social Crisis* (New York: Macmillan, 1913), 376–77.

67. Ibid., 413.

68. Ibid., 186.

69. Ibid., 185–86.

70. Ibid., 184.

71. Ibid.

72. Ibid., 183.

73. Wilson, "Address to the Federal Council of Churches, Columbus, Ohio," PWW, 35:334.

74. Ibid.

75. Woodrow Wilson, "Luncheon Address in Buffalo [to Ellicott Club]," November 1, 1916, PWW, 38:576–77.

76. Ibid., 38:577.

77. Wilson, "Address to the Federal Council of Churches, Columbus, Ohio," PWW, 35:334.

78. Ibid., 35:334–35.

79. Ibid., 35:335.

80. Woodrow Wilson, "Remarks to the Maryland Annual Conference of the Methodist Protestant Church," April 8, 1915, PWW, 32:495.

81. Ibid.

82. Ibid.

Chapter Three

1. *The Individual and the Social Gospel* (New York: Missionary Education Movement of the United States and Canada, 1914), 66–67; also quoted in Gary Dorrien, *Soul in Society: The Making and Renewal of Social Christianity* (Minneapolis: Fortress, 1995), 49.

2. See Robert Gerwarth and Erez Manela, *Empires at War, 1911–1923* (New York: Oxford University Press, 2014).

3. A. Scott Berg, *Wilson* (New York: Putnam, 2013), 334–35; John Milton Cooper Jr., *Woodrow Wilson: A Biography* (New York: Vintage Books, 2009), 260–61.

4. For more on the history of the Alley Dwelling Act, see Margaret E. Farrar, "Making the City Beautiful: Aesthetic Reform and the (Dis)placement of Bodies," in *Embodied Utopias: Gender, Social Change, and the Modern Metropolis*, eds. Amy Bingaman, Lise Sanders, and Rebecca Zorach (New York: Routledge, 2003), 37–54. For more on Ellen Wilson's reform efforts, see Kathryn Lynnell Beasley, ""I Think We Have an Angel in the White House": First Lady Ellen Axson Wilson and Her Social Activism Concerning the Washington, D.C., Slums, 1913–1914" (master's thesis, Valdosta State University, 2012).

5. Quoted in John Milton Cooper, Jr., *Woodrow Wilson: A Biography* (New York: Vintage, 2009), 261; "Woodrow Wilson to Mary Hulbert," August 7, 1914, PWW, vol. 30, *May–September, 1914*, ed. Arthur S. Link (Princeton, NJ: Princeton University Press, 1979), 30:357.

6. Quoted in Cooper, *Woodrow Wilson*, 266; "Edward M. House, Diary Entry November 6, 1914," PWW, vol. 31, *September 6–December, 1914*, 31:274.

7. As quoted in Cooper, *Woodrow Wilson*, 263; "Woodrow Wilson to Mary Allen Hulbert," August 23, 1914, PWW, 30:437. See also, Berg, *Wilson*, 336.

8. Woodrow Wilson, "Statement August 18, 1914," PWW, 30:394.

9. Ibid.

10. Woodrow Wilson, "A Luncheon Address to the Chamber of Commerce of Columbus, Ohio," December 10, 1915, PWW, vol. 35, *1915–1916*, 35:327–28.

11. Ibid.

12. Woodrow Wilson, "Address to the Federal Council of Churches in Columbus, Ohio," December 10, 1915, PWW, 35:335.

13. Ibid., 35:335–36.

14. "Charles S. Macfarland to Woodrow Wilson, December 14, 1915," PWW, 35:354.

15. Ibid.

16. Ibid., PWW, 35:354n2.

17. See, for example, Ray Abrams, *Preachers Present Arms: The Role of the American Churches and Clergy in World War I* (New York: Roundtable Press, 1933), 21n.

18. See Richard M. Gamble, *The War for Righteousness: Progressive Christianity, the Great War, and the Rise of the Messianic Nation* (Wilmington, DE: ISI Books, 2003); Philip Jenkins, *The Great and Holy War: How World War I Became a Religious Crusade* (San Francisco: HarperOne, 2014); Andrew Preston, "To Make the World Saved: American Religion and the Great War," *Diplomatic History* 38, no. 4 (2014): 813–25.

19. Jenkins, *The Great and Holy War*, 5.

20. See also, Gamble, *The War for Righteousness*, 80; Preston, "To Make the World Saved." Phillip Jenkins illustrates how this thinking did not belong to Americans alone in *Great and Holy War*.

21. For more, see Patricia Appelbaum, *Kingdom to Commune: Protestant Pacifist Culture Between World War I and the Vietnam Era* (Charlotte: University of North Carolina Press, 2009), 46.

22. Washington Gladden, *Forks of the Road* (New York: Macmillan, 1916), 21.

23. Sidney Lewis Gulick and Federal Council of the Churches of Christ in America Commission on Peace and Arbitration, *The Fight for Peace: An Aggressive Campaign for American Churches* (New York: F. H. Revell, 1915), 64.

24. Ibid., 191.

25. Ibid.

26. Ibid., 183–84.

27. Washington Gladden, *The Nation and the Kingdom: Annual Sermon Before the American Board of Commissioners for Foreign Missions* (Boston: Board of Commissioners for Foreign Missions: 1909), 9.

28. Shailer Mathews, *Patriotism and Religion* (New York: The Macmillan Company, 1918), 28.

29. See David Sehat, *Myth of American Religious Freedom* (New York: Oxford University Press, 2011).

30. David Sehat outlines the history of this myth in *Myth of American Religious Freedom*; Andrew Preston demonstrates how Christian and American missions became intertwined in *Sword of the Spirit, Shield of Faith: Religion in American War and Diplomacy* (New York: Knopf, 2012).

31. Charles Macfarland, *Christian Service and the Modern World* (New York: Fleming H. Revell Company, 1915), 132.

32. Ibid.

33. Ibid.

34. Ibid., 138–39.

35. For insights on this process, see David Chidester, "Colonialism," in *Guide to the Study of Religion*, eds. Willi Braun and Russell T. McCutcheon (New York: Cassell, 2000), 423–37.

36. *The Rights of Man: A Study in Twentieth Century Problems* (Boston: Houghton, Mifflin and Company, 1902), 343.

37. Ibid., 336.

38. Ibid., 336.

39. Ibid., 335.

40. Ibid., 354.

41. Ibid., 368–69.

42. Gamble, *The War for Righteousness*; Michael McGerr, *A Fierce Discontent: The Rise and Fall of the Progressive Movement in America, 1870–1920* (New York: Oxford University Press US, 2005); Jenkins, *Great and Holy War*; T. Jackson Lears, *Rebirth of a Nation: The Making of Modern America, 1877–1920* (New York: Harper, 2009).

43. See Emily Conroy-Krutz, *Christian Imperialism: Converting the World in the Early Republic* (New York: Cornell University Press, 2015); Ian Tyrell, *Reforming the World: The Creation of America's Moral Empire, America in the World* (Princeton, NJ: Princeton University Press, 2010).

44. Preston, *Sword of the Spirit*, 250.

45. "From the Diary of Nancy Saunders Toy, January 2, 1915," PWW, vol. 32, *January 1–April 16, 1915*, 32:7–9.

46. "Edith Bolling Galt to Annie Stuart Litchfield Bolling, March 23, 1915," PWW, 32:423; for details about Edith and Wilson's first encounter see PWW 32:424n3.

47. Woodrow Wilson, "Dedication," [1915?], Edith Bolling Wilson Papers, Box 57, Miscellany, Manuscript Division, Library of Congress, Washington, DC.

48. "Notification Speech of Hon. Ollie M. James," in *Senate Documents*, vol. 43, United States Congressional serial set. No. 6953 (Washington: GPO, 1916), 3–4.

49. "Convention Roused by James's Speech," *New York Times*, June 16, 1916, 1, ProQuest Historical Newspapers: The New York Times (03624331).

50. Ibid.

51. Ibid.

52. Ibid.

53. Woodrow Wilson, "A Speech in Long Branch, N.J., Accepting the Presidential Nomination," September 2, 1916, PWW, vol. 38, *August 7–November 19, 1916*, 38:132.

54. "An Address to the Senate, January 22, 1917," PWW, vol. 40, *November 20, 1916–January 23, 1917*, 40:536.

55. George Davis Herron, *Woodrow Wilson and the World's Peace* (New York: Mitchell Kennerley, 1917), 77.

56. (Original emphasis) Herron, *Woodrow Wilson and the World's Peace*, 10.

57. "The War Message to Congress, April 2, 1917," PWW, vol. 41, *January 24–April 6, 1917*, 41:525.

58. Ibid., 41:526–27.

59. "[Poem] To the United States from Poet Laureate Robert Seymour Bridges," May 3, 1917, PWW, vol. 42, *April 7–June 23, 1917*, 42:209–10.

60. Historian Ray Abrams gives a fuller account of this meeting in "The Church as Servant of the State," in *Preachers Present Arms*, 77–92.

61. Commission on the Church and Social Service, *Christian Duties in Conserving Spiritual, Moral and Social Forces of the Nation in Time of War* (New York: Federal Council of Churches of Christ in America, 1917).

62. Samuel Zane Batten, ed. *The Moral Meaning of the War: A Prophetic Interpretation* (Philadelphia: American Baptist Publication Society, 1918), 62.

63. Ibid., 81.

64. As quoted in Ibid.

65. The strategies and execution of federal propaganda can be read about in detail in George Creel's *How We Advertised America: The First Telling of the Amazing Story of the Committee on Public Information that Carried the Gospel of Americanism to Every Corner of the Globe* (New York: Harper Brothers, 1920).

66. Abrams, *Preachers Present Arms*, 82.

67. Ibid., 80.

68. "40,000 Cheer for War and Religion Mixed by Sunday: Sermons Brought Up to Date to Link the Kaiser with the Devil as an Enemy Alien," *The New York Times*, April 9, 1917, 1, ProQuest Historical Newspapers: The New York Times (99947774).

69. "War to be Keynote of Sunday Opening: Evangelist Will Adapt his Sermon, 'God's Grenadiers,' to Fit the Occasion," *The New York Times*, April 7, 1917, 12, ProQuest Historical Newspapers: The New York Times (99976212).

70. Theodore Roosevelt, *The Foes of Our Own Household* (New York: George Doran, 1917), 288, 298.

71. Ibid., 288, 15.

72. Andrew Carnegie, *A League of Peace: A Rectorial Address Delivered to the Students in the University of St. Andrews, 17th October, 1905* (Boston: Ginn & Company, 1906), 11.

73. Jane Addams, *The Second Twenty Years at Hull House* (New York: Macmillan, 1930), 45.

74. Ibid.

75. See Abrams, *Preachers Present Arms*, 164–65.

76. Abbott Lawrence Lowell, *A League to Enforce Peace*, World Peace Foundation Series, vol. 5, no. 1, part I (Boston: World Peace Foundation, 1915); William Howard Taft, "League to Enforce Peace," in *Collected Works of William Howard Taft*, vol. 7, *Taft Papers on League of Nations*, ed. Frank X. Gerrity (Athens: Ohio University Press, 2004), 1–4.

77. For more on Rauschenbusch's concerns about the war, see Gary Dorrien, *Soul in Society*, 52–54; Paul M. Minus, *Walter Rauschenbusch, American Reformer* (London: Collier Macmillan, 1988), 182–84.

78. "Woodrow Wilson to Guy Tresillian Helvering," April 19, 1917, PWW, 42:97–98.

79. "Obligation to Serve," *Christian Century* 34, no. 25 (1917), 13.

80. Ibid.

81. Ibid.

82. Christine Heyrman, *Southern Cross: The Beginnings of the Bible Belt* (Chapel Hill: University of North Carolina Press, 1998); Jon Pahl, "Shifting Sacrifices: Christians, War, and Peace in America," in *American Christianities*, eds. Catherine Brekus and W. Clark Gilpin (Chapel Hill: University of North Carolina Press, 2011), 445–65.

83. Pahl, "Shifting Sacrifices," 455.

84. "John Milton Waldron to Woodrow Wilson, April 12, 1917," PWW, 42:50.

85. Ibid., 42:51.

86. See Nicholas Patler, *Jim Crow and the Wilson Administration: Protesting Federal Segregation in the Early Twentieth Century* (Denver: University of Colorado Press, 2004); Eric S. Yellin, *Racism in the Nation's Service: Government Workers and the Color Line in Woodrow Wilson's America* (Durham: University of North Carolina Press, 2013).

87. Woodrow Wilson to John Milton Waldron, April 19, 1917, PWW, 42:98.

88. Chad L. Williams, *Torchbearers of Democracy: African American Soldiers in the World War I Era* (Chapel Hill: University of North Carolina Press, 2010), 7.

89. As quoted in Cooper, *Woodrow Wilson*, 408.

90. This is Chad Williams's persuasive argument in *Torchbearers of Democracy*.

91. Cooper, *Woodrow Wilson*, 410.

92. Abrams, *Preachers Present Arms*; H. C. Peterson and Gilbert C. Fite, *Opponents of War, 1917–1918* (Madison: University of Wisconsin Press, 1957); Joseph Kip Kosek, *Acts of Conscience: Christian Nonviolence and Modern American Democracy* (New York: Columbia University Press, 2011).

93. "Peace Council Asks If Wilson Supports Mobs," *The Evening News* [San Jose, CA], October 13, 1917, 2; for the history of middle-class evangelicals opposing labor activists, see Heath Carter's *Union Made: Working People and the Rise of Social Christianity in Chicago* (New York: Oxford University Press, 2015).

94. "Peace Council Asks If Wilson Supports Mobs," 2; Abrams, *Preachers Present Arms*, 216–17; Peterson and Fite, Opponents of War, 115–17.

95. National Civil Liberties Bureau, *The Case of the Christian Pacifists at Los Angeles, Cal.* (New York: National Civil Liberties Bureau, 1918), 9, University of Colorado-Boulder Libraries Archives, World War I Collection.

96. *The Case of the Christian Pacifists*, 12–13.

97. *The Case of the Christian Pacifists*, 15.

98. Cary T. Grayson, "The Religion of Woodrow Wilson" (n.p.: unpublished manuscript, 1924), Cary T. Grayson Papers, Woodrow Wilson Presidential Library, Staunton, Virginia.

Chapter Four

1. "An Address to the Senate, July 10, 1919," in *Papers of Woodrow Wilson* (PWW), vol. 61, *June 18–July 25, 1919*, ed. Arthur Link (Princeton, NJ: Princeton University Press, 1989), 61:436.

2. Edith Benham Helm, *The Captains and the Kings* (New York: Putnam, 1954), 54.

3. Ibid.

4. See Jonathan Ebel, *Faith in the Fight: Religion and the American Soldier in the Great War* (Princeton, NJ: Princeton University Press, 2010); Ebel, "Of the Lost and the Fallen: Ritual and the Religious Power of the American Soldier," *Journal of Religion* 92, no. 2 (2012): 224–50; Philip Jenkins, *The Great and Holy War: How World War I Became a Religious Crusade* (San Francisco: HarperOne, 2014).

5. Historian John Milton Cooper Jr. advances this argument best in "To Draft the Covenant," in *Breaking the Heart of the World: Woodrow Wilson and the Fight for the League of Nations* (New York: Cambridge University Press, 2010), 10–54.

6. Wilson learned of Pope Benedict's appeals through Robert Lansing. See "From Robert Lansing, with Enclosure, August 13, 1917," PWW, 43:438–39; and, "Walter Hines Page to Robert Lansing, August 15, 1917," PWW, 43:482–517.

7. For a fuller explication of this view and an example of the importance of interweaving American religious history with the history of America in the world, see Peter R. D'Agostino, "The Great War: 'Keep the Roman Question Alive,' 1914–1920," in *Rome in America: Transnational Catholic Ideology from the Risorgimento to Fascism* (Chapel Hill: The University of North Carolina Press, 2004), 103–30.

8. The administration's deliberations over the reply can be found PWW, 43:438–39, 482–83, 487–88. For the final reply, see PWW, 44:57–59; Cooper, *Breaking the Heart*, 418; Berg, *Wilson*, 462.

9. As quoted in Cooper, *Woodrow Wilson*, 418.

10. Cooper, *Woodrow Wilson*, 419; Berg, *Wilson*, 463–69.

11. See "From the Diary of Colonel House," January 4, 1918, PWW, 45:458–59; "A Memorandum by Sidney Mezes, David Hunter Miller, and Walter Lippman: The Present Situation: The War Aims and Peace Terms It Suggests, Our Objectives," PWW, 45:459–74.

12. See PWW, 45:534–39.

13. David Lloyd George, *British War Aims: Statement by the Right Honourable David Lloyd George, January Fifth, Nineteen Hundred and Eighteen* (New York: George Doran Company, 1918), 15, University of North Carolina at Greensboro, Special Collections: World War I Pamphlet Collection, https://archive.org/details/britishwaraimsst00lloy.

14. Erez Manela, "Global Anti-Imperialism in the Age of Wilson," in *Empire's Twin: U.S. Anti-Imperialism from the Founding Era to the Age of Terrorism*, eds. Ian Tyrell and Jay Sexton, The United States in the World (New York: Cornell University Press, 2015), 137–52.

15. Ibid.

16. See Andrew Preston, "The Wilsonian Creed," in *Sword of the Spirit, Shield of Faith: Religion in American War and Diplomacy* (New York: Anchor, 2012), 275–90.

17. See Preston, "The Wilsonian Creed"; Cara Burnidge, "The Business of Church and State: Social Christianity in Woodrow Wilson's White House," *Church History: Studies in Christianity and Culture* 82, no. 3 (2013): 659–66.

18. Sidney Lewis Gulick and Charles S. Macfarland, eds., *The Church and International Relations: Report of the Commission on Peace and Arbitration, Parts II and IV* (New York: Federal Council of the Churches of Christ in America Missionary Education Movement, 1917), 2.

19. Eugene Clyde Brooks and Woodrow Wilson, *Woodrow Wilson as President* (Chicago: Row, Peterson and Company, 1916), 167–68.

20. Richard Theodore Ely, *The World War and Leadership in a Democracy*, The Citizen's Library of Economics, Politics and Sociology, ed. Richard T. Ely (New York: Macmillan, 1918), 126–27.

21. Ibid., 162.

22. Ibid., 160–61 (original emphasis).

23. W. E. B. Du Bois, *Darkwater: Voices from Within the Veil* (New York: Harcourt, Brace and Howe, 1920), 50.

24. Ibid. See Sylvester Johnson, *African-American Religions, 1500–2000: Colonialism, Democracy, and Freedom* (New York: Cambridge University Press, 2015).

25. "From the Diary of Colonel House, September 16, 1918," PWW, 51:23.

26. "A Memorandum by William Howard Taft [c. March 29, 1918]," PWW, 47:200–01; Cooper, *Woodrow Wilson*, 429.

27. As quoted in Cooper, *Woodrow Wilson*, 451; see also "Paris, November 11, 1918," PWW, 53:34.

28. "A Statement," November 11, 1918, PWW, 53:34.

29. "An Address to a Joint Session of Congress," November 11, 1918, PWW, 53:35–43.

30. See Leonard V. Smith, "Empires at the Paris Peace Conference," in *Empires at War, 1911–1923*, eds. Robert Gerwarth and Erez Manela (New York: Oxford University Press, 2014), 257.

31. See editor's note PWW, 50:773n2.

32. As quoted in Cooper, *Breaking the Heart of the World*, 41; the full speech is also in *Congressional Record*, 65th Congress, 3rd session, December 18, 1918, 603–06.

33. Helm, *The Captains*, 68.

34. Ibid., 68, 69.

35. Ibid., 66, 67.

36. Ibid., 68.

37. See "John Sharp Williams to Woodrow Wilson, January 15, 1919," PWW, 54:90–91, 90n1.

38. Helm, *The Captains*, 68.

39. Irwin Hood Hoover, *Forty-Two Years in the White House* (Boston: Houghton Mifflin Company, 1934), 79.

40. "Wilson in Italy: A Photographic Journey," curated by John D. Powell, courtesy of the Woodrow Wilson House, a National Trust Historic Site, Washington, DC; "From the Diary of Dr. Grayson's, Sunday, January 5, 1919," PWW, 53:614; for a history of this propaganda, see Daniela Rossini, *Woodrow Wilson and the American Myth in Italy: Culture, Diplomacy, and War Propaganda, Harvard Historical Studies,* trans. Antony Shugaar (Cambridge, MA: Harvard University Press, 2008).

41. Helm, *The Captains*, 94.

42. See Gerwarth and Manela, *Empires at War*.

43. Described in Cooper, *Woodrow Wilson*, 440; Berg, *Wilson*, 463–69.

44. For more on the different conceptions of a league of nations, see Stephen Wertheim, "The League That Wasn't: American Designs for a Legalist-Sanctionist League of Nations and the Intellectual Origins of International Organization, 1914–1920," *Diplomatic History* 35, no. 5 (2011): 797–836.

45. "A Memorandum by Robert Lansing: The President's Draft of a Covenant for a League of Nations," January 11, 1919," PWW, 54:3.

46. Ibid.

47. Ibid.

48. Jan Christiaan Smuts, *War-time Speeches: A Compilation of Public Utterances in Great Britain* (New York: George H. Doran, 1917), 39.

49. "From the Most Reverend Randall Thomas Davidson to Woodrow Wilson, December 14, 1918," PWW, 53:388.

50. "To the Most Reverend Randall Thomas Davidson from Woodrow Wilson," December 17, 1918, PWW, 53:412.

51. "To the Most Reverend Randall Thomas Davidson from Woodrow Wilson," December 20, 1918, PWW, 53:451.

52. See also Preston, *Sword of the Spirit*, 280.

53. Désiré-Joseph Mercier to Woodrow Wilson, March 25, 1919, PWW, 56:258.

54. Ibid.

55. Ibid.

56. *Wilsonian Moment: Self-Determination and the International Origins of Anti-Colonial Nationalism* (New York: Oxford University Press, 2009), 7.

57. Frederick R. Dickinson, "Toward a Global Perspective of the Great War: Japan and the Foundations of a Twentieth-Century World," *American Historical Review* 119, no. 4 (October 2014): 1163.

58. See Frederick Dickinson, *War and National Reinvention: Japan in the Great War, 1914–1919*, Harvard East Asian Monographs (Cambridge, MA: Harvard East Asia Center, 2001), 236, 210.

59. Frederick R. Dickinson, *World War I and the Triumph of a New Japan, 1919–1930* (New York: Cambridge University Press, 2013), 8.

60. "Supplementary Article VI" in "A Draft of a Covenant" (January 8, 1919), PWW 53:678–686.

61. This article appears as "Supplementary Agreements VII" in Wilson's "Second 'Paris Draft' of Covenant" (January 18, 1919, PWW 54:147), but it is often cited as "Article 21" in State Department records; *Papers Related to the Foreign Relations of the United States, Paris Peace Conference, 1919* (Washington, DC: USGPO, 1942–1947), III:397.

62. Naoko Shimazu, *Japan, Race and Equality: The Racial Equality Proposal of 1919* (London: Routledge, 1998), 20.

63. For a sense of the breadth of documents under consideration, see the thirteen volumes pertaining to the Paris Peace Conference in the U.S. State Department's official record of U.S. diplomacy (*Paris Peace Conference*, vols. 1–13, in *Papers Relating to the Foreign Relations of the United States* (Washington, DC: GPO, 1945–1947). These documents do not include private publications of specific national delegates or their support staff.

64. David Hunter Miller, *My Diary at the Conference of Paris*, vol. I (New York: Appeal, 1924), I:114.

65. Ibid., I:116.

66. Ibid.

67. See David Chidester, *Savage Systems: Colonialism and Comparative Religion in Southern Africa*, Studies in Religion and Culture (Charlottesville: University of Virginia Press, 1996); Chidester, *Empire of Religion: Imperialism and Comparative Religion* (Chicago: University of Chicago Press, 2014).

68. Miller, *My Diary*, I:186.

69. Ibid., I:245,

70. Ibid., I:243.

71. "Remarks upon the Clause for Racial Equality, April 11, 1919," PWW, 57:269.

72. For a summary of these positions, see Frederick Dickinson, "Versailles in the Context of National Renovation: Wilson Arrives in Japan," in *War and National Reinvention* (Cambridge, MA: Harvard University Asia Center, 1999), 204–38.

73. Jonathan Z. Smith, "Religion, Religions, Religious," in *Critical Terms for Religious Studies*, ed. Mark C. Taylor (Chicago: University of Chicago Press, 1998), 281.

74. Jason Ananda Josephson's *The Invention of Religion in Japan* (Chicago: University of Chicago Press, 2012). See also Ian Buruma, *Inventing Japan: 1853–1964* (New York: Modern Library Chronicles, 2004); Tomoko Masuzawa, *The Invention of World Religions: Or How European Universalism Was Preserved in the Language of Pluralism* (Chicago: University of Chicago Press, 2012).

75. See Josephson, *The Invention of Religion in Japan*; Buruma, *Inventing Japan*.

76. See Shimazu, *Japan, Race, and Equality*; Dickinson, *War and National Reinvention*.

77. See Bruce Elleman, *Wilson and China: A Revised History of the Shandong Question* (New York: M. E. Sharpe, 2002).

78. "Senior Chaplain C. H. Brent to Woodrow Wilson, April 11, 1919," PWW, 57:284.

79. "Woodrow Wilson to Senior Chaplain C. H. Brent, April 15, 1919," PWW, 57:371.

80. "Remarks upon the Clause for Racial Equality, April 11, 1919," PWW, 57:269.

81. Helm, *The Captains*, 119.

82. Ibid.

83. "From the Diary of Ray Stannard Baker, Saturday the 5th [April 1919]," PWW, 57:5.

84. Ibid.

85. John Maynard Keynes, *The Economic Consequences of the Peace* (New York: Harcourt, Brace & Howe, 1920), 6.

86. "An Address to the Senate July 10, 1919," PWW, 61:427.

87. "An Address to the Senate July 10, 1919," PWW, 61:436.

88. Wilson was the first president to schedule regular press conferences. For more on his relationship to the press corps and how it changed, see Robert C. Hildebrand, ed., *The Complete Press Conferences, 1913–1919*, vol. 50, *Papers of Woodrow Wilson*, ed. Arthur S. Link (Princeton, NJ: Princeton University Press, 1985).

89. "Press Conference, July 10, 1919," PWW, 50:793.

Chapter Five

1. Henry Cabot Lodge, *"The Essential Terms of Peace" Speech to US Senate 23 August 1918* (Washington, DC: Government Printing Office, 1918), 5, Wallace McClure Pamphlet Collection, Woodrow Wilson Presidential Library (WWPL), Staunton, Virginia.

2. Sidney Lewis Gulick and Federal Council of the Churches of Christ in America Commission on Peace and Arbitration, *The Fight for Peace: An Aggressive Campaign for American Churches* (New York: F. H. Revell, 1915), 64.

3. Majority and minority leaders were not identified in 1919 because the practice began in 1920. Lodge is often retroactively credited for having the title in 1919 since he served in that role from 1920 until his death in 1924.

4. Coined by Oliver Wendell Holmes, "Boston Brahmin" refers to the upper echelon of New England families who for several generations shaped the development of elite culture, especially academic institutions like Harvard University, and politics in New England. Some families, like the Winthrops, could trace their heritage to the Puritans.

5. Woodrow Wilson, *A History of the American People*, 5 vols. (New York: Harper, 1902–1903); Wilson, *George Washington* (New York: Harper Brothers, 1903); Henry Cabot Lodge, *George Washington* (Boston: Houghton Mifflin, 1889); Wilson, *A Short History of the English Colonies in America* (New York: Harper Bros., 1881); Wilson, *The Story of the Revolution* (New York: Charles Scribner's Sons, 1898); Wilson, *The Democracy of the Constitution and Other Addresses and Essays* (New York: Charles Scribner's Sons, 1915).

6. Henry Cabot Lodge, *Alexander Hamilton* (Boston: Houghton Mifflin, 1898); Lodge, *Daniel Webster* (Boston: Houghton Mifflin, 1883); for more on Lodge's attention to American history as well as his approach as a historian, see William C. Widenor, "The Attractions and Uses of History," in *Henry Cabot Lodge and the Search for an American Foreign Policy* (Berkeley: University of California Press, 1980), 1–43.

7. See Henry Cabot Lodge and Abbott Lawrence Lowell, *A Joint Debate on the Covenant of the League of Nations: Lodge Vs. Lowell Symphony Hall, Boston March 19, 1919* (Boston: Boston Evening Transcript, 1919).

8. See Ralph A. Stone, *The Irreconcilables: The Fight Against the League of Nations* (Lexington: University Press of Kentucky, 1970); Christopher McKnight Nichols, "Irreconcilables," in *Promise and Peril: America at the Dawn of a Global Age* (Cambridge, MA: Harvard University Press, 2011).

9. For more on these debates, see Markku Ruotsila, *The Origins of Christian Anti-Internationalism: Conservative Evangelicals and the League of Nations* (Washington, DC: Georgetown University Press, 2008).

10. William Edgar Borah, *Closing Speech of Hon. William E. Borah on the League of Nations* (Washington, DC: GPO, 1919), 10.

11. Ibid.

12. Ibid., 11.

13. Ibid.

14. Ibid., 16.

15. Albert B. Fall, 58; Cong. Rec. 3499 (1919), Friday, August 1, 1919, 3499.

16. Asle J. Gronna, 58 Cong. Rec. 7427 (1919), Friday, October 24, 1919, 7427.

17. Ibid.

18. Ibid.

19. Ruotsila, *Origins of Christian Anti-Internationalism*, 130.

20. Henry Cabot Lodge and Abbott Lawrence Lowell, *A Joint Debate on the Covenant of the League of Nations: Lodge Vs. Lowell Symphony Hall, Boston March 19, 1919* (Boston: Boston Evening Transcript, 1919), 13.

21. Philander Knox, *The Altar of Our Nationality: Address of Hon. Philander C. Knox Delivered at Independence Square, Philadelphia, July 4, 1921* (Washington, DC: Government Printing Office, 1921), 5, Internet Archive, http://www.archive.org/details/altarofournation00knox.

22. Ibid.

23. George Norris, 58 Cong. Rec. 2595 (1919), Tuesday, July 15, 1919, 2595.

24. George Norris, 58 Cong. Rec. 6818 (1919), Monday, October 13, 1919, 6818.

25. George Norris, 58 Cong. Rec. 6826 (1919), Monday, October 13, 1919, 6826.

26. George M. Marsden, *Fundamentalism and American Culture* (New York: Oxford University Press, 2006), 141–42.

27. Marsden, *Fundamentalism and American Culture*, 159. Matthew Avery Sutton, *American Apocalypse: A History of Modern Evangelicalism* (Cambridge, MA: Belknap Press, 2014), x–xiv.

28. As quoted in Marsden, *Fundamentalism and American Culture*, 155.

29. See Marsden, *Fundamentalism in American Culture*, chapter 16.

30. For analysis of the connection between white Protestants and nativism, see John Higham, *Strangers in the Land: Patterns of American Nativism, 1860–1925* (New Brunswick, NJ: Rutgers University Press, 2002); for the Ku Klux Klan specifically, see Kelly J. Baker, *Gospel According to the Klan: The KKK's Appeal to Protestant America, 1915–1930* (Lawrence: University Press of

Kansas, 2011); Manfred Berg, *Popular Justice: A History of Lynching in America* (Lanham: Ivan R. Dee, 2011); Thomas Pegram, *One Hundred Percent American: The Rebirth and Decline of the Ku Klux Klan in the 1920s* (Lanham: Ivan R. Dee, 2011).

31. Cary T. Grayson, "Crusaders: Reflections on Woodrow Wilson," Cary T. Grayson Papers, WWPL. This sentiment that Wilson's idealism was actually a form of realism can also be found in Arthur Link's *The Higher Realism of Woodrow Wilson, and Other Essays* (Nashville, TN: Vanderbilt University Press, 1971).

32. "From the Diary of Edith Benham," January 14, 1919, *Papers of Woodrow Wilson*, vol. 54, *January 7–February 7, 1919*, ed. Arthur Link (Princeton, NJ: Princeton University Press, 1986), 54:63; Edith Benham Helm, *The Captains and the Kings* (New York: Putnam, 1954), 89–90.

33. "From the Diary of Edith Benham," January 14, 1919, PWW, 54:63; Helm, *The Captains*, 89–90.

34. Ibid.

35. Gulick, *The Fight for Peace*, 173.

36. "Negroes, Race Equality, and Protection of, Etc.," in *Treaty of Peace with Germany: Hearings Before the Committee on Foreign Relations United States Senate Sixty-Sixth Congress, First Session on the Treaty of Peace with Germany, Signed at Versailles on June 28, 1919 and Submitted to the Senate on July 10, 1919, By the President of the United States* (July 31–Sept. 12, 1919), United States Congress Senate Foreign Relations Committee (Washington, DC: Government Printing Office, 1919), 687.

37. For the widespread appeal of "righteousness" as a wartime impulse, see Richard M. Gamble, *The War for Righteousness: Progressive Christianity, the Great War, and the Rise of the Messianic Nation* (Wilmington, DE: ISI Books, 2003) and Philip Jenkins, *The Great and Holy War: How World War I Became a Religious Crusade* (San Francisco: HarperOne, 2014).

38. "Negroes, Race Equality, and Protection of, Etc.," *Treaty of Peace with Germany*, 687.

39. Ibid.

40. Ibid., 688.

41. Ibid., 691.

42. Ibid., 681.

43. Ibid.

44. "Statement of Mr. Allen W. Whaley," *Treaty of Peace with Germany*, 682.

45. Ibid., 683.

46. The other speakers were Joseph H. Stewart, J. H. Neill, J. T. Thomas, W. H. Jernagan, Charles S. Williams, and J. A. Lankford (*Treaty of Peace with Germany*, 3).

47. Stops included the home states for William Borah (Idaho), Asle Gronna (North Dakota), Hiram Johnson (California), George Norris (Nebraska), Miles Poindexter (Washington), James A. Reed (Missouri), and Charles S. Thomas (Colorado).

48. John Milton Cooper, *Woodrow Wilson: A Biography* (New York: Alfred A. Knopf, 2009), 521.

49. Woodrow Wilson, "An Address in Sioux Falls," September 8, 1919, PWW, *September–November 5, 1919*, ed. Arthur S. Link (Princeton, NJ: Princeton University Press, 1990), 63:113.

50. Ibid.

51. Woodrow Wilson, "An Address in Pueblo, Colorado," September 25, 1919, PWW, 63:512.

52. Ibid., 63:513.

53. Cary T. Grayson, "The Religion of Woodrow Wilson" (n.p.: unpublished manuscript, 1924), Cary T. Grayson Papers, WWPL.

Chapter Six

1. Joseph Tumulty, "War or Peace: Address by Joseph P. Tumulty for the Woman's International League for Peace and Freedom [radio address]," December 18, 1934, Joseph P. Tumulty Collection, Manuscript Division, Library of Congress, Washington, DC

2. Bernard Baruch, "Text of Talk by Bernard Baruch Lauding Ideals of Woodrow Wilson," *New York Times*, November 11, 1947.

3. Edward A. Martin to Woodrow Wilson, February 28, 1921, WWP, Series 9, vol. 5, Manuscript Division, LOC.

4. Ibid.

5. "Republican Party Platform of 1920," June 8, 1920, courtesy of The American Presidency Project, University of California, Santa Barbara, http://www.presidency.ucsb.edu/ws/index .php?pid=29635.

6. Ibid.

7. "Statistics of the Congressional and Presidential Election of November 2, 1920," http:// clerk.house.gov/member_info/electionInfo/1920election.pdf; W. E. B. Du Bois, "Why I Won't Vote," *The Nation*, October 20, 1956.

8. "Democratic Party Platform of 1920," June 28, 1920, via The American Presidency Project, University of California, Santa Barbara, http://www.presidency.ucsb.edu/ws/index .php?pid=29592.

9. For more on Isolationism and its intellectual changes, see Christopher McKnight Nichols, "The Irreconcilables," in *Promise and Peril: America at the Dawn of a Global Age* (Cambridge, MA: Harvard University Press, 2011), 229–72.

10. Matthew Avery Sutton, *American Apocalypse: A History of Modern Evangelicalism* (Cambridge, MA: Belknap Press of Harvard, 2014), xi–xii; See also Joel A. Carpenter, *Revive Us Again: The Reawakening of American Fundamentalism* (New York: Oxford University Press, 1997); George Marsden, *Fundamentalism in American Culture*, 2nd edition (New York: Oxford University Press, 2006); Leo P. Ribuffo, *The Old Christian Right: The Protestant Far Right from the Great Depression to the Cold War* (Philadelphia: Temple University Press, 1988); Ernest R. Sandeen, *The Roots of Fundamentalism: British and American Millenarianism, 1800–1930*, Reprint edition (London; Chicago: University of Chicago Press, 2008).

11. Harry Emerson Fosdick, "Shall the Fundamentalists Win?" in *American Religions: A Documentary History*, ed. R. Marie Griffith (New York: Oxford University Press, 2007), 423.

12. Ribuffo, *The Old Christian Right*, 82–86; Sutton, *American Apocalypse*, 51–53.

13. Elesha J. Coffman provides a compelling history and analysis of the development of "mainline" in *The Christian Century and the Rise of the Protestant Mainline* (New York: Oxford University Press, 2013).

14. "A Radio Address [November 10, 1923]," *The Papers of Woodrow Wilson* (hereafter PWW), ed. Arthur Stanley Link, vol. 68, *April 8, 1922–February 6, 1924* (Princeton, NJ: Princeton University Press, 1993), 68:467n1.

15. "A Radio Address [November 10, 1923]," PWW, 68:466–67.

16. "A News Report: Wilson Overcome Greeting Pilgrims; Predicts Triumph [New York Times], November 11, 1923," PWW, 68:470.

17. Ibid.

18. Ibid., 68:469.

19. "James M. Cox to Woodrow Wilson, November 13, 1923," PWW, 68:473–74.

20. Ibid.

21. Ray Stannard Baker, "The True Secret of Woodrow Wilson," *New York Times,* February 10, 1924, XX1, ProQuest Historical Newspapers: The New York Times (103298489).

22. Ibid.

23. Ray Stannard Baker to Woodrow Wilson, [1923], Ray Stannard Baker Papers, LOC.

24. *A Declaration of Ideals and Policy Looking Toward a Warless World: A Program Adopted by the Federal Council of Churches of Christ in America* (New York: Federal Council of the Churches of Christ in America, 1921), n.p.

25. Ibid.

26. Ibid.

27. "Federal Council of Churches to Woodrow Wilson, [1921]," WWP, Series 9, vol. 5, Manuscript Division, LOC.

28. Wilsonians were one part of a larger effort to memorialize war efforts. See Jay Winter, "Approaching the History of the Great War: A User's Guide," in *The Legacy of the Great War: Ninety Years On* (Columbia: University of Missouri Press, 2009); Paul Faussell, *The Great War and Modern Memory* (1975; repr. New York: Oxford University Press, 2000).

29. "Mrs. Gertrude Farrell Kelly to Joseph Tumulty, November 1, 1920," WWP, Series 9, vol. 5, Manuscript Division, LOC.

30. "Woodrow Wilson Theme of Sermon: Dr. John W. Frazer, Pastor of Central Methodist Church Delivered Eulogy on the Retiring President," February 28, 1921, (newspaper clipping) in WWP, Series 9, vol. 5, Manuscript Division, LOC.

31. "A Great President" in *The Jewish World*, March 2, 1921 (clipping) in WWP, Series 9, vol. 5, LOC.

32. Ibid.

33. Rabbi Stephen Wise and Rabbi Samuel Schulman, "War, Religion, and Preparedness," *Peace Advocate* 78, no. 5 (May 1916), 137, JSTOR, http://www.jstor.org/stable/20667505.

34. See Michael Alexander, *Jazz Age Jews* (Princeton, NJ: Princeton University Press, 2001); Leonard Dinnerstein, *Antisemitism in America* (New York: Oxford University Press, 1995); Jonathan D. Sarna, *American Judaism: A History* (New Haven, CT: Yale University Press, 2005).

35. Wilson's support of the Balfour Declaration, and the American Jewish Congress's appeals to him, can be found in "From Stephen Samuel Wise, with Enclosures, March 2, 1919," PWW 55:368–86.

36. "Albert Kaufman to Woodrow Wilson, November 24, 1923," PWW, 68:485.

37. "Grand Eulogy by Rabbi Wise: Magnificent Tribute Paid Dethroned Wilson at Rotary Dinner," March 1921, (clipping) in WWP, Series 9, vol. 5, Manuscript Division, LOC.

38. Carlton J. Hayes, *A Brief History of the Great War* (New York: Macmillan, 1922), 410–11.

39. PWW 68: 393–95; *Atlantic Monthly* CXXXII, August 1923, 145–46.

40. Ibid.

41. "A Report of Two Interviews," PWW, 68:588.

42. Ibid.

43. Ibid., 68:589.

44. "Reverend Francis C. Young to Cary T. Grayson, February 19, 1924," Cary T. Grayson Papers, Condolence Letters, Woodrow Wilson Presidential Library (hereafter WWPL), Staunton, Virginia.

45. "Mr. and Mrs. Samuel Gompers to Mrs. Wilson, February 3, 1924," (telegram) WWP, Series 9, vol. 5, Manuscript Division, LOC.

46. Arthur Link's magisterial and indispensable *Papers of Woodrow Wilson,* which informs most scholarly works on Wilson's presidency, includes notable telegrams and notes, but the

extent of condolence and sympathy notes can only be found via the Library of Congress' Woodrow Wilson Papers (Series 9: Scrapbooks, vols. 6–11, Manuscript Division, LOC).

47. David Hunter Miller, "Woodrow Wilson: Memorial Address Delivered at the Madison Avenue Presbyterian Church," 2, Cary T. Grayson Papers, WWPL.

48. Ibid., 3.

49. Wilson as quoted by Miller, ""Woodrow Wilson: Memorial Address," 3.

50. Edith Bolling Galt Wilson Papers, Misc. folder, Manuscript Division, LOC.

51. James H. Taylor, "A Great Man Has Fallen," Memorial Service at Central Presbyterian Church, Washington, DC, in Honor of Woodrow Wilson, President of the United States (February 10, 1924), 7, Presbyterian Historical Society, Philadelphia.

52. Ibid., 8.

53. "Breckinridge Long to Cary Grayson, February 12, 1924," Cary T. Grayson Papers, WWPL.

54. This theme is unavoidable in WWP, Series 9: Scrapbooks, vols. 6–11.

55. Cary T. Grayson, *Woodrow Wilson: An Intimate Memoir* (New York: Holt, Rinehart and Winston, 1960), 69.

56. Ibid., 93.

57. See Kelly J. Baker, *Gospel According to the Klan: The KKK's Appeal to Protestant America, 1915–1930* (Lawrence: University Press of Kansas, 2011).

58. Shailer Mathews, *The Validity of American Ideals* (Nashville: The Abingdon Press, 1922).

59. Henry Frederick Ward, *The Religion of Democracy* (New York: Federal Council of Churches of Christ in America, 1922), http://catalog.hathitrust.org/Record/009041723/Home.

60. Richard Wightman Fox, *Reinhold Niebuhr: A Biography* (New York: Harper & Row, 1985), 47.

61. See William Hutchinson, *Modernist Impulse in American Protestantism* (Durham: Duke University Press, 1992); Kathryn Lofton, "The Methodology of the Modernists: Process in American Protestantism," *Church History: Studies in Christianity and Culture* 75, no. 2 (2006): 374–402; Matthew S. Hedstrom, *The Rise of Liberal Religion: Book Culture and American Spirituality in the Twentieth Century* (New York: Oxford University Press, 2013).

62. Kevin M. Schultz, *Tri-Faith America: How Catholics and Jews Held Postwar America to Its Protestant Promise* (New York: Oxford University Press, 2011), 30.

63. See Schultz, *Tri-Faith America*, 28–31.

64. As quoted in Schultz, *Tri-Faith America*, 32.

65. See Schultz, *Tri-Faith America*, 32.

66. "Baker Hails Wilson as Guiding Us Now: Depression Halted Tendency to Discount 'Idealism,'" *New York Times*, April 14, 1932, 1, ProQuest Historical Newspapers: New York Times (99621481).

67. Ibid.

68. Ibid.

69. Newton D. Baker, Carlton J. H. Hayes, and Roger Straus, eds. *The American Way: A Study of Human Relations Among Protestants, Catholics, and Jews* (Chicago: Willett, Clark, & Co., 1936), vii–viii.

70. Baker, *The American Way*, 10.

71. Schultz, *Tri-Faith America*, 59.

72. Schultz uses this phrase in *Tri-Faith America*, 58.

73. "Annual Message to Congress on the State of the Union, January 6, 1941" in "State of the Union Addresses and Messages," *The American Presidency Project,* University of California-Santa Barbara, http://www.presidency.ucsb.edu/ws/index.php?pid=16092.

74. "Isolation Seen Repudiated in U.S.," *New York Times,* May 12, 1942.

75. David Lawrence, "The Crusade That Failed But Lives On: This Is the Story of Woodrow Wilson's Last Efforts to Prevent the War We Now Fight," *New York Times,* November 14, 1943, SM3, ProQuest Historical Newspapers: New York Times (106725018).

76. Ibid.

77. Ibid.

78. "Address of the Honorable Huston Thompson, Former Assistant Attorney General of the United States, at the Tomb of President Wilson in the Washington Cathedral at 3:15 pm, on Armistice Day, November 11, 1943," in Josephus Daniels Papers, Box 682, Manuscript Division, LOC.

79. Arthur Sweetser, "Wilson," in *America's Reception of "Wilson," The Screen Dramatization of the Life and Times of a Great American: Woodrow Wilson* (New York: Woodrow Wilson Foundation, [1944/45]) in Josephus Daniels Papers, Memorials—Woodrow Wilson file, Manuscript Division, LOC.

80. Arthur Sweetser "Wilson," written for *Changing World,* September 1944, Josephus Daniels Papers, WWF materials, Manuscript Division, LOC.

81. Ibid.

82. "New York Post, 3 August [1944]" in *America's Reception of "Wilson," The Screen Dramatization of the Life and Times of a Great American: Woodrow Wilson* (New York: Woodrow Wilson Foundation, [1944/45]) in Josephus Daniels Papers, Memorials—Woodrow Wilson file, Manuscript Division, LOC.

83. Ibid.

84. Ibid.

85. Ibid.

86. "August 7," compiled in *America's Reception of "Wilson," The Screen Dramatization of the Life and Times of a Great American: Woodrow Wilson* (New York: Woodrow Wilson Foundation, [1944/45]) in Josephus Daniels Papers, Memorials—Woodrow Wilson file, Manuscript Division, LOC.

87. Anthony Burke Smith, *The Look of Catholics: Portrayals in Popular Culture from the Great Depression to the Cold War* (Lawrence: University of Kansas Press, 2010), 1.

88. See John McGreevy, *Parish Boundaries: The Catholic Encounter with Race in the Twentieth Century Urban North* (Chicago: University of Chicago Press, 1998).

89. For more on this process, see Lila Corwin Berman, *Speaking of Jews: Rabbis, Intellectuals, and the Creation of an American Public Identity* (Berkeley: University of California Press, 2009); Michael Alexander, *Jazz Age Jews* (Princeton, NJ: Princeton University Press, 2001); Jenna Weissman Joselit, *The Wonders of America: Reinventing Jewish Culture 1880–1950* (New York: Picador, 2002); Jonathan D. Sarna, *American Judaism: A History* (New Haven, CN: Yale University Press, 2005).

90. "Albert Hall Speech [London]," January 17, 1946, in *The Eleanor Roosevelt Papers* (hereafter ERP), vol. 1, *The Human Rights Years: 1945–1948,* ed. Allida Black (New York: Charles Scribner's Sons, 2007), 216.

91. Eleanor's version of the quote can be found in "Albert Hall Speech [London]," ERP 1:217. According to the editor, Eleanor is specifically quoting the King James Version of Luke 9:24, but a similar verse can be found in Matthew, Mark, and John (ERP 1:218n8).

92. See Matthew Avery Sutton, "Was FDR the Antichrist? The Birth of Fundamentalist Anti-liberalism in a Global Age," *Journal of American History* 98, no. 4 (March 1, 2012): 1052–74; Sutton, *American Apocalypse.*

Conclusion

1. "An Address to a Joint Session of Congress," November 11, 1918, PWW, 53:35–43.

References

Archival Sources

Woodrow Wilson Presidential Library, Staunton, Virginia [WWPL]
William D. Hoyt Jr. Papers
   Cary T. Grayson Papers
Joseph P. Tumulty Papers
   Wallace McClure Pamphlet Collection
Woodrow Wilson Papers, Manuscript Division, Library of Congress
   Woodrow Wilson Papers [WWP]
   Ray Stannard Baker Papers
   Josephus Daniels Papers
   Edith Bolling Galt Wilson Papers
   Robert Lansing Papers
Papers Related to the Foreign Relations of the United States, Paris Peace
   Conference, 1919
Presbyterian Historical Society [PHS]
ProQuest Historical Newspapers: New York Times
America's Historical Newspapers

Published Primary Sources

Abbott, Lyman. *The Rights of Man: A Study in Twentieth Century Problems.* Boston: Houghton,
   Mifflin and Company, 1902.
Addams, Jane. *Democracy and Social Ethics.* New York: Macmillan, 1905.
———. *Peace and Bread in Time of War.* New York: Macmillan, 1922.
———. *The Second Twenty Years at Hull House.* New York: Macmillan, 1930.
———. *Twenty Years at Hull House: With Autobiographical Notes.* New York: Macmillan, 1912.
Alderman, Edwin Anderson. "Woodrow Wilson: Memorial Address Delivered Before a
   Joint Session of the Two Houses of Congress December 15, 1924, in Honor of Woodrow

Wilson Late President of the United States." Washington: Government Printing Office, 1924.

American Rights League. *No False Peace: A Warning by American Religious Leaders.* New York: American Rights League, 1917. Library of Congress Internet Archive. http://www.archive.org/details/nofalsepeace00amer.

Babcock, Maltbie. *The Success of Defeat.* New York: Charles Scribner's Sons, 1905.

Baker, Newton D., Carlton J. H. Hayes, and Roger Straus, eds. *The American Way: A Study of Human Relations Among Protestants, Catholics, and Jews.* Chicago: Willett, Clark, & Co., 1936.

Barton, Bruce. *The Man Nobody Knows.* Indianapolis: Bruce-Merrill, 1925.

Baruch, Bernard. "Text of Talk by Bernard Baruch Lauding Ideals of Woodrow Wilson." *New York Times,* November 11, 1947.

Batten, Samuel. *The Christian State: The State, Democracy and Christianity.* Philadelphia, PA: Griffith & Rowland Press, 1909.

———. *If America Fail: Our National Mission and Our Possible Future.* Philadelphia, PA: The Judson Press, 1922.

———. *The Moral Meaning of the War: A Prophetic Interpretation.* Philadelphia, PA: American Baptist Publication Society, 1918.

———. *The Social Task of Christianity: A Summons to the New Crusade.* New York: Fleming H. Revell Company, 1911.

Batten, Samuel Z. et al. *A Social Service Catechism.* New York: Federal Council of Churches of Christ in America, 1912.

Bellamy, Edward. *Looking Backward.* London: William Reeves, 1887.

Borah, William Edgar. *Closing Speech of Hon. William E. Borah on the League of Nations.* Washington, DC: GPO, 1919.

Brooks, Eugene Clyde, and Woodrow Wilson. *Woodrow Wilson as President.* Chicago: Row, Peterson and Company, 1916.

Bryan, William Jennings. *A Tale of Two Conventions: Being an Account of the Republican and Democratic National Conventions of June, 1912, with an Outline of the Progressive National Convention of August in the Same Year.* New York: Funk & Wagnalls, 1912.

Calvin, John. *Institutes of the Christian Religion.* Vol. 1. Translated by John Allen. 6th American ed. Philadelphia: Presbyterian Board of Education, [184?]). HathiTrust Digital Library, http://hdl.handle.net/2027/mdp.39015022384443.

Carnegie, Andrew. *A League of Peace: A Rectorial Address Delivered to the Students in the University of St. Andrews, 17th October 1905.* Boston: Ginn & Company, 1906.

Church Peace Union. *The Church and International Peace.* The Church Peace Union IV: Europe's War, America's Warning. New York: The Church Peace Union, [1914].

Creel, George. *How We Advertised America: The First Telling of the Amazing Story of the Committee on Public Information that Carried the Gospel of Americanism to Every Corner of the Globe.* New York: Harper Brothers, 1920.

Davison, Randall Thomas. *Christ: And the World at War; Sermons Preached in War-time.* Edited by Basil Mathews. London: James Clarke & Company, 1917.

Du Bois, W. E. B. *Darkwater: Voices from Within the Veil.* New York: Harcourt, Brace and Howe, 1920.

———. *The Souls of Black Folk.* 5th ed. Chicago: A. C. McClurg, 1904.

———. "Why I Won't Vote." *The Nation* (October 20, 1956).

Ely, Richard Theodore. *Social Aspects of Christianity: And Other Essays.* New York: T. Y. Crowell & Company, 1880.

———. *The Social Law of Service*. New York: Eaton & Mains, 1896.

———. *The Universities and the Churches: An Address Delivered at the 31st University Convocation, Senate Chamber, Albany, N.Y., July 5, 1893*. Albany: University of the State of New York, 1893.

———. *The World War and Leadership in a Democracy*. Edited by Richard T. Ely. The Citizen's Library of Economics, Politics and Sociology. New York: Macmillan, 1918.

Federal Council of the Churches of Christ in America. *A Plan of Social Work for the Federal Council of the Churches of Christ in America*. New York: The Council, 1912.

———. "The Proclamation of the President of the United States of America to the American People and the Message of the Federal Council to the Churches and Christians of America." New York: Federal Council of Churches of Christ in America, 1916.

Federal Council of the Churches of Christ in America. Commission on the Church and Social Service. *A Social Service Catechism*. New York: Federal Council of Churches of Christ in America, n.d.

———. Commission on the Church and Social Service. *Christian Duties in Conserving Spiritual, Moral and Social Forces of the Nation in Time of War*. New York: Federal Council of Churches of Christ in America, 1917.

———. Commission on International Justice and Goodwill. *The Proposal to Renounce War: A Four Week's Study Course of the Multilateral Anti-War Pact of Paris*. New York: Federal Council of Churches of Christ in America, 1928.

———. Commission on Peace and Arbitration. *The Church and International Relations: Report of the Commission on Peace and Arbitration, Parts I-IV*. New York: Federal Council of the Churches of Christ in America, 1917.

———. General War-Time Commission of the Churches. *War-time Agencies of the Churches: Directory and Handbook*. New York: Federal Council of the Churches of Christ in America, 1919.

Fosdick, Harry Emerson. *Christianity and Progress*. New York: Fleming H. Revell Company, 1922.

———. *The Challenge of the Present Crisis*. New York: Association Press, 1917.

———. *The Meaning of Faith*. New York: Association Press, 1922.

———. *The Meaning of Service*. New York: Association Press, 1920.

Gardner, Augustus Peabody. "Our Inadequate National Defenses: Speech of Hon. Augustus P. Gardner of Massachusetts." Washington: Government Printing Office, December 10, 1914.

George, David Lloyd. *British War Aims: Statement by the Right Honourable David Lloyd George, January Fifth, Nineteen Hundred and Eighteen*. New York: George Doran Company, 1918.

Gladden, Washington. *A Plea for Pacifism*. Columbus, OH: Champlin Press, 1915.

———. *Applied Christianity*. New York: Houghton, Mifflin, and Company, 1886.

———. *The Forks of the Road*. New York: Macmillan, 1916.

Gladden, Washington, and American Board of Commissioners for Foreign Missions. *The Nation and the Kingdom: Annual Sermon Before the American Board of Commissioners for Foreign Missions*. Boston: The Board, 1909.

Gore, Charles. *The League of Nations: The Opportunity of the Church*. New York: G. H. Doran, 1918.

Grayson, Cary Travers. "The Religion of Woodrow Wilson" [n.p.: unpublished manuscript, 1924]. Cary T. Grayson Papers. Woodrow Wilson Presidential Library and Museum.

———. *Woodrow Wilson: An Intimate Memoir*. New York: Holt, Rinehart, and Winston, 1960.

Gulick, Sidney Lewis, and Federal Council of the Churches of Christ in America. Commission on International Justice and Goodwill. *The Christian Crusade for a Warless World*. New York: Macmillan, 1922.

Gulick, Sidney Lewis, and Federal Council of the Churches of Christ in America Commission on Peace and Arbitration. *The Fight for Peace: An Aggressive Campaign for American Churches.* New York: F. H. Revell, 1915.

Gulick, Sidney Lewis, and Charles S. Macfarland, eds. *The Church and International Relations: Report of the Commission on Peace and Arbitration, Parts II and IV.* New York: Federal Council of the Churches of Christ in America, Missionary Education Movement, 1917.

Hayes, Carlton J. *A Brief History of the Great War.* New York: Macmillan, 1922.

Helm, Edith Benham. *The Captains and the Kings.* New York: Putnam, 1954.

Herron, George Davis. *The Defeat in the Victory.* London: C. Palmer, 1921.

———. *Woodrow Wilson and the World's Peace.* New York: Mitchell Kennerley, 1917.

Hoover, Irwin Hood. *Forty-Two Years in the White House.* Boston: Houghton Mifflin Company, 1934.

Keppler, Udo J. "The Good Samaritan," *Harper's Weekly* 72, no. 1858 (October 9, 1912), centerfold. Library of Congress Prints and Photographs Division. Washington, DC. LC-DIG-ppmsca-27883.

Keynes, John Maynard. *The Economic Consequences of the Peace.* New York: Harcourt, Brace & Howe, 1920.

Knox, Philander. *The Altar of Our Nationality: Address of Hon. Philander C. Knox Delivered at Independence Square, Philadelphia, July 4, 1921.* Washington, DC: Government Printing Office, 1921.

Lansing, Robert. "A Definition of Sovereignty." *Proceedings of the American Political Science Association* 10 (1913): 61–75.

Lawrence, David. *The True Story of Woodrow Wilson.* New York: George H. Doran Company, 1924.

Lodge, Henry Cabot. *Alexander Hamilton.* Boston: Houghton Mifflin, 1898.

———. *Daniel Webster.* Boston: Houghton Mifflin, 1883.

———. *The Democracy of Abraham Lincoln: Address by Henry Cabot Lodge Before the Students of Boston University School of Law on March 14, 1913.* Washington, DC: Government Printing Office, 1913.

———. *"The Essential Terms of Peace" Speech to US Senate 23 August 1918.* Washington, DC: Government Printing Office, 1918.

Lodge, Henry Cabot, and Abbott Lawrence Lowell. *A Joint Debate on the Covenant of the League of Nations: Lodge Vs. Lowell Symphony Hall, Boston March 19, 1919.* Boston: Boston Evening Transcript, 1919.

Low, A. Maurice. *Woodrow Wilson: An Interpretation.* Boston: Little, Brown, and Company, 1918.

Lowell, Abbott Lawrence. *A League to Enforce Peace.* World Peace Foundation Series, vol. 5, no. 1, part I. Boston: World Peace Foundation, 1915.

Macfarland, Charles S. *Christian Service and the Modern World.* New York: Fleming H. Revell Company, 1915.

———. *Spiritual Culture and Social Service.* New York: Fleming H. Revell Company, 1912.

———. *Woodrow Wilson: Prophet of a New Era of Humanity, An Address by Rev. Charles S. Macfarland, D. D. at Staunton, Va., the Birthplace of Woodrow Wilson.* [Staunton, VA?: 1924].

Machen, J. Gresham. *Christianity and Liberalism.* New York: Macmillan, 1923.

Mathews, Shailer. *Patriotism and Religion.* New York: Macmillan, 1918.

———. "The Church's Stake in the League to Enforce Peace." New York: League to Enforce Peace, 1916.

———. *The Gospel and the Modern Man.* New York: Macmillan, 1910.

————. *The Individual and the Social Gospel.* New York: Missionary Education Movement of the United States and Canada, 1914.

————. *The Validity of American Ideals.* Nashville: The Abingdon Press, 1922.

McAdoo, Eleanor Wilson, and Margaret Y. Gaffey. *The Woodrow Wilsons.* New York: Macmillan, 1937. HathiTrust Digital Library. http://hdl.handle.net/2027/uc1.b62115.

McConnell, Francis J. *Democratic Christianity: Some Problems of the Church in the Days Just Ahead.* New York: Macmillan, 1919.

McCulloch, James Edward, ed. *The Call of the New South: Addresses Delivered at the Southern Sociological Congress, Nashville, Tennessee, May 7 to 10, 1912.* Nashville: Southern Sociological Congress, 1912.

Miller, David Hunter. *My Diary at the Conference of Paris,* 21 vols. New York: Appeal, 1924.

Morgenthau, Henry. *Ambassador Morgenthau's Story.* New York: Doubleday, Page & Company, 1918.

National Civil Liberties Union. *The Case of the Christian Pacifists at Los Angeles, Cal.* New York City: National Civil Liberties Bureau, 1918.

Papers Related to the Foreign Relations of the United States, Paris Peace Conference, 1919, vols. 1–13 (Washington, DC: USGPO, 1942–1947).

Rauschenbusch, Walter. *A Gospel for the Social Awakening; Selections from the Writings of Walter Rauschenbusch.* New York: Association Press, 1950.

————. *A Theology for the Social Gospel.* 1917. Reprint, New York: Abingdon Press, 1945.

————. *Christianity and the Social Crisis.* New York: Macmillan, 1913.

————. *Christianizing the Social Order.* New York: Macmillan, 1913.

————. *Dare We Be Christians.* New York: Pilgrim Press, 1914.

————. *The Social Principles of Jesus.* College Voluntary Study Courses 7. New York: Association Press, 1925.

Roosevelt, Theodore. *Americanism and Preparedness: Speeches of Theodore Roosevelt July to November 1916.* New York, Mail and Express Job Print, 1917.

————. *America and the World War.* New York: C. Scribner's Sons, 1915.

————. *Americanism in Religion.* Chicago: Blakely-Onswald, 1908.

————. *The Foes of Our Own Household.* New York: George H. Doran Company, 1917.

Roosevelt, Theodore, and Progressive Party National Convention. *Theodore Roosevelt's Confession of Faith Before the Progressive National Convention, August 6, 1912.* New York: Allied Printing, 1912.

Root, Elihu. *League of Nations: Letter from Hon. Elihu Root to Senator Henry Cabot Lodge Relative to the League of Nations.* Washington, DC: Government Printing Office, 1919.

————. *Words Without Deeds, Moral Treason: Extracts from an Address Delivered by Elihu Root in Carnegie Hall, New York City, February 15, 1916.* Cambridge, MA: Harvard University Press, 1916.

Riley, William Bell. *A Divided House: A Statement put forth by the World's Christian Fundamentals Association in its Seventh Annual Convention at Memphis, Tennessee, May 3–10, 1923.* [Memphis?: Rawlings Print Company, 1923]. http://server16120.contentdm.oclc.org/u?/riley,4316.

Scott, James Brown. *Foreign Policy of President Wilson: Messages, Addresses and Papers,* 1918.

Sheldon, Charles. *In His Steps: What Would Jesus Do.* Chicago: Advance, 1896.

Smith, Gerald Birney. "Making Christianity Safe for Democracy: I. The Moral Meaning of Democracy." *The Biblical World* 53, no. 1 (January 1919): 3–13.

————. "Making Christianity Safe for Democracy: II. Democracy and Religious Experience." *The Biblical World* 53, no. 2 (March 1919): 133–145.

———. "Making Christianity Safe for Democracy: III. Democracy and Church Organization." *The Biblical World* 53, no. 3 (May 1919): 245–58.

Smuts, Jan Christaan. *War-time Speeches: A Compilation of Public Utterances in Great Britain.* New York: George H. Doran, 1917.

Stelzle, Charles. *American Social and Religious Conditions.* New York: Fleming H. Revell Company, 1912.

Stelzle, Charles, Jane Addams, Charles Patrick Neill, Graham Taylor, and George Peck Eckman. *The Social Application of Religion.* Cincinnati: Jennings and Graham, 1908.

Taft, William Howard. *Collected Works of William Howard Taft, vol. 7, Taft Papers on League of Nations.* Edited by Frank X. Gerrity. Athens: Ohio University Press, 2004.

———. *Service with Fighting Men: An Account of the Work of the American Young Men's Christian Associations in the World War.* New York: Association Press, 1922.

———. *Taft Papers on League of Nations.* New York: Macmillan, 1920.

Taft, William Howard, Abbott Lawrence Lowell, and Henry Waters Taft. *The Covenanter: An American Exposition of the Covenant of the League of Nations.* New York: Doubleday, Page & Company, 1919.

Taft, William Howard, and William Jennings Bryan. *World Peace: A Written Debate Between William Howard Taft and William Jennings Bryan.* New York: George H. Doran Company, 1917.

Taylor, Graham. *Religion in Social Action.* New York: Dodd, Mead, 1913.

Taylor, James, ed. *Woodrow Wilson in Church: His Membership in the Congregation of The Central Presbyterian Church, Washington, D.C., 1913–1924.* Charleston, SC: Walker, Evans, and Cogswell Company, 1952.

Taylor, Stephen Earl, and Halford Edward Luccock. *The Christian Crusade for World Democracy.* New York: The Methodist Book Concern, 1918.

Tippy, Worth. "The Church and Social Service: Social Work of the Federal Council of Churches." *The Journal of Social Forces* 1, no. 1 (November 1922): 36–38.

Treaty of Peace with Germany: Hearings Before the Committee on Foreign Relations United States Senate Sixty-Sixth Congress, First Session on the Treaty of Peace with Germany, Signed at Versailles on June 28, 1919 and Submitted to the Senate on July 10, 1919, by the President of the United States (July 31–Sept. 12, 1919). United States Congress Senate Foreign Relations Committee. Washington, DC: Government Printing Office, 1919.

Tumulty, Joseph P. *Woodrow Wilson as I Know Him.* New York: Doubleday, Page & Company, 1921.

Ward, Harry Frederick. *The New Social Order: Principles and Programs.* New York: Macmillan, 1920.

———. *The Social Creed of the Churches.* New York: The Abingdon Press, 1914.

Ward, Harry Frederick, and Methodist Episcopal Church Board of Sunday Schools Committee on Curriculum. *Poverty and Wealth, from the Viewpoint of the Kingdom of God.* New York: Methodist Book Concern, 1915.

Ward, Henry Frederick. *The Religion of Democracy.* New York: Federal Council of Churches of Christ in America, 1922. HathiTrust Digital Library. http://catalog.hathitrust.org/Record/009041723/Home.

Wilson, Joseph. *Mutual Relation of Masters and Slaves as Taught in the Bible: A Discourse Preached in the First Presbyterian Church, Augusta, Georgia, January 6, 1861* (Augusta, GA: Steam Press of Chronicle & Sentinel, 1861).

Wilson, Woodrow. *A History of the American People.* 5 vols. New York: Harper & Brothers, 1902.

———. *A Short History of the English Colonies in America.* New York: Harper Bros., 1881.

———. *Address on the Translation of the Bible into English on the Occasion of the Tercentenary Celebration of the Translation of the Bible into the English Language, May 7, 1911.* Washington: Government Printing Office, 1912.

———. *An Old Master and Other Political Essays.* New York: Scribner's and Sons, 1893.

———. *Congressional Government.* Boston: Houghton & Mifflin, 1885.

———. *Democracy Today: An American Interpretation.* New York: Scott Foresman, 1917.

———. "Obligation to Serve." *The Christian Century* 34, no. 25 (June 21, 1917): 13.

———. *On Being Human.* New York: Harper & Brothers, 1916.

———. *Princeton in the Nation's Service.* Princeton, NJ: The Alumni Princetonian, 1896.

———. "Robert E. Lee: An Interpretation." *Journal of Social Forces* 2, no. 3 (March 1924): 321–28.

———. *The Democracy of the Constitution and Other Addresses and Essays.* New York: Charles Scribner's Sons, 1915.

———. *The Minister and the Community.* New York: Association Press, 1912.

———. *The New Freedom: A Call for the Emancipation of the Generous Energies of a People.* New York: Doubleday Page & Company, 1913.

———. *The Papers of Woodrow Wilson.* Edited by Arthur Stanley Link. 69 vols. Princeton, NJ: Princeton University Press, 1966–1993.

———. *The Present Task of the Ministry.* New York: Association Press, 1918.

———. *The President of the United States.* New York: Harper & Brothers, 1916.

———. *The Public Papers of Woodrow Wilson.* Edited by Ray Stannard Baker and William Dodd. 6 vols. New York: Harper & Brothers, 1925–1927.

———. *The Road Away from Revolution.* Boston: Atlantic Monthly Press, 1923.

———. *The State: Elements of Historical and Practical Politics.* Boston: D. C. Heath & Company, 1889.

———. *The Story of the Revolution.* New York: Charles Scribner's Sons, 1898.

———. *The Study of Administration.* New York: Academy of Political Science, 1887.

———. *The Young People and the Church.* Philadelphia: Sunday School Times, 1905.

———. *True Americanism.* [New York City], 1911. HathiTrust Digital Library. http://hdl.handle.net/2027/mdp.39015022403854.

———. *When a Man Comes to Himself.* New York: Harper & Brothers, 1915.

Wilson, Woodrow, and Ronald J. Pestritto. *Woodrow Wilson: The Essential Political Writings.* Lanham, MD: Lexington Books, 2005.

Wise, Stephen S. *Abraham Lincoln, Lincoln and Wilson, Woodrow Wilson.* New York: Free Synagogue House, 1921.

Wise, Rabbi Stephen S., and Rabbi Samuel Schulman. "War, Religion, and Preparedness." *The Advocate of Peace* 78, no. 5 (May 1916): 136–38.

Woodrow, James. *Evolution: An Address Delivered May 7th, 1884, Before the Alumni Association of the Columbia Theological Seminary.* Columbia, SC: Presbyterian Publishing House, 1884.

Woods, Robert A. et al. *The Poor in Great Cities: Their Problems and What Is Being Done to Solve Them.* Poverty New York: Charles Scribner's Sons, 1895.

Secondary Sources

Abrams, Elliott, ed. "Religion in the History of U.S. Foreign Policy." *The Influence of Faith: Religious Groups and U.S. Foreign Policy.* Lanham, MD: Rowman & Littlefield Publishers, 2001.

Abrams, Ray Hamilton. *Preachers Present Arms.* New York: Round Table Press, 1933.

———. *Preachers Present Arms.* Rev. ed. Scottdale, PA: Herald Press, 1969.

Ahlstrom, Sydney E. *A Religious History of the American People.* 2nd ed. New Haven, CT: Yale University Press, 2004.

Albanese, Catherine. *America: Religion and Religions,* 3rd ed. Belmont, CA: Wadsworth, 1999.

———. *A Republic of Mind and Spirit: A Cultural History of American Metaphysical Religion.* New Haven, CT: Yale University Press, 2008.

Alexander, Michael. *Jazz Age Jews.* Princeton, NJ: Princeton University Press, 2001.

Ambrosius, Lloyd E. *Wilsonian Statecraft: Theory and Practice of Liberal Internationalism During World War I.* Lanham, MD: Rowman & Littlefield, 1991.

———. *Wilsonianism: Woodrow Wilson and His Legacy in American Foreign Relations.* New York: Palgrave Macmillan, 2002.

———. *Woodrow Wilson and the American Diplomatic Tradition: The Treaty Fight in Perspective.* New York: Cambridge University Press, 1990.

Appelbaum, Patricia Faith. *Kingdom to Commune: Protestant Pacifist Culture Between World War I and the Vietnam Era.* Chapel Hill: University of North Carolina Press, 2009.

Asad, Talal. *Formations of the Secular: Christianity, Islam, Modernity.* Stanford: Stanford University Press, 2003.

Babik, Milan. "George D. Herron and the Eschatological Foundations of Woodrow Wilson's Foreign Policy, 1917–1919." *Diplomatic History* 35, no. 5 (November 2011): 837–57.

———. *Salvation and Statecraft: Wilsonian Liberal Internationalism as Secularized Eschatology.* Waco, TX: Baylor University Press, 2013.

Baker, Kelly J. *Gospel According to the Klan: The KKK's Appeal to Protestant America, 1915–1930.* Lawrence: University Press of Kansas, 2011.

Baker, Ray Stannard. *Woodrow Wilson: Life and Letters.* 8 vols. Garden City, NY: Doubleday, Page & Company, 1927–1939.

Beasley, Kathryn Lynnell. "'I Think We Have an Angel in the White House': First Lady Ellen Axson Wilson and Her Social Activism Concerning the Washington, D.C., Slums, 1913–1914." Master's thesis, Valdosta State University, 2012.

Bebbington, David. *Evangelicalism in Modern Britain: A History from the 1730s to the 1980s.* New York: Routledge, 1989.

Benbow, Mark. *Leading Them to the Promised Land: Woodrow Wilson, Covenant Theology, and the Mexican Revolution, 1913–1915.* Kent, OH: Kent State University Press, 2010.

Bender, Daniel E. "Perils of Degeneration: Reform, the Savage Immigrant, and the Survival of the Unfit." *Journal of Social History* (2008): 5–29.

Berg, A. Scott. *Wilson.* New York: Putnam, 2013.

Berg, Manfred. *Popular Justice: A History of Lynching in America.* Lanham: Ivan R. Dee, 2011.

Berman, Lila Corwin. *Speaking of Jews: Rabbis, Intellectuals, and the Creation of an American Public Identity.* Berkeley: University of California Press, 2009.

Bingaman, Lise Sanders, and Rebecca Zorach, eds. *Embodied Utopias: Gender, Social Change, and the Modern Metropolis.* New York: Routledge, 2003.

Bivins, Jason C. *The Fracture of Good Order: Christian Antiliberalism and the Challenge to American Politics.* Chapel Hill: University of North Carolina Press Books, 2003.

Blum, Edward J. *Reforging the White Republic: Race, Religion, and American Nationalism, 1865–1898.* Baton Rouge: Louisiana State University Press, 2007.

———. *W. E. B. Du Bois: American Prophet.* Philadelphia: University of Pennsylvania Press, 2009.

Blum, Edward J., and Paul Harvey. *The Color of Christ: The Son of God & the Saga of Race in America.* Chapel Hill: University of North Carolina Press, 2012.

Blumenthal, Henry. "Woodrow Wilson and the Race Question." *The Journal of Negro History* 48, no. 1 (January 1963): 1–21.

Bowman, Matthew. "Sin, Spirituality, and Primitivism: The Theologies of the American Social Gospel, 1885–1917." *Religion and American Culture* 17, no. 1 (2007): 95–126.

———. *The Urban Pulpit: New York City and the Fate of Liberal Evangelicalism*. New York: Oxford University Press, 2014.

Brekus, Catherine, and W. Clark Gilpin, eds. *American Christianities*. Chapel Hill: University of North Carolina Press, 2011.

Brittain, Michelle. *The Politics of Whiteness: Race, Workers, and Culture in the Modern South*. Athens: University of Georgia Press, 2004.

Brown, Candy Gunther. *The Word in the World Evangelical Writing, Publishing, and Reading in America, 1789–1880*. Chapel Hill: University of North Carolina Press, 2004.

Bullitt, William, and Sigmund Freud. *Thomas Woodrow Wilson: Twenty-Eighth President: A Psychological Study*. Boston: Houghton Mifflin, 1966.

Burnidge, Cara. "Protestant Liberalism." In *Encyclopedia of Religion in America*, edited by Charles Lippy and Peter Williams, 3:1782–90. Washington, DC: CQ Press, 2010.

———. "The Business of Church and State: Social Christianity in Woodrow Wilson's White House." *Church History: Studies in Christianity and Culture* 82, no. 3 (2013): 659–66.

Buruma, Ian. *Inventing Japan: 1853–1964*. New York: Modern Library Chronicles, 2004.

Butler, Jon. *Awash in a Sea of Faith: Christianizing the American People*. Harvard University Press, 1990. *Becoming America: The Revolution Before 1776* Cambridge, MA: Harvard University Press, 2001.

Butler, Leslie. *Critical Americans: Victorian Intellectuals and Transatlantic Liberal Reform*. Durham, NC: University of North Carolina Press, 2007.

Carpenter, Joel. *Revive Us Again: The Reawakening of American Fundamentalism*. New York: Oxford University Press, 1997.

Carson, Mina. *Settlement Folk: Social Thought and the American Settlement Movement, 1885–1930*. Chicago: University of Chicago Press, 1990.

Carter, Heath. *Union Made: Working People and the Rise of Social Christianity in Chicago*. New York: Oxford University Press, 2015.

Cashman, Sean Dennis. *America in the Age of the Titans: The Progressive Era and World War I*. New York: New York University Press, 1988.

Chaplin, Jonathan. *God and Global Order: The Power of Religion in American Foreign Policy*. Waco, TX: Baylor University Press, 2010.

Chidester, David. *Savage Systems: Colonialism and Comparative Religion in Southern Africa*. Studies in Religion and Culture. Charlottesville: University of Virginia Press, 1996.

———. *Empire of Religion: Imperialism and Comparative Religion*. Chicago: University of Chicago Press, 2014.

———. "Colonialism." In *Guide to the Study of Religion*, edited by Willi Braun and Russell T. McCutcheon, 423–37. New York: Cassell, 2000.

Coffman, Edward M. *The War to End All Wars: The American Military Experience in World War I*. Lexington: University Press of Kentucky, 1998.

Coffoman, Elesha J. *The Christian Century and the Rise of the Protestant Mainline*. New York: Oxford University Press, 2013.

Cohen, Nancy. *The Reconstruction of American Liberalism, 1865–1914*. Chapel Hill: University of North Carolina Press, 2002.

Conroy-Krutz, Emily. *Christian Imperialism: Converting the World in the Early Republic*. The United States in the World. New York: Cornell University Press, 2015.

Cooper, John Milton. *Woodrow Wilson: A Biography*. New York: Alfred A. Knopf, 2009.

———. *Breaking the Heart of the World: Woodrow Wilson and the Fight for the League of Nations*. New York: Cambridge University Press, 2001.

Cooper, John Milton, and Woodrow Wilson International Center for Scholars. *Reconsidering Woodrow Wilson: Progressivism, Internationalism, War, and Peace*. Washington, DC: Woodrow Wilson Center Press, 2008.

Curtis, Heather. *Faith in the Great Physician: Suffering and Divine Healing in American Culture, 1860–1900*. Baltimore: Johns Hopkins University, 2007.

Curtis, Susan. *A Consuming Faith: The Social Gospel and Modern American Culture*. Columbia: University of Missouri Press, 2001.

D'Agostino, Peter R. *Rome in America: Transnational Catholic Ideology from the Risorgimento to Fascism*. Chapel Hill: The University of North Carolina Press, 2004.

Davis, Allen. *Spearheads for Reform: The Social Settlements and the Progressive Movement, 1890–1914*. New York: Oxford University Press, 1967.

Dennis, Michael. "The Southern Evangelicalism of Woodrow Wilson." *Fides Et Historia* 33, no. 1 (2001): 57–72.

Detweiler, Robert. *Uncivil Rites: American Fiction, Religion, and the Public Sphere*. Chicago: University of Chicago Press, 1996.

Dickinson, Frederick. "Toward a Global Perspective of the Great War: Japan and the Foundations of a Twentieth-Century World." *American Historical Review* 119, no. 4 (October 2014): 1154–83.

———. *War and National Reinvention: Japan in the Great War, 1914–1919*. Cambridge, MA: Harvard University Asia Center, 1999.

———. *World War I and the Triumph of a New Japan, 1919–1930*. New York: Cambridge University Press, 2013.

DiNunzio, Mario. *Woodrow Wilson: Essential Writings and Speeches of the Scholar-President*. New York: New York University Press, 2006.

Dinnerstein, Leonard. *Antisemitism in America*. New York: Oxford University Press, 1995.

Dochuk, Darren. *From Bible Belt to Sunbelt: Plain-folk Religion, Grassroots Politics, and the Rise of Evangelical Conservatism*. New York: W. W. Norton, 2012.

Dolan, Jay. *In Search of American Catholicism: A History of Religion and Culture in Tension*. New York: Oxford University Press, 2002.

Dorn, Jacob H. "The Social Gospel and Socialism: A Comparison of the Thought of Francis Greenwood Peabody, Washington Gladden, and Walter Rauschenbusch." *Church History* 62, no. 1 (March 1993): 82–100.

———. *Washington Gladden: Prophet of the Social Gospel*. Columbus: Ohio State University Press, 1968.

Dorrien, Gary J. *Social Ethics in the Making: Interpreting an American Tradition*. Malden, MA: Wiley-Blackwell, 2009.

———. *Soul in Society: The Making and Renewal of Social Christianity*. Minneapolis: Fortress Press, 1995.

———. *The Making of American Liberal Theology*. 3 vols. Louisville, KY: Westminster John Knox Press, 2001–2006.

Dubin, Martin David. "Elihu Root and the Advocacy of a League of Nations, 1914–1917." *The Western Political Quarterly* 19, no. 3 (September 1966): 439–55.

Duke, David Nelson. "Harry F. Ward: Social Gospel Warrior in the Trenches: The Social Gospel's Staying Power During the War and Its Aftermath." In *Perspectives on the Social Gospel: Papers from the Inaugural Social Gospel Conference at Colgate Rochester Divinity School*, edited by Charles Hodge Evans. Lewiston, NY: Edwin Mellen Press, 1999.

Ebel, Jonathan H. *Faith in the Fight: Religion and the American Soldier in the Great War*. Princeton, NJ: Princeton University Press, 2010.

———. "Of the Lost and the Fallen: Ritual and the Religious Power of the American Soldier." *Journal of Religion* 92, no. 2 (2012): 224–50.

———. "The Great War, Religious Authority, and the American Fighting Man." *Church History: Studies in Christianity and Culture* 78, no. 1 (March 2009): 99–133.

Eisner, Marc Allen. *From Warfare State to Welfare State: World War I, Compensatory State Building, and the Limits of the Modern Order*. University Park, PA: Pennsylvania State University Press, 2000.

Elleman, Bruce. *Wilson and China: A Revised History of the Shandong Question*. New York: M. E. Sharpe, 2002.

Esposito, David M. *The Legacy of Woodrow Wilson: American War Aims in World War I*. Westport, CT: Praeger, 1996.

Espinosa, Gastón. *Religion and the American Presidency: George Washington to George W. Bush with Commentary and Primary Sources*. New York: Columbia University Press, 2009.

Esposito, David M. *The Legacy of Woodrow Wilson: American War Aims in World War I*. Westport, CT: Praeger, 1996.

Farwell, Byron. *Over There: The United States in the Great War, 1917–1918*. New York: W. W. Norton & Company, 2000.

Faussell, Paul. *The Great War and Modern Memory*. New York: Oxford University Press, 2000.

Ferrell, Robert H. *Woodrow Wilson and World War I, 1917–1921*. New York: Harper & Row, 1985.

Fessenden, Tracy. *Culture and Redemption: Religion, the Secular, and American Literature*. Princeton, NJ: Princeton University Press, 2006.

Flanagan, Maureen A. *America Reformed: Progressives and Progressivisms, 1890s–1920s*. New York: Oxford University Press, 2007.

Flehinger, Brett. *The 1912 Election and the Power of Progressivism: A Brief History with Documents*. The Bedford Series in History and Culture. Boston: Bedford/St. Martin's, 2003.

Fleming, Thomas. *The Illusion of Victory: America in World War I*. New York: Basic Books, 2004.

Franchot, Jenny. *Roads to Rome: The Antebellum Protestant Encounter with Catholicism*. Berkeley: University of California Press, 1994.

Fenton, Elizabeth. *Religious Liberties: Anti-Catholicism and Liberal Democracy in Nineteenth-Century U.S. Literature and Culture*. New York: Oxford University Press, 2011.

Fitzgerald, Timothy. *Religion and Politics in International Relations: The Modern Myth*. New York: Continuum, 2011.

———. *Religion and the Secular: Historical and Colonial Formations*. London: Routledge, 2007.

Foucault, Michel. *Discipline and Punish: The Birth of the Prison*. New York: Pantheon, 1977.

Fox, Richard Wightman. *Reinhold Niebuhr: A Biography*. New York: Harper & Row, 1985.

Fox, Richard Wightman. "The Liberal Ethic and the Spirit of Protestantism." In *Community in America: The Challenge of Habits of the Heart*, edited by Charles H. Reynolds and Ralph V. Norman, 238–49. Berkeley: University of California Press, 1988.

Freidel, Frank Burt. *Over There: The Story of America's First Great Overseas Crusade*. Philadelphia: Temple University Press, 1990.

Gamble, Richard M. "Savior Nation: Woodrow Wilson and the Gospel of Service." *Humanitas* 14, no. 1 (2001): 4–22.

———. *The War for Righteousness: Progressive Christianity, the Great War, and the Rise of the Messianic Nation.* Wilmington, DE: ISI Books, 2003.

Gassaway, Brantley. *Progressive Evangelicals and the Pursuit of Social Justice.* Chapel Hill: University of Northern Carolina Press, 2014.

Geertz, Clifford. *The Interpretation of Cultures.* New York: Basic Books, 1973.

Gerwarth, Robert, and Erez Manela, eds. *Empires at War: 1911–1923.* The Greater War. New York: Oxford University Press, 2014.

Ginzburg, Carlo. *The Cheese and the Worms: The Cosmos of a Sixteenth-Century Miller.* London: Routledge, 1976.

Gordon, Linda. *The Great Arizona Orphan Abduction.* Cambridge, MA: Harvard University Press, 1999.

Griffith, R. Marie, ed. *American Religions: A Documentary History.* New York: Oxford University Press, 2007.

———. *Born Again Bodies.* Berkeley: University of California Press, 2004.

Guglielmo, Thomas A. *White on Arrival: Italians, Race, Color, and Power in Chicago, 1890–1945.* New York: Oxford University Press, 2004.

Gunn, T. Jeremy. *Spiritual Weapons: The Cold War and the Forging of an American National Religion.* Westport, CT: Praeger Publishers, 2009.

Gutjahr, Paul. *Popular American Literature of the 19th Century.* New York: Oxford University Press, 2001.

Haberski, Raymond J. *God and War: American Civil Religion Since 1945.* New Brunswick, NJ: Rutgers University Press, 2012.

Hall, David D. *Worlds of Wonder, Days of Judgment: Popular Religious Belief in Early New England.* Cambridge, MA: Harvard University Press, 1990.

Handy, Robert T. *A Christian America: Protestant Hopes and Historical Realities.* New York: Oxford University Press, 1984.

———. *The Social Gospel in America, 1870–1920.* New York: Oxford University Press, 1966.

———. *Undermined Establishment: Church–State Relations in America, 1880–1920.* Princeton, NJ: Princeton University Press, 1991.

Harvey, Paul. *Freedom's Coming: Religious Culture and the Shaping of the South from the Civil War through the Civil Rights Era.* Chapel Hill: University of North Carolina Press, 2007.

Haynes, Jeffrey. *Introduction to International Relations and Religion.* New York: Pearson, 2007.

Hedstrom, Matthew. *The Rise of Liberal Religion: Book Culture and American Spirituality in the Twentieth Century.* New York: Oxford University Press, 2013.

Henry, Andrew. *Southern Crucifix, Southern Cross: Catholic-Protestant Relations in the Old South.* Tuscaloosa: University of Alabama Press, 2012.

Herzog, Jonathan P. *The Spiritual-Industrial Complex: America's Religious Battle Against Communism in the Early Cold War.* Oxford; New York: Oxford University Press, 2011.

Heyrman, Christine Leigh. *Southern Cross: The Beginnings of the Bible Belt.* Chapel Hill: University of North Carolina Press, 1998.

Higham, John. *Strangers in the Land: Patterns of American Nativism, 1860–1925.* New Brunswick, NJ: Rutgers University Press, 2002.

Hodgson, Godfrey. *Woodrow Wilson's Right Hand: The Life of Colonel Edward M. House.* New Haven: Yale University Press, 2006.

Hoeveler, J. David, Jr. "The University and the Social Gospel: The Intellectual Origins of the 'Wisconsin Idea." *The Wisconsin Magazine of History* 59, no. 4 (1976): 282–98.

Hofstadter, Richard. *The Age of Reform: From Bryan to F.D.R.* New York: Knopf, 1955.

Hogan, Michael. *Woodrow Wilson's Western Tour: Rhetoric, Public Opinion, and the League of Nations.* College Station: Texas A&M University Press, 2006.

Hoover, Dennis, and Douglas Johnston, eds. *Religion and Foreign Affairs: Essential Readings.* Waco, TX: Baylor University Press, 2012.

Hurd, Elizabeth Shakman. *The Politics of Secularism in International Relations.* Princeton, NJ: Princeton University Press, 2008.

Hutchinson, William R. *Between the Times: The Travail of the Protestant Establishment in America, 1900–1960.* New York: Cambridge University Press, 1992.

———. *Errand to the World: American Protestant Thought and Foreign Missions.* Chicago: University of Chicago Press, 1993.

———. *The Modernist Impulse.* Durham, NC: Duke University Press, 1976.

Inboden, William. *Religion and American Foreign Policy, 1945–1960: The Soul of Containment.* New York: Cambridge University Press, 2008.

Ikenbery, John G., ed. *The Crisis of American Foreign Policy: Wilsonianism in the Twenty-First Century.* Princeton, NJ: Princeton University Press, 2009.

Jackson, Gregory S. *The Word and Its Witness: The Spiritualization of American Realism.* Chicago: University of Chicago Press, 2009.

Jacobson, Matthew Frye. *Whiteness of a Different Color: European Immigrants and the Alchemy of Race.* Cambridge, MA: Harvard University Press, 1999.

Jenkins, Phillip. *The Great and Holy War: How World War I Became a Religious Crusade.* San Francisco: HarperOne, 2014.

Jennings, Francis. *The Invasion of America: Indians, Colonialism, and the Cant of Conquest.* Chapel Hill: University of North Carolina Press, 1975.

Johnson, Sylvester. *African-American Religions, 1500–2000: Colonialism, Democracy, and Freedom.* New York: Cambridge University Press, 2015.

Johnston, Robert D. "Re-Democratizing the Progressive Era: The Politics of Progressive Era Political Historiography." *Journal of the Gilded Age and Progressive Era* 1, no. 1 (January 1, 2002): 68–92.

Joselit, Jenna Weissman. *The Wonders of America: Reinventing Jewish Culture 1880–1950.* New York: Picador, 2002.

Josephson, Jason Ananda. *The Invention of Religion in Japan.* Chicago: University of Chicago Press, 2012.

Kane, John. *Between Virtue and Power: The Persistent Moral Dilemma of U.S. Foreign Policy.* New Haven: Yale University Press, 2008.

Katz, Michael B. *In the Shadow of the Poorhouse: A Social History of Welfare in America.* 10th ed. New York: Basic Books, 1996.

Keene, Jennifer D. *Doughboys, the Great War, and the Remaking of America.* Baltimore: John Hopkins University Press, 2003.

Kennedy, David M. *Over Here: The First World War and American Society.* New York: Oxford University Press, 2004.

Kirby, Dianne. *Religion and the Cold War.* New York: Palgrave, 2003.

Kalb, Deborah, Gerhard Peters, and John T. Woolley. *State of the Union: Presidential Rhetoric from Woodrow Wilson to George W. Bush.* Washington, DC: CQ Press, 2006.

Kennedy, Ross A. *The Will to Believe: Woodrow Wilson, World War I, and America's Strategy for Peace and Security.* Kent, OH: Kent State University Press, 2009.

Kennedy, Ross A., ed. *A Companion to Woodrow Wilson*. Malden, MA: Wiley-Blackwell, 2013.

Klassen, Pamela. *Spirits of Protestantism: Medicine, Healing, and Liberal Christianity*. Berkeley: University of California Press, 2011.

Kloppenberg, James T. *Uncertain Victory: Social Democracy and Progressivism in European and American Thought, 1870–1920*. New York: Oxford University Press, 1988.

Knock, Thomas J. *To End All Wars: Woodrow Wilson and the Quest for a New World Order*. New York: Oxford University Press, 1992.

Kosek, Joseph Kip. *Acts of Conscience: Christian Nonviolence and Modern American Democracy*. New York: Columbia University Press, 2011.

Kraig, Robert Alexander. *Woodrow Wilson and the Lost World of the Oratorical Statesman*. College Station: Texas A&M University Press, 2004.

Lancaster, James L. "The Protestant Churches and the Fight for Ratification of the Versailles Treaty." *The Public Opinion Quarterly* 31, no. 4 (1967): 597–619.

Lasch-Quinn, Elisabeth. *Black Neighbors: Race and the Limits of Reform in the American Settlement House Movement, 1890–1945*. Chapel Hill: University of North Carolina Press, 1993.

Lears, Jackson. *Rebirth of a Nation: The Making of Modern America, 1877–1920*. New York: Harper, 2009.

Lincoln, Bruce. *Discourse and the Construction of Society: Comparative Studies of Myth, Ritual, and Classification*. New York: Oxford University Press, 1992.

———. *Holy Terrors: Thinking about Religion after September 11*. 2nd ed. University of Chicago Press, 2006.

Lindley, Susan Hill. "Neglected Voices and Praxis in the Social Gospel." *Journal of Religious Ethics* 18, no. 1 (2001): 75–102.

Link, Arthur Stanley. *The Higher Realism of Woodrow Wilson, and Other Essays*. Nashville: TN: Vanderbilt University Press, 1971.

———. "The Negro as a Factor in the Campaign of 1912." *The Journal of Negro History* 32, no. 1 (January 1947): 81–99.

———. *Wilson the Diplomatist: A Look at His Major Foreign Policies*. Chicago: Quadrangle, 1965.

———. *Woodrow Wilson: A Biography*. Chicago: Quadrangle, 1963.

———. *Woodrow Wilson: Revolution, War, and Peace*. Arlington Heights, IL: AHM Pub. Corp., 1979.

———. "Woodrow Wilson: The American as Southerner." *The Journal of Southern History* 36, no. 1 (February 1970): 3–17.

Lofton, Kathryn. "The Methodology of the Modernists: Process in American Protestantism." *Church History: Studies in Christianity and Culture* 75, no. 2 (2006): 374–402.

Luker, Ralph. "The Social Gospel and the Failure of Racial Reform, 1877–Present," *Church History* 46, no. 1 (1977): 80–99.

———. *The Social Gospel in Black and White American Racial Reform, 1885–1912*. Chapel Hill: University of North Carolina Press, 1991.

Lynch, Allen. "Woodrow Wilson and the Principle of 'National Self-Determination': A Reconsideration." *Review of International Studies* 28 (2002): 419–36.

Maffly-Kipp, Laurie F., Leigh E. Schmidt, and Mark Valeri. *Practicing Protestants: Histories of Christian Life in America, 1630–1965*. Baltimore: The Johns Hopkins University Press, 2006.

Magee, Malcolm D. *What the World Should Be: Woodrow Wilson and the Crafting of a Faith-Based Foreign Policy*. Waco, TX: Baylor University Press, 2008.

Mamdani, Mahmood. *Good Muslim, Bad Muslim: America, the Cold War, and the Roots of Terror*. New York: Pantheon Books, 2004.

Manela, Erez. *The Wilsonian Moment: Self-Determination and the International Origins of Anti-colonial Nationalism*. New York: Oxford University Press, 2007.

Marsden, George M. *Fundamentalism and American Culture*. New York: Oxford University Press, 2006.

———. "The Gospel of Wealth, the Social Gospel, and the Salvation of Souls in Nineteenth-Century America." *Fides Et Historia: Official Publication of the Conference on Faith and History* 5, no. 1 (1973): 10–21.

Masuzawa, Tomoko. *The Invention of World Religions: Or How European Universalism Was Preserved in the Language of Pluralism*. Chicago: University of Chicago Press, 2012.

McKillen, Elizabeth. *Making the World Safe for Workers: Labor, the Left and Wilsonian Internationalism*. Urbana: University of Illinois Press, 2013.

Mead, Walter. *Special Providence: American Foreign Policy and How It Changed the World*. New York: Knopf, 2001.

Marty, Martin E. *Modern American Religion*. 3 vols. Chicago: University of Chicago Press, 1997–1999.

———. *Righteous Empire: The Protestant Experience in America*. New York: Dial Press, 1970.

Maxwell, Angie. *The Indicted South: Public Criticism, Southern Inferiority, and the Politics of Whiteness*. Chapel Hill: University of North Carolina Press, 2014.

McDannell, Colleen. *Material Christianity: Religion and Popular Culture in America*. New Haven, CT: Yale University Press, 1995.

McGreevy, John. *Parish Boundaries: The Catholic Encounter with Race in the Twentieth-Century Urban North*. Chicago: University of Chicago Press, 1998.

Minus, Paul M. *Walter Rauschenbusch, American Reformer*. London: Collier Macmillan, 1988.

Modern, John Lardas. *Secularism in Antebellum America*. Chicago: University of Chicago Press, 2011.

Moore, R. Laurence. *Religious Outsiders and the Making of Americans*. New York: Oxford University Press, 1987.

Morgan, William M. *Questionable Charity: Gender, Humanitarianism, and Complicity in U.S. Literary Realism*. Hanover: University Press of New England, 2004.

McGerr, Michael. *A Fierce Discontent: The Rise and Fall of the Progressive Movement in America, 1870–1920*. New York: Oxford University Press, 2005.

Muehlenbeck, Philip E., ed. *Religion and the Cold War: A Global Perspective*. Nashville: Vanderbilt University Press, 2012.

Noll, Mark A. *America's God: From Jonathan Edwards to Abraham Lincoln*. New York: Oxford University, 2002.

———. *Scandal of the Evangelical Mind*. Grand Rapids, MI: Eerdmans, 1995.

Noll, Mark A., and Luke E. Harlow. *Religion and American Politics: From the Colonial Period to the Present*. New York: Oxford University Press, 2007.

Nichols, Christopher McKnight. *Promise and Peril: America at the Dawn of a Global Age*. Cambridge, MA: Harvard University Press, 2011.

Ninkovich, Frank A. *The Wilsonian Century: U.S. Foreign Policy Since 1900*. Chicago: University of Chicago Press, 2001.

O'Connor, Brendon. *American Foreign Policy Traditions*. 4 vols. Los Angeles: SAGE, 2010.

Orsi, Robert A. *The Madonna of 115th Street*. Rev. ed. New Haven, CT: Yale University Press, 2002.

Ownby, Ted. *Subduing Satan: Religion, Recreation, and Manhood in the Rural South, 1865–1920*. Chapel Hill: The University of North Carolina Press, 1993.

Pahl, Jon. *Empire of Sacrifice: The Religious Origins of American Violence*. New York: New York University Press, 2010.

Painter, Nell Irvin. *Standing at Armageddon: The United States, 1877–1919*. New York: W. W. Norton, 1987.

———. *The History of White People*. New York: W. W. Norton & Co., 2011.

Pascoe, Peggy. *Relations of Rescue: The Search for Female Moral Authority in the American West, 1874–1939*. New York: Oxford University Press, 1990.

Park, Miles Adam. "'The Greatest Scrapper Who Ever Lived': The Historiography of American Muscular Christianity." Unpublished essay, 2010.

Patler, Nicholas. *Jim Crow and the Wilson Administration: Protesting Federal Segregation in the Early Twentieth Century*. Denver: University of Colorado Press, 2004.

Pegram, Thomas. *One Hundred Percent American: The Rebirth and Decline of the Ku Klux Klan in the 1920s*. Lanham: Ivan R. Dee, 2011.

Perry, Elisabeth Israels. "Men Are from the Gilded Age, Women Are from the Progressive Era." *The Journal of the Gilded Age and Progressive Era* 1, no. 1 (January 1, 2002): 25–48.

Peterson, H. C., and Gilbert C. Fite. *Opponents of War, 1917–1918*. Madison: University of Wisconsin Press, 1957.

Phillips, Paul T. *A Kingdom on Earth: Anglo-American Social Christianity, 1880–1940*. University Park: Pennsylvania State University Press, 1996.

Pierce, Anne. *Woodrow Wilson and Harry Truman: Mission and Power in American Foreign Policy*. Westport, CT: Praeger, 2003.

Piott, Steven L. *American Reformers, 1870–1920*. Lanham, MD: Rowman & Littlefield Publishers, 2006.

Piper, John F. *The American Churches in World War I*. Athens: Ohio University Press, 1985.

Pittenger, Mark. "A World of Difference: Constructing the 'Underclass' in Progressive America." *American Quarterly* 49, no. 1 (1997): 26–65.

Porterfield, Amanda. *The Transformation of American Religion*. New York: Oxford University Press, 2001.

Preston, Andrew. *Sword of the Spirit, Shield of Faith: Religion in American War and Diplomacy*. New York: Anchor Books/Random House, 2012.

———. "To Make the World Saved: American Religion and the Great War." *Diplomatic History* 38, no. 4 (2014): 813–25.

Price, Matthew C. *The Wilsonian Persuasion in American Foreign Policy*. Youngstown, NY: Cambria Press, 2007.

Putney, Clifford. *Muscular Christianity: Manhood and Sports in Protestant America, 1880–1920*. Cambridge, MA: Harvard University Press, 2001.

Raboteau, Albert J. *Slave Religion: The "Invisible Institution" in the Antebellum South*. New York: Oxford University Press, 1978, 2004.

Remillard, Art. *Southern Civil Religions: Imagining the Good Society in the Post-Reconstruction Era*. Athens: University of Georgia Press, 2011.

Renda, Mary. *Taking Haiti: Military Occupation and the Culture of U.S. Imperialism, 1915–1940*. Chapel Hill: University of North Carolina Press, 2001.

Reynolds, David S. *Faith in Fiction: The Emergence of Religious Literature in America*. Cambridge, MA: Harvard University Press, 1981.

Ribuffo, Leo P. *The Old Christian Right: The Protestant Far Right from the Great Depression to the Cold War*. Philadelphia: Temple University Press, 1988.

Roediger, David. *Working Toward Whiteness: How America's Immigrants Became White: The Strange Journey from Ellis Island to the Suburbs*. New York: Basic Books, 2006.

Roof, Wade Clark, and William McKinney. *American Mainline Religion: Its Changing Shape and Future*. New Brunswick, NJ: Rutgers University Press, 1987.

Ross, Dorothy. "American Modernities, Past, and Present." *The American Historical Review* 116, no. 3 (June 2011): 702–14.

Rossini, Daniela. *Woodrow Wilson and the American Myth in Italy: Culture, Diplomacy, and War Propaganda*. Harvard Historical Studies 161. Translated by Antony Shugaar. Cambridge, MA: Harvard University Press, 2008.

Ruotsila, Markku. "Conservative American Protestantism in the League of Nations Controversy." *Church History: Studies in Christianity and Culture* 72, no. 3 (September 2003): 593–616.

———. *The Origins of Christian Anti-internationalism: Conservative Evangelicals and the League of Nations*. Washington, DC: Georgetown University Press, 2008.

Ryan, Susan M. *The Grammar of Good Intentions: Race and the Antebellum Culture of Benevolence*. New York: Cornell University Press, 2005.

Salzman, Raymond. *Reform and Revolution: The Life and Times of Raymond Robins*. Kent, OH: Kent State University Press, 1991.

Sandeen, Ernest. *The Roots of Fundamentalism: The Roots of British and American Millenarianism, 1800–1930*. Reprint, Chicago: University of Chicago Press, 2008.

Sarna, Jonathan D. *American Judaism: A History*. New Haven, CT: Yale University Press, 2005.

Schaffer, Ronald. *America in the Great War: The Rise of the War Welfare State*. New York: Oxford University Press, 1991.

Schmidt, Leigh. *Restless Souls: The Making of American Spirituality*. San Francisco: Harper, 2005.

Schmidt, Leigh, and Sarah Promey. *American Religious Liberalism*. Indianapolis: Indiana University Press, 2012.

Schmidt, Peter. "Walter Scott, Postcolonial Theory, and New South Literature." *The Mississippi Quarterly* 56, no. 4 (2003): 545–54.

Schultz, Kevin M. *Tri-Faith America: How Catholics and Jews Held Postwar America to Its Protestant Promise*. New York: Oxford University Press, 2011.

Scott, Joan. *Gender and the Politics of History*. New York: Columbia University Press, 1988.

Seales, Chad. *The Secular Spectacle: Performing Religion in a Southern Town*. New York: Oxford University Press, 2013.

Sehat, David. *Myth of American Religious Freedom*. New York: Oxford University Press, 2011.

Settje, David E. *Faith and War: How Christians Debated the Cold and Vietnam Wars*. New York: New York University Press, 2011.

Shah, Timothy Samuel, Alfred C. Stepan, and Monica Duffy Toft, eds. *Rethinking Religion and World Affairs*. New York: Oxford University Press, 2012.

Shimazu, Naoko. *Japan, Race and Equality: The Racial Equality Proposal of 1919*. London: Routledge, 1998.

Sklar, Kathryn Kish. "'Some of Us Who Deal with the Social Fabric': Jane Addams Blends Peace and Social Justice, 1907–1919." *Journal of the Gilded Age and Progressive Era* 2, no. 1 (January 2003): 80–96.

Smith, Anthony Burke. *The Look of Catholics: Portrayals in Popular Culture from the Great Depression to the Cold War*. Lawrence: University of Kansas Press, 2010.

Smith, Erin A. *What Would Jesus Read? Popular Books and Everyday Life in Twentieth-Century America*. Chapel Hill: University of North Carolina Press, 2015.

Smith, Gary Scott. *Faith and the Presidency: From George Washington to George W. Bush*. New York: Oxford University Press, 2006.

———. *The Search for Social Salvation: Social Christianity and America, 1880–1925*. Lanham, MD: Lexington Books, 2000.

Smith, Page. *America Enters the World: A People's History of the Progressive Era and World War I*. New York: McGraw-Hill, 1985.

Smith, Jonathan Z. "Religion, Religions, Religious." In *Critical Terms for Religious Studies*, edited by Mark C. Taylor. Chicago: University of Chicago Press, 1998.

Stevens, Jason W. *God-Fearing and Free: A Spiritual History of America's Cold War*. Cambridge, MA: Harvard University Press, 2010.

Steigerwald, David. *Wilsonian Idealism in America*. Ithaca, NY: Cornell University Press, 1994.

Stone, Ralph. *The Irreconcilables: The Fight Against the League of Nations*. Lexington: University Press of Kentucky, 1970.

Stuckey, Mary E. "'The Domain of Public Conscience': Woodrow Wilson and the Establishment of a Transcendent Political Order." *Rhetoric & Public Affairs* 6, no. 1 (Spring 2003): 1–23.

Sutton, Matthew A. *American Apocalypse*. Cambridge, MA: Harvard University Press, 2014.

———. "Was FDR the Antichrist? The Birth of Fundamentalist Antiliberalism in a Global Age." *Journal of American History* 98, no. 4 (February 19, 2012): 1052–74.

Szasz, Ferenc M. *The Divided Mind of Protestant America, 1880–1930*. Tuscaloosa: University of Alabama Press, 2002.

Toft, Monica Duffy. *God's Century: Resurgent Religion and Global Politics*. New York: W. W. Norton, 2011.

Tucker, Robert W. *Woodrow Wilson and the Great War: Reconsidering America's Neutrality, 1914–1917*. Charlottesville: University of Virginia Press, 2007.

Tyrell, Ian. *Reforming the World: The Creation of America's Moral Empire*. Princeton, NJ: Princeton University Press, 2010.

Tyrell, Ian, and Jay Sexton. *Empire's Twin: U.S. Anti-Imperialism from the Founding Era to the Age of Terrorism*. The United States in the World. New York: Cornell University Press, 2015.

Walworth, Arthur. *Wilson and His Peacemakers: American Diplomacy at the Paris Peace Conference, 1919*. New York: W. W. Norton & Company, 1986.

Wells, Jonathan Daniel, and Jennifer R. Green, eds. *The Southern Middle Class*. Baton Rouge: Louisiana State University, 2011.

Weiss, Nancy J. "The Negro and the New Freedom: Fighting Wilsonian Segregation." *Political Science Quarterly* 84, no. 1 (March 1969): 61–79.

Wertheim, Stephen. "The League That Wasn't: American Designs for a Legalist-Sanctionist League of Nations and the Intellectual Origins of International Organization, 1914–1920," *Diplomatic History* 35, no. 5 (2011): 797–836.

White, Christopher. *Unsettled Minds: Psychology and the American Search for Spiritual Assurance, 1830–1940*. Berkeley: University of California Press, 2009.

White, Ronald C. *Liberty and Justice for All: Racial Reform and the Social Gospel (1877–1925)*, The Rauschenbusch Lectures. San Francisco: Harper & Row, 1990.

White, Ronald C., and Charles Howard Hopkins. *The Social Gospel: Religion and Reform in Changing America*. Philadelphia: Temple University Press, 1976.

Widenor, William C. *Henry Cabot Lodge and the Search for an American Foreign Policy*. Berkeley: University of California Press, 1980.

Wiebe, Robert. *The Search for Order, 1877–1920*. New York: Hill and Wang, 1967.

Williams, Chad L. *Torchbearers of Democracy: African American Soldiers in the World War I Era*. Chapel Hill: University of North Carolina Press, 2010.

Williams, Joseph. *Spirit Cure: A History of Pentecostal Healing*. New York: Oxford University Press, 2013.

Williams, Peter. *America's Religions: From Their Origins to the Twenty-first Century*. Champaign: University of Illinois Press, 2008.

Wilson, Erin K. *After Secularism: Rethinking Religion in Global Politics*. Basingstoke, Hampshire [England]; New York: Palgrave Macmillan, 2012.

Winter, Jay. *The Legacy of the Great War: Ninety Years On*. Columbia: University of Missouri Press, 2009.

Wolgemuth, Kathleen. "Woodrow Wilson and Federal Segregation," *The Journal of Negro History* 44, no. 2 (1959): 158–73.

Woodward, David R. *Trial by Friendship: Anglo–American Relations, 1917–1918*. Lexington, KY: University Press of Kentucky, 2003.

Wray, Matt. *Not Quite White: White Trash and the Boundaries of Whiteness*. Durham, NC: Duke University Press, 2006.

Wyatt-Brown, Bertram. *The Shaping of Southern Culture: Honor, Grace, and War, 1760s–1880s*. Chapel Hill: The University of North Carolina Press, 2000.

Yellin, Eric Steven. *Racism in the Nation's Service: Government Workers and the Color Line in Woodrow Wilson's America*. Chapel Hill: University of North Carolina Press, 2013.

Zieger, Robert H. *America's Great War: World War I and the American Experience*. Lanham, MD: Rowman & Littlefield, 2001.

Index